MW01625497

Land's Polaroid

Land's Polaroid

A COMPANY AND THE MAN WHO INVENTED IT

Peter C. Wensberg

A PETER DAVISON BOOK

Houghton Mifflin Company / Boston 1987

Library of Congress Cataloging-in-Publication Data

Wensberg, Peter C.
Land's Polaroid.

"A Peter Davison book."
Includes index.
1. Land, Edwin Herbert, 1909– . 2. Polaroid Corporation — History. 3. Polaroid Land camera — History.
I. Title.
TR140.L28W46 1987 338.7'681418'0924 87–2806
ISBN 0-395-42114-4

Printed in the United States of America

A 10 9 8 7 6 5 4 3 2 1

Author's Note

This book recounts many conversations held over a long period of time and reconstructed from memory. In each instance the substance and tone of these conversations are accurate; the dialogue is as precise as memory permits.

Unless otherwise credited, all photographs are courtesy of Polaroid Corporation.

To Andrea

Every man has his basic worth,
from which must be subtracted his vanity.

BISMARCK

An idea isn't responsible for the people who believe in it.

DON MARQUIS

Any problem can be solved using the materials in the room.

EDWIN H. LAND

Contents

Land's Polaroid

Prologue

Polaroid

Santa Barbara, 1986

Polaroid is a word coined in 1934 by Clarence Kennedy, a Smith College professor. It first described Edwin Land's first commercial product, a synthetic polarizing material made of plastic; later it became the name of Land's company when it was reorganized. Polaroid, a name known throughout the world, compares in recognition value with Ford, Sony, Boeing, Shell, Mercedes, and other corporate names that have originated in different ways but become a part of the international vocabulary of products and commerce.

Ford, of course, is the name of a man, as are Boeing, Bell, Edison, and hundreds of other familiar company names. Mercedes was named after the daughter of Emile Jellinek, an early associate of Gottlieb Daimler. It has survived as a trademark because it is more euphonious than Jellinek, Daimler, or Benz and certainly more so than Emile, Gottlieb, or Carl, Herr Benz's first name. Sony is a contrived name, made up by Akio Morita, its founder, for the same reason that George Eastman created Kodak: it is easy to say, easy to remember, and not closely related to any other names or words in any language.

In hindsight, Polaroid seems a fortunate choice. When the word was first used it suggested another plastic substance, celluloid, which was enjoying a brief but considerable success. *Polar* denotes polarization. The suffix *-oid* indicates likeness, similarity, having the shape or nature of. Land considered other name suggestions in 1937. One of them, Epibolipol, would have made life difficult, perhaps terminally so, for a struggling enterprise. Polaroid, however, now stands for a company.

Sometimes people use the name, incorrectly, to identify the company's current principal products, which are instant cameras and instant pictures. The resident lawyers are quick to point out that "a Polaroid" is an incorrect use of a registered trademark, and Polaroid does not correctly refer to a camera or a self-developing picture.

Polaroid as a company was for forty-five years virtually synonymous with Edwin Land. He was its founder. He invented its first products and indeed many of its products and processes throughout the five decades of the company's history. His titles, during most of the period from 1937 to 1982, included Chairman of the Board, President, Chief Executive Officer, Chief Operating Officer, and Director of Research. Although he assiduously cultivated a legend of privacy and inaccessibility to the press, he remained far and away the best-known member of the company, for many years the only one familiar to the public except for such people as Steve Allen, Garry Moore, Perry Como, Laurence Olivier, Danny Kaye, and the duo of James Garner and Mariette Hartley, all of whom demonstrated Polaroid cameras on television. Advertising makes strange bedfellows. Land would go well out of his way to avoid meeting Polaroid's video representatives in person. He stayed aloof from the company's advertising so long as his friends and intimates told him Polaroid's advertising was good. The moment he suspected it was verging on the mediocre — the natural habitat of advertising — he descended from Olympus clothed in a mantle of righteousness.

Since for many years advertising was included among my marketing responsibilities at Polaroid, my relationship with Land was alternately very close and moderately distant. It was always, however, friendly and informal. For a combination of reasons, among them a twenty-year difference in our ages and my own lack of scientific credentials, I always felt comfortable speaking my mind to him. Many of his employees did not. He was revered to an extraordinary extent by most of the people who worked for him — a situation that of course made communication difficult. Most men of Land's stature, particularly those to whom great success has come in the business world, earn their share of detractors. Land's were primarily, but not exclusively, outside the company, principally in the ranks of financial analysts and reporters. Within the company, particularly among employees who had been with him for many years, he seemingly could do no wrong. This gave rise to the almost universal practice of addressing him as Dr. Land or sometimes simply Doctor.

Land did not earn a college degree, either as an undergraduate or a graduate student, from Harvard, the only university he attended. The list of institutions from which he received honorary degrees, however, includes Harvard, Yale, Columbia, Carnegie Institute of Technology, New York University, Williams College, Tufts College, Washington University, Polytechnic Institute of Brooklyn, University of Massachusetts, Brandeis University, and others. He has received more medals and scientific honors, including the Presidential Medal of Freedom and the National Medal of Science, than most living Americans. The full list of his honors runs to three pages. He holds 533 patents, second only to Thomas Edison's 1,093, and he was inducted into the National Inventors Hall of Fame in Washington in 1977.

For years I called him Dr. Land. He often asked me to call him Din, a nickname used since his childhood by close friends and associates. I finally was able to comply. No friend, associate, or acquaintance ever called him Ed. The *Wall Street Journal* called him Mr. Land. It felt the Doctor title was false and a sham. It has traditionally been critical of him, and the animosity was returned. For the purposes of this book, I have chosen to call him simply Land.

I joined Polaroid in 1958 with little knowledge of the company, but with a sense that I was embarking on an adventure, a notion amply justified. I began in advertising and promotion, went to Europe to assist some of the new subsidiary companies then being organized, returned to head advertising and later marketing for the parent company. I was a member of the policy group called the management executive committee. In 1980 I became executive vice president and was given responsibility for technical and industrial photography. In 1982, Land cut the last but one of his ties with his company and retired to devote full time to his laboratory and foundation on the Charles River, the Rowland Institute for Science. Two months later I left Polaroid as well. The subject of this book is Polaroid and Land. The span is 1926 to 1982, the period when the company and the man were inseparable, virtually indistinguishable.

Land was an inventor throughout his career and will remain so throughout his life which, since he is in excellent health, appears to promise many productive years ahead. One of his most interesting inventions — his company — was not patentable, though it has proved very difficult to copy. More case histories have been written about it at the Harvard Business School than about almost any other corporation. It is widely known and studied in Japan, as is its inventor. It has had an impact on American culture as well as American industry. It successfully defended a technological monopoly, not only against Kodak and other American competitors, but against the Russians, who tried unsuccessfully to copy the early Polaroid camera with a line-for-line version called the Moment, which they "invented" in 1955.

This book is intended as neither a biography of Land nor a history of Polaroid. It was not "authorized" by Land or by the company. Land has not participated in its writing, nor, I suspect, will he be satisfied with the results. This book, for better or worse, reflects my memory and understanding of events, conversations, and personalities. It has benefited enormously, in addition, from the contributions, corrections, and amplifications of many who were part of Polaroid during the Landian era. For those events which occurred between 1958 and 1982, I have relied on my own memory and those of others who were present. For the years prior to 1958, I have used conversations with and tapes of many of the participants, as well as printed sources. Polaroid has kindly given me access to the corporate archive. I am immensely grateful to the many people who assisted me in the preparation of this book.

Authorized it was not, but Land's persona has been hovering about me as I write. "You can't say that!" it admonishes me. "How do you know what people think? How do you know what they said if you weren't there?" And "Don't split infinitives." Land was and is meticulous about syntax. The persona is much more comfortable when I quote Land's words precisely from a transcript or a letter to his shareholders than when I attempt to recreate a conversation. It heaves gusty sighs of relief that its owner hewed to a lifelong habit of rarely writing or replying to letters. Nothing Land ever committed to paper has had less than his complete concentration. This persona, I fear, itches to snatch the pencil from my fingers and edit, improve, and, above all, delete. I am one of the very few who ever tried to edit Land. My editing successes, however, were few. Now I feel a powerful editorial force surging to and fro in my workroom. It rages and frets at my naiveté, my inexactitude, my habit of generalization, and my lack of sophisticated technical knowledge. Yet it was these traits and my willingness to tell him the truth that made me useful to Land. Once he flattered me by introducing me as "one of the architects of Polaroid." I allowed as how I was actually one of the carpenters. There was only one architect.

Edwin H. Land deserves and requires a scientific biography. His career in science has been a long one, including some achievements that will last well beyond the products of his company. I am not that author and this is not that book. This is a portrait of a man and a company who occupied the same space, and often, but not always, spoke with the same voice. If it is an admiring portrait, I do not apologize. I did not see Land as a legend, a tycoon, a genius, or a tyrant, although he was certainly all of these and more. From the first day I met him, however, he impressed me as a person who lived his life more intensely than the rest of us. His lifelong friend, adviser, and sometime mentor, Julius Silver, who first met the twelve-year-old Land at a summer camp where Silver was a counselor, described Land as "the most extraordinary person I have ever met." Since Silver has known Einstein, Baruch, Harriman, Israel's great leaders, and many other of the twentieth century's most interesting minds, egos, and personalities, his judgment is significant.

Land's life seemed to me primarily a life of the mind. His great dramas were largely self-created, played on the stage, Polaroid, which he constructed for himself. If those productions did not begin or end as the supporting cast would have them, small matter to the principal player. His interest in our reactions was minimal — polite, sometimes kind, but limited by the great drain of energy necessary to sustain his own part.

As I watched Laurence Olivier working on an empty stage in Paris, rehearsing, playing to the most critical of audiences, himself, I was reminded irresistibly of Land. No one could care more than he about the nuances, about the polish, about the details that contributed to an elegant performance. And yet in Land's case, as in my exposure to Olivier, the humanity of the figure on the stage made him an object of the most intense interest. I knew Land as a man who could proclaim with serious demeanor, "Anything worth doing is worth doing to excess," and struggle unsuccessfully to contain a smile. His ideas, his achievements, his mistakes, were indeed excessive. But the smile will last in my memory.

1

The Optical Society

New York, 1947

The storm could be heard above the noise of the crowded lobby. The Hotel Pennsylvania was jammed. Big, shabbily comfortable, moderately ornate, once among the best of the midtown hotels, across Seventh Avenue from Penn Station at the corner of Thirty-third, the Pennsylvania relied on the garment trade. During the buying off-seasons it often hosted small conventions such as that of the Optical Society of America, six hundred and fifty of whose members were there or trying to get there on the evening of February 21 for their winter meeting.

Land stood among a noisy, impatient crowd in the lobby waiting for an elevator. He had traveled down from Boston on the Merchants Limited the day before. Now the world outside had turned chaotic. A storm was jeopardizing his career, his plans, his company, and the future he had been painstakingly reconstructing for the past three and a half years. "Nature doesn't care," he told his young laboratory assistants. By that he meant that nothing in nature would help or hinder their progress to a solution except their own ingenuity, which admittedly was itself a condition of nature. Nature offered no bar to the elegant solution over the awkward compromise if they had the imagination to seek it and the wit to discover it. Nature, serene or savage in their eyes, had no concern for the affairs of men. That included the weather.

The worst blizzard in six years was roaring down Seventh Avenue like the Merchants Limited, driving people, cabs, buses, everything not fastened to the street, before it. The radio attributed six deaths to the storm so far. The steaming lobby of the Pennsylvania could not hold another person. Cold, wet, impatient scientists and journalists besieged the registration desk, hunted down bellboys, pushed into the bar, and argued with the head waiter in the dining room. The group in front of the elevators waited with growing annoyance. One of the four cars was out of service, and fifteen minutes had elapsed since the last elevator door had opened. Alarmed by the sound of the wind a few minutes earlier, Land had stepped out through the revolving door and tasted the violence of the storm. Nature was rude and uncaring. The snow, driven like white rope past the marquee of the hotel, piling up against mailboxes and bus stop signs, showed no signs of abating. Even at four in the afternoon the street was dark as night, the stately columns of the Baths of Caracalla across the street blurred and indistinct.

Land agonized about the truck being driven down from Cambridge with equipment essential to the evening's demonstration. If it was late or didn't arrive — but he couldn't contemplate such a disaster. Howie Rogers had also chosen to drive down that afternoon. Land bitterly regretted that he had not told him to take the train. Howie might not make it. Land *required* him to be there. In two hours Land would be standing on the edge of the abyss, and he wanted his own people supporting him. They were his most important audience. He had worked with them for months to prepare for this night, the demonstration rehearsed a hundred times, two hundred times, each iteration honing the pace, the order, the equipment, the words, the dramatic effect, until the last twenty times were identically perfect. He needed the support of this group to whom he had played a season of midnight performances. He needed them *tonight!*

He especially needed Howie Rogers, the short, unassuming man who had become indispensable to Land. Completely without pretension, Rogers was Land's perfect laboratory foil and of late had produced surprises on his own. Ten years earlier, with one year of Harvard behind him, broke and pumping gas at a Jenney station in Brighton, Massachusetts, he had met Land at the insistence of his brother, Nickerson Rogers. Land hired Howie, taught him, and made him a first-class scientist. No, a world-class scientist, Land thought, looking impatiently at the elevator indicator, whose arrow seemed petrified in place on the fourteenth floor: one of the most imaginative explorers of the territory, the domain, of colloids in supersaturated solutions, the domain of diffusion transfer. That might be made into an acceptable introduction for Howie, if he were to introduce him, which he would not, since Howie did not want to stand up in front of a crowd of Ph.D.s and seemed unlikely to arrive anyway.

Bill McCune and Otto Wolf had come down with Land on Thursday, the previous day, with some of the cameras, the lights, the film, and the tools. They set up the equipment in Land's small hotel room after they checked in, did a dry run, discovered a short circuit in the connections of the electric motor that drove the processing rollers, worked for several hours to rewire it, then tested everything once again.

Otto had studied aeronautical engineering at MIT and after his graduation in 1933 hung around the Land-Wheelwright Laboratories on Dartmouth Street in Boston until Land discovered Otto could design, build, and repair any piece of machinery that could be described to him. With Maxfield Parrish, Jr., Otto had supervised the modification of the big 8 x 10 view camera that would be the centerpiece of tonight's demonstration, as well as the 4 x 5 Speed Graphic, the classic news photographer's camera, that would be used as a backup. Otto knew every screw and hairspring in both cameras and had designed and built the film processing units for them in Polaroid's model shop, working under a shroud of secrecy that surpassed that of their wartime activities.

Bill McCune, an automotive engineer who had come from General Motors, was deeply involved with this pair in the design of the prototype Polaroid camera. Several crude models already existed in the SX-70 shop back in Cambridge. At the moment, Otto was having a drink in the lounge, stretching his rangy athlete's frame between two chairs; Bill was in his room, talking on the telephone to Cambridge. They were to meet in the Georgian Room as soon as it was cleared of the people and debris of the afternoon session. The Contributed Papers on spectroscopy had been read, beginning at two o'clock. Land had heard in the lobby that the highlight of the afternoon session was Dr. E. O. Hulbert's paper, "The Upper Atmosphere of the Earth." It concluded with movie footage of captured V-2 rockets being launched from the White Sands Proving Ground in New Mexico. Instruments parachuted at the apogee had provided the measurements and observations for the paper. Spellbound, the audience had watched the awful ascent of projectiles recently expatriated from Peenemünde, soon to bury themselves in the high plains of New Mexico rather than the architecture of London and Birmingham.

Now the chairs in the Georgian Room were being regrouped around dining tables for twelve, with a head table set against the narrow margin of the big room. In one corner a pair of small tables and four chairs were set aside for Land's demonstration. At 5:45 the hotel crew would be finished. Guests would begin to arrive a little before 7:00 for the informal dinner session. If the truck arrived in time, Land, McCune, and Wolf would have an hour to move their equipment in, set it up, run through the procedures once if time allowed, and find their places — Land at the head table, McCune, Wolf, Eudoxia Muller, Meroë Morse, David Grey, and Howie, if he arrived, at a table below the salt. The elevator landed and disgorged four more people than it was intended to carry. Land struggled in, ignoring the crush, his thoughts elsewhere, hoping Bill and Otto were keeping track of the time. I should have kept them with me, he thought.

Eudoxia Muller, Meroë Morse, Dave Grey, and the other members of Land's inner circle would meet in the Georgian Room. Doxie and Meroë, next to Howie the most brilliant of Land's students, were by all odds the most beautiful. Both liberal arts graduates of Smith, they had been steered to Polaroid by Clarence Kennedy, an art historian and eminence of the Smith faculty. Meroë, named after the ancient city on the Nile, had proved beyond dispute Land's contention that a bright, eager, young person with little technical training could become a first-rate scientist. She and Doxie had come to Polaroid fresh from Smith, and Doxie had been assigned by Land to begin the first chemical experiments on his instant photography project, given the code name SX-70, under Land's daily guidance. The two women differed strikingly. Meroë's chestnut-haired beauty, charm, and quiet manner masked a reservoir of determination and ambition, while Doxie, a humorous, cynical blond sprite, talked tough, but was content to be directed rather than director. David Grey, Land's leading optical scientist, distinguished, academic in demeanor, was already recognized as one of Harvard's and the Optical Society's young stars.

Land had planned for almost every contingency except a snowstorm. He knew the outcome of this evening could characterize the new field, his field, forever after. He and Dick Kriebel had made sure that the press knew that an unusual announcement was to be made at this otherwise prosaic meeting. He hoped William Laurence, the science writer for the *New York Times* whose eyewitness story of the bombing of Nagasaki two years earlier had earned him a second Pulitzer Prize, would attend. Land had been meticulous in his preparations. He had chosen a scientific setting to announce his invention, but this meeting, he was certain, offered no competitive news of consequence. He had designed the presentation with a careful balance between modestly stated claims and an electrically dramatic impact. He knew that the rigorous rehearsals would lift the odds in his favor. Something, many things, could still go wrong, but everything in the demonstration had worked often enough for him to feel that he could achieve the conquest of his audience.

Land remembered the occasion eleven years earlier when, with almost the same intensity of preparation, he had shown an audience of reporters gathered at a New York Museum all the magic his young company had created in the four years since he had abruptly left Harvard, a semester before graduating, to conquer the business world. He was desperate to establish its credentials. The planning had been perfect, the right reporters attended, and the staging of the demonstrations produced an almost overwhelming statement. But the news stories about glareless headlights and three-dimensional movies did not appear the next day, not because the reporters were not won over, not because of any factor within Land's control, but because England's king had had the bad grace to choose the same day in 1936 to broadcast his graceful farewell to his subjects and the world. The abdication blew every other story out of the press.

The storm that was howling outside this afternoon was another ill wind. It could delay the equipment truck, keep important members of the Optical Society away, cause Laurence, or the *New York Herald Tribune* reporter, or *Life* magazine to cancel. It would almost certainly prevent Howie from arriving on time. It constituted a threat, a distraction. It could spoil the concentration of his audience, which he *must* have this evening for precisely one hour. If he had no more than that, he felt he would be in control from then on.

Land was thirty-seven. He had known since he was seventeen that he would be a great figure of science and affairs. He had expected to be playing these roles long before now, but he had ultimately been frustrated each time the moment presented itself. He had chosen, wisely or not, to leave Harvard early, though it was clear that he could have been one of its brilliant graduates. Some faculty members still felt that his decision had been quixotic and foolish. For twenty years, since the night in Times Square when he had conjured the idea out of the dizzying lights of Broadway, he had pursued the dream of a polarizing system to eliminate the glare of automobile headlights, only to be rebuffed time and time again by Detroit. He had tried to adapt the technology of polarization, his for a limited time by the rights of his patents, to product after product with only one modest success, Polaroid sunglasses. He had presented the movie industry with the greatest technical revolution since sound and color, the eerie verisimilitude of three-dimensional photography, only to be ignored and misunderstood by Hollywood. He was proud of the war record of his company, but brilliant as some of his wartime successes had been, he did not want, could not continue, to do research and development for hire now that the national emergency was over.

He had staked the future of the company on an idea he called instant photography. The two years following the war had brought the company close to disaster. Sales had fallen from $16 million in 1945 to $4 million the next year and were running at a rate of less than $2 million in 1947. Profits had evaporated, even with large excess profit tax credits carried forward from the war years. Land feared that in 1947 his company could end up losing as much as $2 million, more than the entire projected sales total for the year. Worst of all, he had been forced to fire people, good people, scientists and engineers, men and women who had worked like galley slaves during the war, men and women he needed to make the photographic project work. From about thirteen hundred employees at war's end, Polaroid had shrunk to fewer than three hundred. All that training, all those marvelous technical competences, were being dissipated, scattered.

Despite his nagging sense of, not failure, but success too long postponed, Land had been noticed, praised, and rewarded more than almost any young scientist in the American industrial community. He had received four medals: the Cresson Medal from the Franklin Institute, the John Scott Medal and Award from the City of Philadelphia Trusts, the Hood Medal from the Royal Photographic Society in London, and the Rumford Medal from the American Academy of Arts and Sciences. He had been named one of America's Modern Pioneers and been fulsomely introduced to the readers of *Fortune* in an early issue of that magazine. His own writings were read and quoted in academic and even government circles.

In 1944, at the height of the war effort, he had written a paper for a forum on the future of industrial research. "I believe quite simply that the small company of the future will be as much a research organization as it is a manufacturing company, and that this new kind of company is the frontier for the next generation." He visualized new fields in chemistry, nuclear physics, radar technics, and color photography. He surmised that "a group of fifty good scientists contemplating one of these fields and inspired by curiosity about them and a determination to make something new and useful can invent and develop an important new field in about two years. . . . This new field will be a monopoly for the group," added Land, and he asked, "Who can object to such monopolies?"

He had found and trained fifty good scientists. He had developed something new and useful, the polarizing sheet Clarence Kennedy had named Polaroid. He had achieved his patents and his monopoly, but the polarizer had not developed into a field of real importance. Detroit was to blame. The automobile manufacturers would not accept an idea so logical, so effective, so inexpensive to implement that it had excited the imagination of even some of the most tough-minded financiers on Wall Street. The automobile industry was lethargic, greedy, insular, suspicious of science, and imbued with distrust for anything NIH, Not Invented Here.

The field of polarization, which Land had chosen as a boy of seventeen, upon which he had staked his scientific career, around which he had built and financed his company, to which he had devoted almost every hour of his energy for the past twenty years, was moribund. At thirty-seven he had achieved everything to which he aspired except success. He was recognized as an attractive prophet, a charismatic example of an area of American business that was more legend than real, the business of high technology. World War II had saved his company and given him the market that Detroit and Hollywood had not. But that was over. He had been searching for a field that he could dominate without dependence on any entity except the American public, and now he believed he had found it. He had found it in an improbable place, Santa Fe, at an unexpected time, a brief week's vacation before Christmas in 1943 when his mind was filled with the problems of making a guided missile fly for the Navy. The new idea, an instant camera, which had been received as a sudden, incredibly comprehensive intuition in which "the camera, the film, and the physical chemistry became so clear to me," had evolved in three years to a working system. Now it was waiting in his hotel room, waiting to be exposed to the Optical Society, waiting to become the field for which he had hungered all his life: *his* field, his alone, his monopoly, his science that would astonish an audience of millions of people all across America, all over the world. The elevator stopped at his floor and Land leaped out, raced down the dark corridor. There was no more time. He heard the wind crying outside, rattling the windows of the hotel.

2

The Picture

New York, 1947

Dr. Max Herzberger and Dr. Mary Warga gave an account of their recent visits to optical spectroscopic laboratories in England and France, and particularly of the Réunion d'Opticiens in Paris at which they represented the Optical Society of America. Dr. W. E. Meggers of the U.S. Bureau of Standards contributed interesting anecdotes, as did Mr. N. A. Esserman of the Australian National Standards Laboratory, who had the distinction of having traveled the greatest distance to attend the meeting." Thus were recorded the reports given during the dessert-and-coffee course of the informal dinner session of the winter meeting of the Optical Society of America on February 21 by O. S. Duffendack, the chairman of the program committee.

The photographer from the *New York Times* was not entertained by Herzberger and Warga, nor was he moved by the account of the latest in European equipment for the recording of infrared spectra, nor by the social highlights of the Réunion d'Opticiens. He was ready to kill for a drink. He had walked, run rather, since the force of the wind had propelled him at a trot, struggling to keep his feet under him, from the IRT to the Hotel Pennsylvania. His shoes were soaked and his overcoat, thrown on a pile of late arrivals' coats, hats, and galoshes, soggy. He plotted revenge on the night photo editor who had handed him this dog of an assignment when he punched in for the evening shift. What a joke! A bunch of beards escaped from a college campus living it up in New York on creamed chicken and Jell-O salad. Even the women had beards to his jaundiced eye as he scanned the Georgian Room, where four hundred diners applauded Duffendack politely while dessert plates were cleared.

The *Times* photographer had noticed with mild surprise, however, that a number of his colleagues were present: Herb Nichols, head photographer of the *Christian Science Monitor;* an Associated Press photographer; a man from *Life;* all with their camera equipment. They looked as bored as he felt, waiting for something to justify their presence or anticipating an opportunity to escape to the bar, the city room, or home. The photographer decided that the coverage of this academic sewing circle was heavy enough to justify another hour. Maybe someone worth shooting would show up. He noticed several reporters standing together near the door at the back of the stuffy room, staring blankly at the three great chandeliers, the peeling gilt, the scarred banquet furniture. Too far away for him to get their attention without making himself conspicuous, he decided, so he leaned back in his chair and shut his eyes.

Duffendack rose to introduce the next speaker. The perfect name for the chairman of this bunch, the *Times* man thought as the toastmaster sat down and a beardless young man stood up to scattered applause. His baby face set in a grim smile of greeting, this person began speaking in a low, toneless voice as the photographer felt blessed sleep overtaking him. He'd give it another half hour, then take a powder, if he had to walk over tables to get out of there. As he drifted off, the word *camera* registered on his consciousness. He opened an eye. The speaker said that photography had been his hobby. He had been studying it during the war when he was working on guided missiles for the Navy. "I don't know much about photography," he said with becoming modesty, his dark gray three-piece suit and conservative diagonally striped tie giving more the appearance of an assistant bank manager than an optical scientist. His eyes, however, belied the bland façade. The mouth smiled, the voice smiled, the eyes were deadly serious. "But as an amateur hobbyist, I have read most of the histories, particularly those dealing with the Fox Talbot experiments." Familiar with neither Fox nor Talbot, the photographer began to drift again, but he revived as the speaker left the podium and crossed the room to a small oak table in the corner surrounded by three metal chairs and a folding screen. Two men stepped forward to collapse the screen, revealing a large portrait camera on a tripod flanked by floodlights. The *Times* photographer prepared to make his getaway. The young guy was going to take pictures of the beards. The photographer reached for his camera case and started for the door.

Land sat down in front of the camera. Wait a minute; he was going to take his own picture. The *Times* man paused in his flight as the floods were switched on, one behind the camera, one to Land's right. Land continued talking, describing to his audience, some of whom stood up to see better, what he was doing. He picked up a photographer's rubber bulb attached to the shutter bezel of the camera by a slender air hose. Land's face contorted in a brief smile as he squeezed the bulb, the click of the shutter clearly audible in the room. "Now I am going to switch on the electric motor that drives the processing rollers," he said. Herb Nichols of the *Monitor* moved closer and took a flash shot of the scene. Gathered around Land and the big camera were several men and women, their expressions, as they stared down at him, ranging from puzzled to skeptical. Another photographer raised his camera and shot the group from the reverse angle, putting Nichols in the background behind Land. Nichols had a puzzled expression, too. A waiter dropped a spoon and the clatter echoed in the room. Land sat looking at a darkroom timer with a large sweep-second hand on the table in front of him. "Fifty seconds," he managed in a voice so tight it croaked.

Otto Wolf opened the gleaming, raw-metal chamber attached to the mahogany back of the beautiful old Deardorff camera and, using a knife, sliced off two sheets of paper the size of letterhead, tightly stuck together. He handed them to Land, who was still seated, still staring at the camera's orb staring back at him. Otto thrust the paper sandwich at him again; he took it and turned to look at the Graflex of the *Monitor* photographer, his face thoughtful, serious, his mouth no longer smiling but compressed in a tight line. Watch me, said his eyes, but he did not speak. Watch me. The room was hushed. Watch me. He peeled the two sheets apart with a crackle and presented them to Nichols's camera, which instantly responded. A gasp rippled around the room.

Land held in his right hand a brilliant sepia image of himself, the face only slightly less than life size. His left hand, resting on the table, gripped the negative image of the same sober face caught by his own squeeze of the bulb just as the smile disappeared. The tableau held for a moment, then the *Times* man tipped over his chair, plunging toward Land, holding his camera high, shoving past guests and waiters. In an instant Land was surrounded by a wall of photographers and reporters clamoring for him to repeat, explain, pose, stand up. He did none of these. He smiled again at Otto, this time a beatific smile of joy and redemption. He waited while Duffendack cleared a space in front of the table so the room could see him once again. When it quieted, Land repeated the process of instant self-portraiture to the accompaniment of a continuous rattle of flash-guns.

The denouement was documented this time by every photographer present. Land repeated the two expressions with uncanny accuracy: the sober image of his face in his own photograph beside the riveting challenge of eyes that commanded the attention of the press cameras. Holding the picture of himself close to his face, he presented two different men separated by a great event, the old Land and the new Land. Between them lay an epiphany, the manifestation of the intuitive experience in Santa Fe three years earlier that had offered him what he had been seeking all his life, a field of his own, a *domain* that he alone could inhabit, command, and control. It did not belong to the man in the picture, the sober, serious, thoughtful man. It belonged to the young wizard who held the magic image, the shaman whose eyes burned into the camera. In an electric instant Land had reinvented photography, his company, and himself.

Never was a birth so vividly recorded. The picture appeared in *Life* magazine one week later as a full page, one of the classic photographs of the decade, reprinted in every photographic retrospective of the forties and fifties subsequently published. It appeared next morning on the front page of the second section of the *New York Times* along with William Laurence's column-long story, more words than the *Times* gave to battles, elections, and the deaths of great men that day. It appeared on the front page of the *Rochester Democrat and Chronicle,* to be viewed with mixed emotions by the management and employees of Eastman Kodak in that company town. It appeared in newspapers and magazines all over America and in most of the world press. Instant photography achieved instant awareness. Everything was explained, everything stated, everything shown, about the man and the process, in one picture. It was recorded over and over again that evening until there could be no doubt that every photographer present had it and had it exactly as Land had rehearsed it.

The informal dinner session of the winter meeting of the Optical Society of America degenerated into a party. Howie Rogers, who had arrived just before dinner, just after the equipment truck, struggling in from the snowbound Merritt Parkway, Bill McCune, Otto Wolf, Meroë Morse, and David Grey took turns shooting pictures of the guests with the Speed Graphic while Land demonstrated the processing with a small set of rollers on the table. The reporters crowded around him. Occasionally the big 8 x 10 winked, sometimes catching Land with his head down as he manipulated the rollers. He was asked repeatedly when it would be on the market and how much it would cost. "It will be several months before we can say." Was the paper negative discarded? "Yes, but we can produce a film-based negative that can be used for making additional prints." "Combinations of different films and different chemical formulations will produce a wide range of speeds, contrasts, and other photographic characteristics." He smiled at Laurence and said, "The new processes are inherently adaptable for making X rays, pictures in color, and motion pictures." Every pen scratched every pad. Howie winced, all too aware of the towering cliffs that must be scaled to achieve color.

Land indicated one of the images that covered the table in front of him, showing only the top of his head and his fingertips. He laughed and said, "This is one of the most significant pictures we have taken this evening. It illustrates a very important point. If you are not satisfied with a picture, this new process allows you to retake" — the word was emphasized — "the picture immediately and correct the fault. You know that you have a perfect picture *on the spot*. You need never be disappointed again." Over and over the process was repeated. No one was disappointed. People crowded close to those fortunate enough to have their pictures taken. But already the distinction between verbs was being discussed. These pictures were not "made," the image recorded, sent to a lab or a darkroom to be developed, fixed, and printed, later to be returned, perhaps to the owner of the face in question, perhaps not. These pictures were *taken*, then given back to the subject; the entire process of pose, exposure, anticipation, and response was shared by both the subject and the picture-taker. It was a new experience, a new pleasure.

Each time Land tripped the shutter on the Speed Graphic or the big Deardorff, light, supplied by a flashbulb in the case of the former or the floodlights for the latter, entered through the lens and fell upon the film, delivering some of its energy to the silver halide crystals coated on the surface. The energy caused a few atoms of pure metallic silver to form within some of the crystals; the more light received by a spot on the film, the more atoms of silver created. When developed, the crystals of silver halide containing pure silver turned black. Thus, the brightest areas of the image, Land's forehead, for instance, were the blackest after development. Dark areas of the scene, such as his eyes and brows, registered on the film by crystals that were not exposed, hence did not turn dark on development. This latent image, which reversed the light and dark values, was the negative. Conventional photography accomplished development by immersion of the negative in a chemical agent, usually hydroquinone, in a darkroom so that no additional light could affect the silver halide record of the original scene. After development the negative was bathed in a solution of sodium thiosulfate, or hypo, which dissolved the unexposed and undeveloped crystals and washed them away. Finally the negative was fixed and dried. To produce a usable picture, one had to repeat the process in a darkroom, exposing a sheet of photosensitive paper through the negative to reverse the reversal, and the resultant print, then a true representation of the natural scene, again had to be developed, fixed, washed, and dried.

Land accomplished his magic in a novel and ingenious way. He used the silver normally washed away by the hypo, the silver that represented the dark areas of the scene, to form the dark areas of the print. All the chemicals needed for the development process, the hydroquinone and the hypo, plus some others, resided in a jelly the consistency of soft butter, encapsulated in a sealed chamber Land called the pod. A pod was attached to each sheet of the positive print paper. After the camera exposed the photosensitive negative paper to the light of the scene, the two sheets were pulled together, face to face, by the processing rollers and wrung out like two towels going through a clothes wringer at once. As they passed through the steel rollers, the pod ruptured and the viscous chemicals extended evenly between them over their entire common surface. The success of the process depended completely on the precision of that chemical delivery system: the absolutely smooth surfaces of the two rollers; the carefully regulated pressure between them; the exactly measured quantity of reagent needed to cover the surface common to negative and positive without missing a corner or leaking beyond the edges. When the chemicals touched the two sheets they began to work quickly. The hydroquinone turned the exposed silver halide crystals into silver on the negative. The hypo gathered into solution the unexposed crystals which, rather than being washed away, transferred with elegant precision to the positive sheet, where the silver deposited the positive image. Thus, Land formed the negative and positive simultaneously.

The developer performed two functions: it held the exposed silver grains to the negative and developed the unexposed silver in the hypo solution on the surface of the positive. The hypo functioned as the bridge, depositing unexposed crystals from the film to the positive until the image was completely formed from the silver ions they contained. The entire process took only fifty seconds for the demonstration at the Hotel Pennsylvania. When stripped apart, the positive print appeared virtually dry, while the negative image, no longer useful in its paper version and slightly damp, would quickly dry on exposure to the air. Land chose not to discuss the other chemicals contained in the pod. He would say only that the sepia images, carefully examined and generally admired by the professional photographers for their tonal quality and lack of grain, were permanent and that tests had shown them to be as resistant to fading as conventional prints.

The press threw themselves at Land's feet. The *Times* called the "one-step" camera "revolutionary." In addition to three subheadlines, a cutaway diagram, a full column of text, and the electrifying picture of Land opening the era of instant photography, it printed an extraordinary editorial entitled "The Camera Does the Rest" on the editorial page of the same edition. The title played on the famous Kodak slogan, "You press the button, we do the rest." "All this seems so simple," the *Times* pundit wrote, "that, as usual, we wonder why it was not done before. . . . In ordinary developing and fixing, silver in the unexposed areas is lost — washed away. This very silver now forms a positive which pops out of the camera when the knob is turned. There is nothing like this in the history of photography."

The editor of *National Photo Dealer,* the trade magazine of photographic equipment dealers and photofinishers, headlined his account "Bombshell in Photography?" After some handwringing about the potential impact of Land's invention on the photographic industry, he cautioned his concerned readers: "We cannot repeat the mistake of the ice-manufacturers who attempted to sweep the electric refrigerator off the market by trying to prove that ice is superior." William Laurence, as usual, was able to recognize the future when he saw it. Watching intently as Land stripped apart the first instant picture, he leaned back for a moment, rolled his eyes to the ceiling, and laughed, saying, "All we need now for our morning edition is a built-in caption writer."

3

Harvard

Norwich, Cambridge, and New York, 1926

Edwin Herbert Land was born in Bridgeport, Connecticut, a cradle of American industry, on May 7, 1909, to Harry and Martha Land. He went to Bridgeport public schools until his family moved to nearby Norwich, where he attended Norwich Academy to prepare for college. At seventeen, a slender boy, handsome and self-possessed, the only child of a stable, loving family, he journeyed to Cambridge, Massachusetts, to enter Harvard. His father had a prosperous salvage and scrap metal business, and the son grew up in a comfortable middle-class home. His nickname, Din, was his own baby pronunciation of Edwin. Land had a shy smile and piercing black eyes under dark, heavy brows. His thick black hair sat above his broad forehead like a cap. He had a quiet self-confidence, enhanced by modest athletic prowess on soccer fields and running tracks and burnished by a brilliant academic career at Norwich Academy. His recent summers had been spent in upstate New York at a boys' camp run by an MIT engineer. Julius Silver, a young camp counselor from New York City, became a friend and confidant. Silver was impressed by Land and another boy, who had installed an electrical system at the camp when Land was only twelve. As he got to know him better, the counselor discovered that Land was deeply interested in something called polarized light. Land's shy explanations of this phenomenon and accounts of experiments conducted in a basement laboratory at home so interested Silver that he resolved not to lose sight of the boy.

Science and invention consumed Land's attention. At seventeen he was deeply concerned with how he should spend his time and intellect and what field he could make his own. He carried to Cambridge a romantic vision of science developed by omnivorous reading and the certainty that he would achieve scientific success, the definition of which was clearly, if broadly, defined in his mind. He was filled with impatience and frustration, as are most seventeen-year-olds, but his were focused on the question of which scientific path he should follow. When Land was a child, a handsome mantel clock, of which his father was inordinately proud and which chimed the hours, the halves, and the quarters, captured his attention. One evening when his parents were out, the boy climbed to the mantelpiece on a living room chair, took the clock down, and, using a fine screwdriver, disassembled it, laying the parts out carefully and methodically on a newspaper spread out on the oriental carpet.

He worked quickly to complete the autopsy and reassemble the corpus, but he was still on his knees among the pieces when his parents returned. His usually indulgent father showed his anger by punishing the boy and collecting the parts of the timepiece in a box and sending them to a clockmaker. Land thought long that night in bed about the experience and would remember it the rest of his life. He had failed; he couldn't complete the experiment, not because he was not capable, but because he didn't have control. He had learned something about the technology of clocks, but more than a little about something more important. What good are knowledge and technique without control? His father told him he could set up a lab in the basement as long as clocks and other household necessities remained out of bounds.

Land admired Michael Faraday, one of the scientific heroes of the nineteenth century. Faraday, the son of a blacksmith, was apprenticed at an early age to a bookbinder and, in addition to mastering the artful mechanics of that trade, read all the scientific volumes that came through the bindery. Michael seized the opportunity to attend a lecture by Sir Humphry Davy, made copious notes, and wrote to the great chemist. Davy granted Michael an audience and, astonished at his intelligence and zeal, became his mentor. He took the youth into his laboratory as an assistant. Faraday, he said, was his greatest discovery.

The young man raced from one achievement to another in chemistry and the exciting new field of electricity. At thirty-four he discovered the hydrocarbon benzene, which opened doors to a new branch of organic chemistry. He developed the process of electrolysis and described electromagnetic induction, which led to the development of the electric generator. Late in his career he demonstrated that the plane of polarized light is deflected by a strong magnetic field. His experiments with electromagnetic force stimulated James Clerk Maxwell and Heinrich Hertz. Radio, television, radar — a host of current inventions — sprang from seeds that were planted by Faraday. The greatest experimental scientist of his era, he became one of the towering figures in the pantheon. The ambition to become another Faraday could heat the blood of a seventeen-year-old aspiring scientist.

In 1926, Thomas Edison was seventy-nine, still creating, ranging widely, trying among other things to develop a source of native rubber in the United States, the subject of the last patent of his life. Edison had invented or perfected an amazing list of devices, among them the stock ticker, the automatic and multiplex telegraph, the incandescent lamp, the phonograph, the motion picture camera and projector, the carbon telephone transmitter, the alkaline storage battery, methods for concentrating iron ore, a manufacturing process for cement, the first central power station, the prototype electric distribution grid, naval equipment, techniques for chemical production — there appeared to be no end to what he could accomplish, although his nonconsumable cigar was not a success. In spite of the fact that he had only three months of formal education, many of the technological artifacts of the twentieth century bore his stamp if not his name. An irate railroad baggagemaster destroyed Edison's hearing by boxing his ears when the boy was twelve. By the time Edison was thirty-two, he had introduced the modern age of light.

Success brought Edison medals "by the quart." A tireless experimenter and an unfailing optimist, he said, when his laboratory in West Orange, New Jersey, burned down, "All of our mistakes have been destroyed," and built a new "invention factory" on the same site. Eccentric, disheveled, with a vocabulary unacceptable in polite society, he was nevertheless viewed as the epitome of American inventive genius, an individual who had changed the conditions of life virtually overnight by the application in appropriate proportion of "perspiration and inspiration." He was a great defender of the patent system. In his eighty-four years he was granted 1,093 patents, more than any man then or since. His first was awarded when he was twenty-two years old.

Alexander Graham Bell had died in 1922. Born within three weeks of Edison, he was one of the few great inventors of the era with a formal education. He attended the University of Edinburgh and University College, London, whereas Edison, Ford, the Wrights, and George Eastman had little or no formal learning. Bell's wife, like Edison, was deaf. Bell spent the early part of his career teaching the deaf and studying the mechanics of hearing. In 1871, he immigrated to Boston to teach at Sarah Fuller's school for the deaf. Helen Keller was among his private pupils. His studies, similar to Edison's in many areas, led Bell to design an "electric speaking telegraph," later called a telephone. In 1876, he made his first voice transmission, the inadvertent "Mr. Watson, come here, I want you," from his laboratory at 5 Exeter Place. Bell made the first "long distance" call in 1876 from Boston to a building on Osborn Street in Cambridge, where Land was to have his personal laboratory and office sixty-six years later. Edison maintained good terms with Bell and made many contributions to telephone technology, including the carbon transmitter. One which was not patented was the expression "Hello," which Edison first used as a substitute for the phrase, then universally in use, "Are you ready to talk?" or in England, "Are you there?" Bell's initial patent application for the telephone — the single most valuable patent ever granted — was received at the patent office on February 14, 1876, just two hours before Elisha Gray filed notice for a similar device.

Henry Ford was sixty-three when Land entered Harvard, sixteen years younger than Edison, whom Ford had idolized ever since he met the inventor in 1895 at an early job as chief engineer of the Detroit Edison Company. In 1926, Ford loomed as the greatest industrial figure in the world. He had built half of all the cars sold in America. River Rouge, newly completed, was the largest integrated industrial complex in any country, its tentacles extending via Ford ships and railroad lines to mines, forests, and subsidiary factories that produced most of the elements of the "universal car," the Tin Lizzie, the Model T. The T was entering its last years, sales down somewhat from the peak in 1923 when 1,700,000 were sold at a price of about $300 apiece. Ford now spent more and more time on political and social activities. Opinionated, inflexible, and bigoted, he had, however, startled the industrial world and his own workers by establishing the $5.00 a day minimum wage, almost twice his own company's former average pay.

In 1926, Ford prepared a celebration in Edison's honor, the Golden Jubilee of Light, to be held in Dearborn, not West Orange. Ford swept up Edison's Menlo Park laboratory and transported every stick to Michigan. He created the Edison Institute there and even brought in the railroad station where young Tom Edison had been thrown off the train when, experimenting with chemicals, he set fire to a baggage car. Ford, the magnate who had changed the face of America from rural villages connected by dirt roads to industrial cities and crowded highways, was obsessed with collecting, preserving in the shadow of his factories the artifacts and architecture of his youth. Edison complied with this fanciful recreation with wry good grace. He allowed as how the rebuilt laboratory was about 99 percent perfect. "What's wrong?" asked his anxious host.

"We never kept the floor this clean," Edison replied.

George Eastman was seventy-two in 1926. His only extravagance in a frugal, hard-working youth went for his hobby, photography. From high school in Rochester, New York, he became a messenger, then a bookkeeper at a local bank. He began experimenting to develop a dry photographic plate after chemicals packed in his trunk had ruined his clothes on a summer trip to Mackinac Island. He was granted a patent in England when he was twenty-five and one in America a year later. He sold the English patent and opened a shop in Rochester to manufacture photographic plates. By 1926 he employed more than fifteen thousand people. Kodak, the name he coined, had become one of the three largest photographic companies in the world. "You press the button, we do the rest" was translated into a dozen languages. Eastman's film was indispensable to Edison for his motion picture work. Genuinely committed to research, Eastman's laboratories had helped make the American chemical industry self-sufficient during the world war, and Kodak was moving toward world leadership in the manufacture of chemicals. The only setback had come at the hands of the courts. Eastman had attempted to circumvent Hannibal Goodwin's patent for flexible film, but in 1913 the federal court found in favor of Goodwin, and Eastman had to pay $5 million to Goodwin's heirs and others.

Harvard Square in 1926 was the center of a small town within a small city. Harvard was an island of privilege in the blue-collar neighborhoods of Cambridge — Irish, Greek, Italian, and German. The stores of Harvard Square outwardly formed a cluster not unlike those that might be found in any small New England community, their clientele predominantly white, Anglo-Saxon, Protestant, and affluent. The Harvard Square tobacconists and tailors rivaled the best in Boston. Trolley cars ran down Massachusetts Avenue to Main Street, the Massachusetts Institute of Technology, the Charles River, and on to Boston. The fare was ten cents; the *Boston Evening Transcript* cost three cents; tuition at Harvard was $300 a year.

Abbott Lawrence Lowell, president of the university, had succeeded Charles William Eliot, a chemist, in 1909. Lowell, an aristocrat from the wealthy New England family of legendary lineage, presided over the largest university library in the world and a faculty renowned for its cultural lions: George Lyman Kittredge, the Shakespearean scholar; Bliss Perry, the editor; John Livingston Lowes, the literary scholar; Roger Bigelow ("Frisky") Merriman, the historian, whom Theodore White, who followed Land as an undergraduate, called "perhaps the most colorful character on Harvard's then vivid faculty of characters." Several new dormitories had just been completed in Harvard Yard and one on the Charles, forerunners of the seven beautiful houses that were to be built along the river, presenting to Boston one of its most majestic vistas.

Harvard's buildings formed an enclave behind walls of brick and wrought iron, shaded by oaks, maples, elms, and chestnuts, indeed draped in ivy. Land was a fortunate young man. His father could afford to send him to the preeminent university in America. Land brought with him a first-rate academic record and a hungry, questioning mind. The circumstances suggested that Land and Harvard were about to begin a relationship that would lead predictably to years of study, degrees, success, possibly wealth. He could hardly have imagined that he was beginning instead an association that was to be intermittent, unorthodox, nontraditional in the extreme, one which would endure throughout his life to the great benefit of both parties.

There was a turmoil within him: he was searching for his field, the field that would make his name known to the world of science. He had read all the scientific literature that was available to him at Norwich. "I was fortunate enough to acquire Robert W. Wood's *Physical Optics,* which I read nightly the way our forefathers read the Bible," he said. Harvard offered him all of science to examine, and from it he sought his opportunity. "As I review the nature of the creative drive in the inventive scientists that have been around me, as well as in myself," he later wrote, "I find the first event is an urge to make a significant intellectual contribution that can be tangibly embodied in a product or process." This owes more to Edison than to Faraday, the great experimenter. "The urge, as pure urge, precedes in a perfectly generalized way the specific contribution — so that the individual hunts for a *domain* in which to utilize the urge."

That search for a domain of science to call his own began before Land was seventeen and continued throughout his life. He precisely described the nuances of his search: "This early stage need not be early in life, it can occur intermittently throughout life. The hunting process is fascinating to contemplate because during it there may be many abortive first approaches at the verbal level to fields which are then rejected as being either not significant enough or not feasible enough — and then, quite suddenly, a field will emerge conceptually so full blown in the creator's mind that the words can scarcely come from his mouth fast enough to describe the new field in its full implication and elaborateness."

The exhilaration of discovery, the sudden rush of ideas, and the struggle to articulate them as soon as possible after the conceptual moment, seemed intuitively known to Land at seventeen. To suspect that such moments lay ahead of him generated an urgency to narrow the choice to that domain which was most likely to yield a great insight. It could not be trivial. It must be significant. It must also be tangible. So much in science had been accomplished! Faraday had moved the world forward a hundred years a hundred years earlier. Edison had compressed genius and energy enough for three lifetimes into his span. Land said, "At the age in which each week seems like a year, I picked field after field before I decided that the great opportunity was polarized light."

The principles of light and how it is transmitted had been studied and debated for more than three hundred years. In the seventeenth century, Christiaan Huygens, a Dutch physicist, advanced the theory that light traveled with a wavelike motion through a weightless invisible medium called luminiferous ether. This ran contrary to Isaac Newton's view that light was composed of minute particles or corpuscles that traveled in straight lines at enormous speed. As early as 1675, Olaus Rømer, a Danish astronomer, had measured the speed of light with surprising accuracy. Huygens's wave theory survived subsequent experiments, although the notion of luminiferous ether did not. Waves of light were believed to travel in a forward direction, vibrating at right angles in every direction from the forward path. Certain substances in nature, such as the semiprecious stone tourmaline or crystals of Iceland spar, also called calcite, could be used to split the light into oppositely polarized beams. In 1808, Étienne-Louis Malus, a French engineer and physicist, observed that the glaring image of the sun reflected in the windows of the Luxembourg Palace was extinguished when he looked through a prism of calcite, the first recorded example of one of the effects of polarization. Jean-Baptiste Biot, another Frenchman, discovered the polarizing powers of tourmaline. These natural polarizers, although rare and expensive, were not uncommon in early optical laboratories.

The crystal device most widely used to demonstrate and experiment with polarization was the Nicol prism, developed from calcite in 1828 by William Nicol, a Scottish physicist, but its fragility and rarity made it as costly as its predecessors. Even though there was as yet no commercial use for polarization outside the laboratory, the "classical problem" — a problem known to exist in science but with no known solution — of producing an artificial polarizer had attracted a good deal of attention and energy. In 1852, William Bird Herapath, an English physician, came close to producing an artificial polarizing material. With the aid of a student named Phelps and a dog whose name has not survived, Herapath discovered that tiny needle-shaped crystals could be formed by combining iodine with quinine salt. Phelps liberally dosed the dog with quinine, then added iodine to its urine; the resultant crystals possessed intriguing properties. Studying them under his microscope, Herapath observed that some crystals seemed transparent and some opaque. As he delicately moved them, he realized that they were all transparent unless they were crossed one on another at an angle of 90 degrees. They were in fact polarizers of light. He tried diligently to create larger and more robust crystals, but with no success. Seventy years of experimentation with iodide-quinine crystals followed, but the art was little advanced. They proved too fragile, too small, and useless in the laboratory, the only venue that needed or wanted them.

Land was seeking something scientifically significant. The problem of creating an artificial polarizer fit that criterion. But he wanted something beyond that. He wanted to make an intellectual contribution "that can be tangibly embodied in a product or a process." What product could a polarizer embody? What was the need? Land discovered his market and his product on Broadway. At seventeen, walking one tumultuous night in Times Square, a day's train ride from Harvard Square with its little trolleys and sober Colonial buildings, Land experienced the conceptual exhilaration of field, product, and process, all rushing into his mind at once. The visual clichés of Broadway stunned the boy from Norwich, Connecticut. He was immersed in light. The great lighted signs were stupendous, brilliant, the headlights of the cabs and buses dazzling. Surrounded by the scintillation of the early twentieth century, Land found the glare of Broadway overpowering, dangerous. He perceived an urgent need to control the light of the scene. The method was polarization, the product some sort of shield or filter, cheap, easy to fabricate. The process — the process remained enigmatic, but it must involve the creation of a crystal, perhaps in a transparent substance such as glass or plastic, to comb out the vibrations of light that produced glare so blinding that you could be run down by a taxi while crossing Times Square if you did not keep your wits about you. But he had isolated the field from the broad spectrum, that was the important thing. He decided not to return to Harvard, but to stay in New York to solve the classical problem.

4

The Window

New York, 1927–1928

Land's parents, pleased with a brilliant beginning to their son's education, were stunned when he told them he was not going back to Harvard for his second year. He planned to study and experiment in New York. He would use his college allowance to pay his expenses in the city. It would be no more expensive than Cambridge, perhaps less if he were careful. Reluctantly, fearfully, they consented. He had already found a room in New York in the basement of an apartment house on West Fifty-fifth Street just off Broadway. It was a shabby block not far from the lights and the theater crowds, a street of small shops, restaurants, and an occasional hotel, dirtier than Boston as all New York streets were, redolent of automobile exhaust and horse manure in about equal measure. Land's room was a tiny, windowless cell situated behind the furnace, but it contained a bed, a chair, a table, and an electric light, the essentials he needed for the first part of the experiment.

He spent his waking hours at the New York Public Library sixteen blocks away. Every morning he walked downtown, stopping for a cup of scalding coffee at a lunch counter on Broadway, to be at the doors when they opened at nine o'clock. The two massive stone lions, Patience and Fortitude, gazed impassively on the boy as he ran up the broad steps and entered the portals of one of the great free libraries of the world. In 1927 it contained over two million volumes, more than Harvard's renowned Widener Library. The scientific collection alone included almost two hundred thousand items. The architects Carrère and Hastings had created this mighty Greco-Roman temple in front of Bryant Park in 1898–1911.

Its main reading room, a lofty chamber with light streaming down from the high clerestory windows on rows of long oak tables, murmured with the sounds of study, the scrape of chairs on the stone floor, pages turning, the wheels of a book cart, the echoing slam of a card catalogue drawer pushed home, an occasional ruffle of snores. Such a library provided an appropriately noble promontory from which to survey the classical problem, and Land, in control of his course of study, began his reading with fierce energy. He planned to devour the entire literature available on the subject of polarization and to reread everything he had already found at Norwich and Harvard, with special attention to the works of William Herapath.

Land had first encountered Herapath in a book by Sir David Brewster, the inventor of the kaleidoscope, the television of 1850. No genteel home lacked one; it reposed on the library table to be passed around for family evenings or shared with guests. Brewster wanted to incorporate the vivid colors produced by polarization with those reflected by the bits of colored glass in his popular device. He hoped to use a crystal of herapathite for the eye lens of the kaleidoscope.

Brewster's mention of Herapath's work caught Land's attention. Herapath was an unusual scientist, not only creative, inquisitive, and persistent, but able in his writings to communicate a sense of personal excitement and enthusiasm. Land discovered a series of articles by Herapath in the British publication *Philosophical Magazine* that chronicled his attempts, while he was actually performing the experiments, to create a larger iodide-quinine crystal, which was to be the first man-made polarizer. Herapath's goal had been to grow a crystalline structure large enough to cover the eyepiece of his microscope, one eighth of an inch in diameter. He ultimately failed to create a large herapathite, as he had optimistically named it. The crystals proved so fragile that they crumbled at the slightest touch, yet his accounts of the struggle proved fascinating. Land later told a group at the Franklin Institute that "though Herapath failed to produce a material in useful form, his vision of what he hoped to accomplish, his enthusiastic and eloquent descriptions of what he thought he was just about to achieve, have been a vital stimulus to all who have in the last eighty years encountered his writings. Herapath did not discover the material, only its polarizing properties. But he took the new polarizer to his heart with the same elation that subsequent readers throughout these eighty years have felt over the material. He felt that it was his very own, even as each successive generation of readers have felt that in discovering his articles they have discovered his polarizer." In a burst of candor Land added, "I confess that no one felt this proprietary interest more keenly than I did upon my first reading of his articles."

Herapath and his successors attempted to make larger crystals. As Land's studies progressed he began to realize that success might lie in the opposite direction. "It is a curious property of research activity," Land told his audience at the Franklin Institute in 1937, "that after the problem has been solved the solution usually seems obvious. This is true not only for those who have not previously been acquainted with the problem, but also for those who have worked over it for years. As they regard their finished work they cannot help wondering why a simple, rational process that can be performed in a day took them, rational people, ten years to develop. In research, as in the whole civilizing process, why does it take so long to learn so little? In our laboratory notebooks, as we review them, it is as hard to find the answer to research slowness as it is difficult to find the answer to civilizing slowness in our history books. There is the same strange interpenetration of methodical, intellectual activity stimulated and interrupted by irrelevant emotional and economic daily problems."

Land had his share of daily problems, which may or may not have seemed irrelevant at the moment, but the abstractions of polarizers and headlights were far more pressing and immediate. He concentrated ferociously on his quest as he alternated between long days in the reference room on Fifth Avenue and Forty-second Street and his walks at night, books in hand, to look at the lights of Broadway. When he settled to his evening reading in the room behind the furnace, his task was as specific to him as any college curriculum. It had begun to dawn on him that the answer to Herapath's problem might be to develop smaller crystals, millions of them, rather than one large "artificial tourmaline." Small crystals aligned in rows like a comb in a transparent medium would form an "optical grain," an "asymmetrical optical texture," as he described it in one of his lab books. He could imagine several ways to construct optical grain.

Among the ideas he wanted to examine was a polarizing device used by François Arago, a French physicist, in 1812, which consisted of a pile of glass plates coated with metal. Light reflected from the plates or transmitted through them at an angle exhibited an appreciable degree of polarization. Land had collected a few rudimentary pieces of equipment in his room, but lack of space, inadequate light, and fear of discovery by the building superintendent severely limited him. His hours in the great vault of the library reading room and the solitude of the stacks had infected him with Herapath's eloquent enthusiasm. His own thinking had been liberated. He believed he knew what none of the other scientists who had struggled with this question for more than a century had guessed. The classical problem seemed in his grasp. He could make his mark high on the tree. But he sat alone in an airless room that vibrated to the combustion of the furnace and the passage of the subway a block away. He had come beyond the point where books alone could help him. He needed a laboratory, equipment, colleagues, everything that Harvard might have offered. But time was short. He was committed to his own plan — New York; now he had to make a success of it. He was stubbornly determined to succeed on his own terms, in his own way. He responded to his need for assistance in unusual fashion for a scholar and an aspiring scientist: he ran an ad in a newspaper.

Land advertised for a "mechanical dentist," a dental technician interested in doing some experimental work. He had no other address to give but that of his apartment, and he was astonished when twenty men knocked at his basement door the day after the advertisement appeared in the classified columns. He invited them in as they arrived and asked them to demonstrate their technical skills with a small gas torch and some gold, which he had each man melt down. Into this Holmesian vignette marched a character who would have done credit to Conan Doyle. Ernest Calabro, a small, dandified man, introduced himself to Land, took in the bizarre scene, and set about organizing it. Each applicant was questioned, tested by Calabro with the torch and the melting pot, and dismissed. When the morning was over, Land was mildly surprised to find that only Ernie was left. He became Land's first employee and stayed with him for twenty-five years. Calabro thought he was answering an ad to assist a dentist. Instead, he found himself in a strange basement workshop with a secretive young man of eighteen who was well dressed but usually disheveled, often highly agitated, prone to long periods of intense activity, rarely volunteering any explanation of what he was trying to accomplish, eating haphazardly, his sleeves rolled up, his shock of dark hair falling in his face as he worked.

Calabro did not have the slightest clue as to what Land was doing. He seemed to have funds, so Calabro called at the basement room regularly for three months, performing tasks that included plating, cutting, forming, and polishing alloy and glass plates. A superb technician with strong hands and an artist's touch, he had indeed helped Land make the right choice of assistants. Calabro was quick, dexterous, and jolly, a man about Broadway who talked confidently about his exploits on the town. Land enjoyed his company, but told him very little, and he made it clear that if Ernie were to speak about the basement room to anyone, the job was finished. One evening as the two of them were walking down Broadway, Land said hesitantly, "Wouldn't it be wonderful if we could have a plate of glass, place another plate over it, rotate it, and have it gradually shut off the light?" Calabro looked at him with a puzzled expression. He had no idea what Land was talking about, but he liked this odd youth; Ernie had a hunch Land was doing something important, they didn't seem to be breaking the law, and, as long as the money was forthcoming, Ernie decided he was going to stick.

The pile of plates proved unproductive. Land returned to the notion that had intrigued him in the library, the idea of not one large crystal but many millions of microscopic crystals uniformly oriented in the same plane. He had given thought to three problems: what crystals to use, what medium to support them, and how to arrange them. Each of these puzzles had an almost infinite number of possible solutions. Land was evolving a way of attacking the imponderables. He described it a few years later: "Of course, the secret that we had then . . . was in knowing that if you dream of something worth doing and then simply go to work on it and don't think anything of personalities, or emotional conflicts, or of money, or of family distractions; if you just think detail by detail of what you have to do next, it is a wonderful dream even though the end is a long way off. . . . If there are about five thousand steps to be taken . . . you start taking the first ten, and . . . twenty after that. . . . It is amazing how quickly you get through . . . 4,990. The last ten steps you never seem to work out. But you keep on coming nearer to giving the world something . . ." Later he wrote, "In my then youthful innocence it seemed to me that these problems could be solved in a rather short time, perhaps a few months."

But it took him almost three years. He found a second colleague, Helen Maislen, a beautiful Smith College graduate whom he met in New York. A bright, attractive, adventuresome brunette whose nickname was Terre, pronounced "Terry," she was an art major who had studied under Clarence Kennedy, but Land set out to make her a scientist. Land's life certainly offered opportunity for adventure. Before long Terre was accompanying him on nocturnal visits to a laboratory building at Columbia University. They climbed up a fire escape and went through a convenient window that was usually left unlocked. There for a few hours each night Land had clandestine access to a well-equipped laboratory.

He had made most of his basic experimental choices. He was attempting to orient herapathite, iodide-quinine crystals, in a small glass cell. He had spent a month grinding the needle-shaped crystals to microscopic fineness with a small hand mill. He then mixed them with a solution of nitrocellulose lacquer, a process that would have caused the Columbia administration grave concern had they been aware of it. He placed the suspension of herapathite in a cylinder of glass a half-inch in diameter and a quarter-inch thick. This hollow lens of reddish-black crystals was then placed in the arms of the device that had brought the two conspirators to Columbia in the first place, a powerful electromagnet that could generate a magnetic field of ten thousand gauss. Terre aimed a bright light at the glass, and Land described the next moment as "the most exciting single event in my life. . . . When the field was turned on . . . slowly and somewhat sluggishly the cell became lighter and quite transparent; when we examined the transmitted light with a Nicol prism, it went from white to black as the prism was turned."

Ernie Calabro would have been amazed. Land had succeeded; he had made the first artificial polarizer. He had done what Herapath had failed to imagine: marshaled millions of tiny iodine needles into perfect linear orientation using magnetic force, so that light shown through them was combed into polarization. It was a vivid moment, a conscious instant of intense personal gratification. They gazed at the tiny glass container glowing in the beam of light. It was useless in any practical sense. It would not do for the headlights of a car. It did not satisfy Land's need for a tangible embodiment of his idea. But it was almost certainly the significant intellectual contribution on which he had staked his New York exile. He had come a thousand steps. The next steps stretched endlessly ahead of him, but he had his first invention in hand. Land and Terre switched off the equipment, pocketed their precious vial, extinguished the lights, and stole out of the window onto the fire escape, into the fragrant night air of Morningside Heights.

5

The Milk Barn

Cambridge and Wellesley Hills, 1929–1932

Land returned to Harvard in 1929. At twenty he had radically altered the circumstances of his life. He was married, and he had made his first major invention. With Terre's help he had progressed beyond the glass capsule of liquid polarizer to the first pieces of hand-formed plastic sheet. Before he left New York he called on Julius Silver for advice about patent protection. Silver, a young corporation lawyer already marked for success on Wall Street and in Washington, questioned Land closely about his work and his plans. He was not surprised to hear that a few years after the twelve-year-old had installed the electric light system at camp he had produced an invention of significance. Silver introduced Land to his friend Donald Brown, a patent attorney. Land and Brown took an immediate liking to each other, and the application for the polarizer patent was initiated. Brown and Silver had a long, thoughtful conversation about the young inventor after he returned to Boston.

The autumn of 1929 brought tumult. The stock market felt its first great shock in late September, just as Land returned to Cambridge. The crash came in October, and the market started a slide that was not to be reversed for eight years. The country's new president, Herbert Hoover, faced a chaotic situation that rapidly worsened with widespread bank failures, foreclosures, and then the first of a series of severe droughts and the beginning of endemic dust storms in the Midwest. Harvard remained an island of relative tranquillity. Land's father had not been a heavy investor in stocks, but his business suffered as the Depression deepened. They had to sacrifice to keep their son in college, but he and his wife were anxious that Land pick up where he had left off three years earlier. A Harvard degree would be even more important in the bad times ahead.

One of the first people Land met on his return to Harvard was George Wheelwright III, a young physics instructor. Wheelwright was in many ways Land's opposite. Tall, sandy-haired, irreverent, loquacious, fond of spirits, cigars, and a funny story, Wheelwright was not at all sure what he wanted to do with his life. Six years older than Land, he had enrolled at Harvard in 1921 with the rather unspecific idea of taking a degree in science, perhaps astronomy. Like Land, he had stayed for only a year, then left to take a job in California with a friend. He was absent from school for five years, enjoyed every minute, and made a considerable amount of money, which was not terribly important to him at the time since he came from a wealthy family. He reentered Harvard in 1927, married his sweetheart, and buckled down to complete his undergraduate work. Astronomy called for physics, and physics demanded math. Wheelwright was bright, and when he applied his considerable talents, he attracted the attention of his professors. In June of 1929, the year Land returned to the university, Wheelwright graduated. He was beginning work in X rays and radium with the thought of a master's degree down the road.

Professor Theodore Lyman, director of the Jefferson Physical Laboratories, asked Wheelwright to teach a course he had taken two years earlier, Electricity and Magnetism, for which he had received a B+. The course was for sophomores and juniors, and Wheelwright thought it might be interesting, even amusing, to become a teacher, so he agreed. A week before the course opened, he mounted the stairs in the old physics building to check the equipment for the experiments he would be using in the course. A young man prowling about the lab seemed bent on the same errand. Wheelwright watched him as he moved rapidly from one setup to another. Wheelwright recalled, "He saw me come in and he rushed to the last experiment, did something, and then came over and said, 'Are you the professor in this course, sir?' I replied, 'I'm the instructor giving it.'

" 'What kind of course are you going to give?'

" 'I'm afraid a dull one. These experiments have been used for a long while. I'd like to see some new ones, but there's no money available. And since they say they still work, I guess we'll have to use them.'

"He looked at me and said, 'What if they don't work?'

" 'Why do you ask?'

" 'Well, I've been trying them and there isn't one here that works any longer. What do you think of that?'

" 'I think it's great.'

"Land's face broke out in a smile, and he said, 'I think we'll get along.' "

They got along very well indeed. Land, for all his reticence, had the ability to charm anyone who interested him, whether it be an Ernie Calabro or a Donald Brown. He and Wheelwright, although opposites in appearance and manner, had much in common. Neither was in awe of Harvard; both had left on their own for an extended period to prove something to themselves and perhaps to their parents. They were brilliant, excited by science, unconventional, and filled with energy. Both were beginning married life in Cambridge in small apartments near the college. Land was the brightest student in Electricity and Magnetism, "the brightest by far," Wheelwright said. Land helped him set up the new equipment Wheelwright had wangled from the department before the course began.

But once into the semester, the instructor experienced some difficulty with his star. "He would cover himself with distinction running the lab and doing the experiment. Then he'd take it home to write it up. When the day came to hand it in it wouldn't be there. I'd call him up and he'd say, 'I'm not quite through.' One day I got his wife on the phone and I said, 'Mrs. Land, can't you do something to get him to finish it?' She said, 'Oh, it's the bane of my existence. He does the same thing when he's fixing things. He works on it as long as he doesn't understand it, but as soon as he understands it, he wants someone else to do it.' " Wheelwright asked her if she could finish the reports on the experiments for Land and send them in. He pointed out that the department required him to lower the grade a point for each day the paper was late. "I know he knows the experiments. He has them letter perfect, but I have to have some proof of it." Terre agreed to finish the papers, and more than once Wheelwright rode his bicycle up Massachusetts Avenue to pick up a paper before the midnight deadline when he'd have to reduce Land's grade.

Wheelwright's classroom style was unconventional. He had, in addition to Land, a nucleus of very bright students. Wheelwright encouraged discussions after the experiments, and if he was asked a question he couldn't answer, which was not infrequently, he wouldn't bluff. "Get

Brooks's *Dictionary of Physics* and look in the second volume. I'm quite sure you'll find it. Then come back and report to us and we'll all know it." This would elicit laughter from the class, but not from Wheelwright's supervisor. He told Wheelwright that he had heard some of the boys in his class say that their instructor didn't know what he was doing. "Well, some of the boys could be right."

"Take a page out of my book. When you don't know something, skim over it." This professor was known for his smoothly delivered lectures.

"Well, I think I'm learning more the other way," Wheelwright replied.

"You're not here to learn, you're here to teach." With that classic admonition, he promised to monitor some of Wheelwright's classes. He did, and Wheelwright began teaching more and learning less.

At the end of the year Wheelwright broached to Land an idea that had been in his mind for some time. He wanted to arrange a laboratory at Harvard in which Land could continue his polarizing work. Land was surprised, flattered, and skeptical. Wheelwright managed a dinner invitation for himself with Professor William Duane, his mentor, and Professor Lyman at Lyman's house. There in his dinner jacket by candlelight he told the two senior Harvard physicists about the young man who was illuminating his class in Electricity and Magnetism. He outlined what Land had accomplished so far in his polarizer work. The three of them lingered at the table over port and cigars. Wheelwright could be very persuasive. One of his associates said George could talk a blue streak. In fact, when he was a small child his mother on more than one occasion had to resort to adhesive tape to stem the flow of her child's conversation. On this occasion he was tactful as well as eloquent. Wheelwright got Land his lab. For the first time in his life, Land was in complete control of the circumstances of his work.

On February 8, 1932, Land presented a paper at a colloquium at Harvard, "A New Polarizer for Light in the Form of an Extensive Synthetic Sheet." The lecture was well attended by an audience of undergraduates, graduates, and not a few professors who filled the seats and lined the periphery of the hall. Wheelwright played, as he described it, Watson to Land's Bell. The audience was attentive and appreciative. Three months later the student-lecturer and the instructor-assistant were walking in Cambridge by Fresh Pond on a chilly spring evening. They had developed a habit of taking long walks, talking in the dark, trying ideas out on each other. Wheelwright had been silent for a while before he said, "You know, Din, what you've got is so important, I think you should have a real laboratory."

"So do I," said the realist at his side.

"Why don't you and I start one? I have some money. I can fund it." There was no response. "Din, how about starting our own lab?" Wheelwright repeated.

"An education without a degree," said Land. It was neither a statement nor a question.

"What the hell does that have to do with anything?" asked his friend.

In June, Land left Harvard for the second and last time. He was one semester short of completing the requirements for graduation. Wheelwright, for his part, was not sorry to forget about his teaching career, if indeed it had been a career, or his erstwhile master's degree. The two of them were filled with ideas for inventions. Wheelwright talked about developing a fuel cell, a self-contained power source, which would be a "prime mover" for farms with no electricity. Land had ideas about stereoscopic movies using polarized light and a hundred other schemes, but the polarizing automobile headlight system was uppermost in his mind. They rented a room on the top floor of the Harvard Square Garage, at the corner of Boylston and Mount Auburn streets, and set up shop. A hand-lettered sign on the door proclaimed it the Land-Wheelwright Laboratories. They were in business. Harvard dozed in the summer sun a few blocks away.

Land had reached a dangerous juncture in his polarizer work. He thought he understood it and therefore, as with repairs on the kitchen plumbing or physics experiments, he was in danger of losing his concentration. There were, however, several thousand steps ahead of him. He had made a number of small polarizer sheets by dipping flat pieces of nitrocellulose into the suspension of iodine needles while it was within the magnetic field, then withdrawing the sheet so as to leave it coated with the crystals. He first dried the sheet in the magnetic field to establish the orientation of the crystals, then gave it a final drying under a heat source to set them. In Harvard Square the heat source was the sun.

During their first month, Land was hanging sheets of nitrocellulose on a line stretched between a chimney and a vent pipe on the garage roof, using clothespins. The owner of the building came up the stairs with Wheelwright in tow to see what his new tenants were up to. Land stopped pinning the nitrate sheets when he saw the man's cigar. In a strained voice Land gave an explanation, largely of whole cloth, of what they were doing, as the afternoon breeze blew the ashes of the cigar around the roof. Wheelwright said later, "I had never seen Din scared before or since. When the man went downstairs, Din wiped his brow and said, 'Jesus, George, we could have blown up Harvard Square.' "

The week following they started taking trips in the country in Wheelwright's Buick, looking for a more private spot for the laboratory. They found it in Wellesley Hills, just across the Weston line. The Jones Farm had been part of an estate that was broken up on the death of the owner. The large dairy barn was empty and could be had on a short-term lease for next to nothing, which was what they could afford. They moved their equipment out from Cambridge into the milk shed, a fine, large room, light and airy, with a cement floor, water, gas, and electricity. Except for a certain agricultural aura that never left the place, the milk barn made an excellent laboratory. It was private, it was within the company's limited means, and if the nitrocellulose blew up it would erase no one but the inventor and his dedicated colleagues. Ernie Calabro made regular trips up from New York to help Land and Wheelwright, and the two wives worked shifts with their husbands. They were developing new ways to make the sheet by means that did not require the difficult electromagnetic orientation.

In spite of the gloomy national news, daily growing darker, Land-Wheelwright Laboratories was off to a flying, joyous start. They had no customers, but Land reminded them that they were creating an industry, not a business. Land and Terre lived in a little house on the grounds of the farm. Land was supporting them on his salary of $2,000 a year, and he built a studio so Terre could paint when she wasn't working in the barn. No one had any regrets, least of all the irrepressible George Wheelwright. "I was much more intrigued by working with Land than in getting another degree from Harvard. I had the strong feeling that if we worked in the lab and it went well, I wouldn't need the degree. And if I had the degree and didn't work in the lab, I'd miss something . . . important."

6

Dartmouth Street

Boston, 1934–1935

Land carried a large cardboard carton folded shut at the top cradled in his arms as he entered the Copley Plaza Hotel. He leaned his shoulder against the heavy doors of the St. James Street entrance, and a doorman hurried over from a departing taxi to open them for him. Land walked with a hesitant step, balancing carefully, down the ornate corridor with its twenty-foot rococo ceiling. The bottom of the carton was wet, and he supported it carefully lest it give way and release its contents on the oriental magnificence of the Copley lobby. He approached the mahogany registration desk beneath the clock. "I want a room this afternoon," he said to the clerk as he settled his damp burden on the counter. "A nice one."

"Yes, sir. Do you wish a single room, a double, or a suite?"

"I think a small suite. How much will it run?" The clerk examined his inventory as Land surreptitiously tested the bottom of the box.

"I can give you a choice parlor suite on the second floor facing Copley Square for ten dollars."

Land scowled. Ten dollars! "That's fine, but it must be on a higher floor and on the west side, overlooking Dartmouth Street."

"That is usually the noisier street."

"I want the western exposure."

"I have a large studio room on the fourth floor that faces Dartmouth for eight dollars."

"Fine." Land signed the register.

"Do you have any other luggage?" the clerk asked with restraint appropriate to the Copley.

"No, just this."

"Then we shall require payment in advance. Do you want a bellboy to assist you with your, ah, parcel?"

"No, thanks. Just give me the key. I'm expecting some of my associates in half an hour. Then at three o'clock there will be a group arriving from Springfield. They'll ask for me, for my room. Please call me first, then send them up." He walked carefully to the elevator, his box making a gurgling sound.

The room was large, airy, and brightly lit by three big windows. Land put the box down and carefully examined the room. He stood in the doorway, looked across to the middle window, then walked to it, parted the drapes, and raised the shade. In two hours the sun would be full upon the windows. The pearl gray granite of the Boston Public Library was already bright with the heat of the afternoon. He opened the window to languid traffic noises. The room would do, he decided. As he was unpacking his box, George Wheelwright arrived. "For Christ's sake, Din, couldn't you find some bigger ones?" Land set the bowl of goldfish on the windowsill.

Land-Wheelwright Laboratories had made its second move, this time from Wellesley back to the city, to a basement workshop at 168 Dartmouth Street, off Copley Square in Boston's Back Bay. They had incorporated, but the addition of an Inc. to their name had not affected the collegial atmosphere. The company resembled nothing so much as a research project run by a group of graduate students hell-bent on their Ph.D.s. Land's first patent for the extensive sheet polarizer had been issued early in 1934, but he had not succeeded in patenting a system for polarizing headlights and automobile windshields to eliminate the glare of night driving. Don Brown had discovered several patents that conflicted with Land's claims in that area. They had hired four people in addition to Terre Land and Emily Wheelwright. One of them, Ernie Calabro, arrived regularly from New York on the Owl, the overnight New Haven sleeper that stopped a stone's throw away at Back Bay Station on Trinity Place. Nickerson Rogers, a young scientist recently graduated from Harvard, had just come on board and asked the two principals to meet his brother, Howard, who had dropped out of Harvard after one year. Howard seemed to fit the Land-Wheelwright pattern in more ways than one.

Although they were struggling to develop a machine that would manufacture plastic polarizer sheet in a continuous strip, their efforts were not continuous because they had gained a reputation for scientific problem solving and were experiencing a modest success consulting for the likes of Harvard, MIT, and Massachusetts General Hospital. Land's growing reputation as a bright and unconventional scientist was their chief stock-in-trade. Wheelwright was increasingly worried that Land might be lured away by one of their clients. When Land returned from a visit to Libbey-Owens-Ford, Wheelwright confronted his partner. "One of their research people told me you want to work there."

"George," Land replied, "I've told you what it's like. They start at eight o'clock and work until four-thirty. Then everything shuts down and they all go home. They don't work on Saturdays or Sundays. They keep taking me out and introducing me to important people and telling me I should work for them. Their lab is on about thirty acres and it's what they call a small research program."

"Well, do you want to?"

"Of course not. How could I get anything done?"

Eastman Kodak had been keeping an eye on Land-Wheelwright through mutual friends at Harvard. On November 30, 1934, it dropped a bombshell on the little company, an order for polarizing camera filters. The Polascreen Filter, as it would be called, increased contrast and removed glare from black-and-white photographs taken in bright sunlight. Land-Wheelwright was to supply the polarizer laminated between two disks of optical glass. Kodak would fit the lens ring and package the filters for sale. It was a $10,000 order.

Eastman Kodak was a huge corporation whose founder had absorbed much of his photographic competition in the United States and, in the best empire-building tradition of the thirties, was expanding rapidly overseas as well as at home. George Eastman, a lonely, reclusive bachelor, had died by his own hand on March 14, 1932, leaving a note that said, "My work is done. Why wait?" But his company continued to grow almost by its own momentum. Balancing their surprise and pleasure at being recognized by Rochester, Land and Wheelwright had to acknowledge that they could not fill the order. They did not have a working machine that could manufacture sheet, they had little experience in lamination of the polarizer to glass, and less in cutting glass disks to a tight specification. Yet they accepted the order with only a moment's hesitation, requested payment in advance of $5,000, and promised delivery in two months with the final $5,000 due on completion of the order. Wheelwright's chutzpah and Land's unbounded optimism had dug them deeply into a hole.

The consulting business ended abruptly. For the first time they had an immutable deadline. They moved cots and air mattresses into the basement shop. George Wheelwright described the scene: "We were approaching, but had not yet achieved, a continuous sheet process. We had various ways of making larger areas than we had ever made before, but they were discontinuous, not a real manufacturing process. Then Land had a bright idea, and we all began working on it for days to try to get it running to fill the Kodak order. I came in the morning before Christmas. None of us of course had time to go out and buy presents, so I brought a quart of champagne to celebrate a little and then go out and do some shopping. I arrived about nine o'clock. The next time either Land or I took our clothes off at all was January eleventh. There is a lot of vague time in there that I don't remember well. The thing that I do remember was early one morning Andy Anderson and I were working on the jaws of the hydraulic press that was going to extrude the sheet. Din was on the floor sort of crying and working with something and not doing very well. He said, 'George, what is the matter? My wife has gone home and your wife has gone. Everyone has gone home and we're not getting anywhere.' I said rather crossly from the corner where I had myself propped up, because if I sat down I'd go to sleep, 'Do you suppose it has anything to do with the fact that we came in here on the twenty-fourth of December and it's now the eleventh of January? Neither of us has taken a shower in eighteen days.' Land said, 'My God, it's the eleventh of January! I've got to do my Christmas shopping. I should be home.' And I said, 'So should I.' But before we left the machine was running and we were making sheet."

Land remembered: "We had to build the machine and get the rolls going and then turn out an awful lot of sheeting from which we were able to cut some to send to Eastman. It was Bob Blake and Ernest and I and my wife and Andy Anderson and George Wheelwright. We packed the whole shipment in a small box, which we carefully wrapped around with black tape and sent to Eastman Kodak with a bill for five thousand dollars. They replied, 'We have received your precious package,' and the company was in business. We delivered in time at that."

The product they delivered had by this time been christened Polaroid. Clarence Kennedy, Terre's professor at Smith, had become a good friend and sometime adviser. Terre had continued her painting at the little studio in Wellesley and later one in Boston. Kennedy was fascinated by the implications of the polarizer work and occasionally dropped in of an evening to visit at Dartmouth Street. He was a tall, slight, awkward-looking man with big ears, a prominent Adam's apple, and gold-rimmed glasses. George Wheelwright told Land that the girls in Kennedy's classes called him the Grecian Urn, but Wheelwright admired both the man and the scholar. One evening Kennedy, Land, and Wheelwright were discussing names. The glass disks, which were being delivered to Kodak and before long might in Land's dream be incorporated in the headlights and windshields of new automobiles rolling out of Detroit, needed a name. It must be unique, said Wheelwright. It must be important, said Land. And it must be classical, said Kennedy. Nominations were invited from the floor. Kennedy proposed Epibolipol, which he insisted was good Greek for "sheet polarizer." They suggested he rethink the question. He then offered Polaroid, and the vote was carried by acclamation.

The big basement room at Dartmouth Street resembled a machine shop more than a laboratory. They had shifted their efforts from the experiments with the composition of the sheet to the design and construction of the means of production. The walls, which occasionally rattled as the New Haven trains rumbled close by, were hung with tools and lined with workbenches. A blackboard proclaimed: "Every night fifty people will die on the highway from headlight glare." Most of the floor space was occupied by a thirty-foot device that resembled a small newspaper press. It was a primitive piece of machinery. A solution of cellulose acetate and crystals was poured into a cast iron vessel at the head of the press. Gas pressure extruded the mixture through the hydraulic jaws below the box, from which it passed through a series of rollers. As the acetate stretched, the crystals were pulled to point all in the same direction, the simplest and most effective of the orientation methods Land had yet devised. When the acetate dried, the needles were locked in place in a brown, semitransparent sheet about two feet wide, as thin as a piece of heavy cellophane.

Much of the design and construction work on this machine had been done by Allan ("Jack") Latham, Land's chief engineer, assisted by a free spirit who had attached himself to the group, a young aeronautical engineering graduate from MIT, Otto Wolf. Looking without much encouragement for a job in Boston's Depression economy after his graduation, he called on his acquaintance George Wheelwright to ask his advice and, fascinated by what was going on at Dartmouth Street, began to spend afternoons there between his infrequent job interviews. Otto had a remarkable creative talent, and it did not take Latham long to realize that he could build anything. He had the rare facility of listening to the description of a problem and then creating a solution on the nearest bench with whatever tools and materials were closest to hand. He was an accomplished mechanic as well as a brilliant mechanical engineer. He never did design an airplane, but he eagerly became one of Land's earliest employees and built the company's production machinery for almost fifty years.

Handsome and well built, Otto was cut from the same cloth as George Wheelwright. He could not resist a joke or a pretty waitress at Levine's Drugstore across Dartmouth Street. He invented a violin called the sonopitch, which surpassed the traditional instrument largely because it was, in the estimation of his unwilling audiences and outspoken critics, much louder. Otto used the sonopitch to relieve tensions — his own, not those of his associates — in the Dartmouth Street dungeon. His arrival was fortuitous. He not only helped build the J-machine, as the press was called, since it produced the formulation that had been christened J-sheet, but he also helped Latham build the first laminator to seal the sheet between the glass disks. This tall, narrow device, in essence a pipe filled with transparent adhesive and a screw-driven plunger to force it onto the sheet as it passed by, was called by someone — probably George Wheelwright — Uncle Dudley. The J-machine and Uncle Dudley ran as long as they were tended assiduously by virtually every free hand available. When sleep overcame a member of the crew, disaster was manufactured instead of sheet. Then the rest of the crew might try to snatch a few precious minutes of sleep themselves before they had to turn to and clean up the mess.

Land and Wheelwright sat facing the door of their Copley Plaza Hotel room. It was a few minutes before three, when the visitors were expected. The Kodak order had seemed like the riches of Araby when the second check arrived from Rochester, but today the stakes were much higher. The market for camera filters was not large. The two entrepreneurs had been examining every possibility they could imagine, looking for a simple consumer product that would provide them with an income base sufficient to allow them to pursue the automotive headlight project. So much had to be done. They needed more people, more lab facilities, more equipment, more space. But most of all they needed more money, more than George Wheelwright or Harry Land could provide.

The American Optical Company was one of the country's largest manufacturers of sunglasses, which were becoming more popular in America every year. They were beginning to be seen on the beach, on lifeguards, and on girls in bathing suits, the legs and skirts of which, in the daring current fashion, barely covered the upper thigh. Sportsmen wore sunglasses as well, as did hunters, fishermen, and boatsmen. Most sunglasses were expensive. Made of tinted glass with metal or plastic frames, they often cost $5.00 or more. Land knew he could produce a pair of sunglasses that would be far superior to tinted glass. Polaroid would eliminate the glare reflected off sand or highway or water, not just darken the overall scene. And he felt they could sell profitably for under $3.00. That combination of product and price might revolutionize the market.

The room telephone rang. Their visitors were on their way up, the train from Springfield evidently having been on time. Land had rejected the idea that they be received at the Dartmouth Street lab. Too much was riding on this meeting to hold it in those Spartan, noisy surroundings. Land did not want to talk about manufacturing techniques and specifications and prices and quantities. He did not want a negotiation. He wanted a victory. He wanted surrender. He wanted applause. There was a knock on the door, and Land rose to open it. The three men walked into a room filled with blinding sunlight. As they squinted against the intensity of light from the windows, Land said in a pleasant voice, "I apologize for the glare. I imagine you can't even see the fish." His visitors, handing their briefcases and coats to George Wheelwright, stared at Land blankly.

"Here, look through this." Land gave each a square of polarizer. As they faced the windows the glare vanished. There was the bowl on the windowsill, the goldfish swimming serenely in their warm environment as if suspended in air. "How many fish do you see?" asked Land in the voice of a kindly professor addressing his young pupils on their first day.

"Six," said the three dutifully.

"This is what your new sunglasses will be made of," said Land. "It's called Polaroid."

7

The World's Fair

Boston and New York, 1936–1939

Having learned how to make Polaroid, Land and Wheelwright set out to invent ways to sell it. Although his thoughts never strayed far from Detroit, Land reluctantly admitted to himself that the headlight idea was far away from realization. Don Brown had searched the patent literature and, to Land's chagrin, discovered that a headlight-windshield system of controlling glare by polarization had been filed upon by not one but two other inventors. One was a young Army lieutenant, Frank Short. The other, a more formidable potential opponent, was a Westinghouse scientist, Lewis W. Chubb. Both had anticipated Land's patent for the system. Neither, however, had the polarizing material that was the essential element. Land had the key, an artificial polarizer that could be manufactured in almost any size and shape, but he could not control the concept of the system itself. It was bitterly discouraging, but he felt the idea was ultimately to be his and that he alone could bring it to fruition. It galled him to know that other inventors had experienced the same revelation as he, but he did not believe Short or Chubb could succeed without him. In the meantime, he had to find uses for his invention. Filters and sunglasses and demonstration kits for schools were not enough to sustain the development work.

Richard Kriebel was called away from his typewriter by a summons from the boss. Kriebel, a short, scholarly-looking young man with black wavy hair and thick glasses, slipped on his coat and adjusted his bow tie in the reflection of the office's single window. His employer, the president of

Sutherland-Abbott, a small industrial advertising agency, had a guest, a familiar figure in the office, a representative for a group of technical magazines who sold space for several of its clients. It took Kriebel a moment to piece the salesman's story together. He was describing a new little company he had visited that morning in the same neighborhood. It wanted to place an advertisement for a teacher's kit in one of his scientific magazines. "What kind of a kit?" asked Kriebel.

"That's what I couldn't quite get," the rep said. "I asked the guy, George Wheelwright is his name, if someone in the place could write the ad."

"What did he say?"

"He said, 'Hell, no. We don't have anyone who can write a letter.' "

The salesman had adjourned to Sutherland-Abbott on Clarendon Street for some assistance. Interested in a new client, however minuscule, his boss sent Kriebel to investigate. After telephoning to make the appointment, Kriebel was ushered into a bare room on the first floor of 168 Dartmouth Street. Below, in the basement, the battle between Land, Otto Wolf, and their cohorts on one side and Uncle Dudley and the J-machine on the other was being waged without significant resolution. Above, the single office contained a desk, one chair, and an empty wastebasket. On the wall a hand-lettered sign said, "This year 20,000 people will die on the highways at night." Land and Wheelwright climbed the stairs from the basement and, as was often the case, Wheelwright began to talk. Kriebel, a thoughtful, imaginative writer with a journalist's instinct, had difficulty in understanding the concept. He was struck by the contrast between the partners: Wheelwright, tall, light-haired, pacing, talking nonstop, using his hands and arms to throw his points across the room; Land, short, silent, almost Latin in appearance, with brooding, piercing eyes that did not long maintain contact. When Wheelwright finished the briefing, Kriebel wasn't any more enlightened than the space salesman who had preceded him.

Land picked up two disks of brown-tinted glass, each six inches in diameter, from the desk. "This is Polaroid glass," he said quietly to Kriebel, holding one disk up between them. "It is transparent, as you see. It transmits almost all the useful light rays." As he talked, the eyes stared intently through the circular window at Kriebel, who couldn't tear his own away. "However, this glass contains a matrix of tiny crystals. It combs out the tangled waves of light so that they are all vibrating on the same plane. The crystals are so small that you cannot see them. They are suspended in cellulose, all oriented in precisely the same direction." Land's voice was soft, and Kriebel strained to hear him even in the otherwise silent room. The eyes burned at him through the pale glass. "There are one thousand billion of these crystals in every square inch."

Kriebel tried to imagine one thousand billion as Land lifted the second disk and held it over the first, the image of his face slightly more greenish brown in hue now, still riveting in the intensity of his gaze. "As I said, the crystalline structure is invisible, but observe that as I turn one of these disks the crystal lines begin to cross and the transmitted light is reduced." To Kriebel's surprise, the fierce Indian visage began to grow darker. The voice continued its hypnotic narrative, but Kriebel was no longer listening. He stared at the eyes as the face around them was eclipsed, and finally the two sparks themselves were extinguished as the disk went completely black. Then Land slowly rotated the second disk to its original position and reappeared, smiling. "Now do you understand what Polaroid is?"

Kriebel understood that he had witnessed a magic trick and that Land was an impressive and original magician. He promised to write the advertisement, which was to appear in the *Review of Scientific Instruments*. He walked back to Clarendon Street disconcerted. It was a great trick, an unforgettable demonstration, but was it more than that? Kriebel was a conservative, rather skeptical young man, conscious of the increasing weight of his responsibilities, which at that moment included a wife expecting their first child, a pressing need to move from their tiny house in Dover to larger quarters that could accommodate a nursery, and his steady, rather undemanding job at Sutherland-Abbott. He felt that another responsibility had somehow been offered. Copley Square looked in an indefinable way different from what it had seemed an hour earlier. I've been polarized, he thought.

Dick Kriebel organized Polaroid's first press conference on January 30, 1936, in a meeting room at the Waldorf-Astoria Hotel in New York. The preparations were barely completed in time by the group of a dozen from Land-Wheelwright, which included for the first time the rather forbidding presence of Dr. Martin Grabau, a Harvard professor recruited by George Wheelwright, who felt the company needed a Ph.D. Kriebel did his job well. The audience included a surprising representation of newspaper and magazine writers as well as executives from Kodak, American Optical, and Bausch & Lomb, a recent sunglass licensee. Kriebel was jittery. He had quickly traveled a long way from fusty Back Bay and the problems of selling shoe machinery and conveyor belts. Everyone whom he had asked for advice had warned him away from Land-Wheelwright. His lawyer had told him flatly that he would be crazy to take a job that came with a significant reduction in salary, but his fascination with the magic of the crossed polarizers prevailed over his wife's misgivings and his own common sense.

The moment Kriebel committed himself to Land-Wheelwright, Land demanded that he produce an audience, a national audience. The means to that audience was rapidly filling the meeting room at the Waldorf. Kriebel recognized some of the press people. He was elated and terminally nervous by turns. Land had planned a three-ring circus. The room was lined with tables displaying a bewildering array of objects: laboratory equipment, baby bottles, a miniature skyscraper of plastic, two automobile grilles complete with headlights and a pair of windshields, several oil paintings, a movie screen with two projectors, lamps of various sizes and configurations, and a coil of clothesline. Kriebel began by thanking the press a little too warmly for coming. He told them they were about to witness the first public demonstration of a new material called Polaroid and the phenomenon of polarized light. Then he stepped aside as the inventor approached the podium. Determined to overcome his inhibitions at facing an audience, Land had worked for a month with Wheelwright and the crew to arm himself for this encounter. From the moment he walked to the microphone, he was determined to stay at least one step ahead of his audience. He reviewed his battle plan on the notes in front of him. George Wheelwright would not have to come forward to salvage the presentation as he had once or twice in the past. Land noticed that Kriebel had added a note at the top of his script: "Smile at your audience." Land frowned in his usual reaction to unasked advice.

As it transpired, Land left his audience floundering in his wake. He demonstrated the polarizing headlight system while the writers crouched behind first one windshield and then the other as headlight beams cut across the darkened room. A three-dimensional color film of puppeteer Tony Sarg's "Polaroid Marionettes" was shown to the audience, who were wearing Polaroid spectacles. They gaped at the sight of puppets dancing out in the space between the screen and the audience. They stared at the face of a handsome model under a polarizing lamp while Land explained that they were looking beneath the surface of the "patient's" skin to see the "true perfection of her complexion." A polariscope showed the stress points of a large gear wheel made of plastic, then the skyscraper model, then a baby bottle, then a miniature dirigible skeleton. Land created garish colors by projecting polarized light through cellophane and touted this as the new era in stage lighting. Reporters donned Polaroid sunglasses to peer at fish in a tank and girls in summer dresses. The fascinated newsmen looked through a window facing another window ten feet away and were told, "No longer will apartment dwellers have to pull down the shades or watch their conduct if windows are equipped with the clear, colorless Polaroid glass demonstrated today." Reporters sat behind each window, able to see clearly what lay between the two, but unable, no matter how hard they peered, to observe the conduct of the other group.

By the time Land had finished his lecture on polarization as a tool for the conservation of priceless old masters and Dr. Grabau had launched into his technical description of the nature of light, using a length of clothesline down which he sent vigorous ripples representing the vibrations of a light wave, the press had capitulated. When the house lights went up for the last time, they accepted Dick Kriebel's thirteen-page press release gratefully. Most of their notes had been scratched in the dark about matters they barely understood. The handout was, for once, a godsend. As the newsmen left, the crew gathered around Land at one of the automobile mock-ups. Grabau still clutched the end of his rope. Land looked drained, Wheelwright elated. Kriebel was a little stunned at what he had loosed on an unsuspecting world. Julie Silver, smiling broadly, walked up from the audience to join them.

This performance, with variations, was repeated twice more in 1936, eleven months later, on November 30, at the National Academy of Sciences in Washington and on December 10 at the New York Museum of Science and Industry at Rockefeller Center. On this occasion the vice president of the museum, Felix Warburg, introduced Land. R. W. Wood, professor of experimental physics at Johns Hopkins University, one of Land's early heroes, spoke briefly. American Optical and Bausch & Lomb sent their presidents. Silver took advantage of this third performance, which was smoother, less frenetic, and perhaps less exciting than the first, to invite several Wall Street acquaintances, including James A. Warburg, a cousin of Felix, and Bernard Baruch. Afterward he introduced them to Land. James Warburg was animated by the excitement of the show and enchanted by Land who, he was told, had just won the Hood Medal from the Royal Photographic Society in London. He told Silver he wanted to introduce Land to some other friends of his, including Union Pacific board chairman W. Averell Harriman. The day flew by in a haze of euphoria. Baruch invited Land to walk across the street to his office to hear a special radio broadcast. As they listened to Edward VIII of England explain that he could no longer continue to govern without Wallis Simpson at his side, Land realized with a sinking heart that the newspaper stories they were anticipating about Polaroid headlights and movies would vanish without a trace in a tidal wave of news as Parliament prepared to pass a bill of abdication on December 11.

None of the new product ideas they had demonstrated promised real commercial substance except sunglasses. Polaroid lamps, whether used for study, drafting, dermatology, or oil paintings, were expensive and generated little excitement. Polaroid windows never became a product, perhaps because of their cost, perhaps because people could not confidently believe their conduct would be invisible to their neighbors.

The hit of the press conferences, however, was three-dimensional movies. The film was made with two movie cameras held with their lenses about six inches apart to simulate the interocular, the distance between human eyes. One camera was equipped with a vertically oriented polarizing filter, the other with a horizontal. The scene was shot simultaneously by both cameras, which saw it from slightly different angles. After being developed, the film was shown by two synchronous projectors using filters identical to those on the recording cameras. The resulting images, shown one on the other on a single screen, looked to the unaided eye like a single, somewhat out-of-focus picture. However, to a viewer with a pair of Polaroid glasses, one lens vertically, one horizontally oriented, objects leaped out from the screen. Bodies walked into the audience. The screen itself became a room, a tunnel, a perspective; flatness gave way to a remarkable sense of reality. Where motion pictures had been accepted by an audience as visual shorthand for human action and dimension, they now assumed a resemblance to life that was uncanny, often unsettling. No one had seen anything like it outside of a stereopticon, and never before, of course, in motion. Success of the three-dimensional effect depended on precision in both taking and projecting the film. If one of the two images was shot or projected slightly out of focus or, worse still, running a frame or two behind the other one, the viewer's eyes would send conflicting signals to the brain which, instead of integrating them into a semblance of reality, would begin to ache with the strain.

In 1937, Land saw two great opportunities for Polaroid. Both New York City and San Francisco were to have fairs opening in 1939. The one in New York, christened The World of Tomorrow, would feature spectacular technology and architecture, including an obelisk called the Trylon and a giant globe, which would accommodate crowds of spectators inside its circumference, called the Perisphere. The New York fair, under construction on a former garbage dump in Flushing Meadows, had the energy and ambition of New York's formidable park commissioner, Robert Moses, behind it, as well as the sanction of the governing body of world fairs. The San Francisco fair, a free-spirited outlaw, was pressing to open before New York's.

Land saw 1939 as a chance to present headlight technology to the greatest audience in American history and perhaps make the sale to the automakers that had eluded him so far. Polaroid's press presentations, with their weeks of preparation and rehearsal, added to the erratic and demanding production schedule, had strained Land-Wheelwright's limited resources of time, space, and money. The peripatetic little company had moved twice more in 1936, once to larger quarters above the basement on Dartmouth Street, then four blocks away to a building on Columbus Avenue. Land kept hiring people: a chemist, a machinist, a crystallographer. Lack of space presented a continuing problem, but lack of money pressed even harder. The company needed funds that could come only from a much larger source of investment than any to which they had access. Land and Julie Silver conferred often in Boston and New York.

George Wheelwright's father had been at Harvard with John Pierpont Morgan. Wheelwright remembered: "When Father decided that Din and I had got far enough along and were really doing something, he gave us a very informal letter on cheap letter paper and sent us down to see Morgan. It was just after they had that 1936 bomb attack on 23 Wall

Street. Land and I turned up in midafternoon, armed with all sorts of strange-looking packages to show Mr. Morgan. We walked in the door and were greeted by four men with shotguns, sawed-off shotguns. After a lot of clamor I finally got Mr. Morgan's secretary to come out. He was an Englishman, a bit la-di-da, with a handkerchief up his sleeve, and he said, 'Oh, gentlemen, what a pity, I don't believe Mr. Morgan can see you today, he's very busy.' That made me mad and I said, 'My father happens to be a close personal friend and I think you'd better take this letter into him.' He took it as though it were a poisoned polecat and went in and came out in about a minute and a half and said, 'Gentlemen, come in and bring everything you have. Mr. Morgan wants to see you.' We went in and it was all very posh, very correct, and we felt sort of silly with all those butlers carrying our packages. Din was scared stiff."

If Land was intimidated by the lions of Wall Street he did not show it, and they did not realize it. Nothing concrete came of the Morgan interview, but Julie Silver had been busy. Under the enthusiastic sponsorship of Jimmy Warburg, a group came together that included W. Averell Harriman, Lewis Strauss and Strauss's partners at Kuhn, Loeb, and several members of Schroder-Rockefeller. The group put up $375,000 and clearly demonstrated what they were investing in by granting Land control of a voting trust of the stock that guaranteed him complete command of the company for ten years. Neither Baruch nor Morgan was among the original group of investors, but both kept an eye on the fledgling. The new company, called Polaroid Corporation, was incorporated in September of 1937, acquiring all the assets of Land-Wheelwright Laboratories, Inc.

The board of directors included Warburg, Harriman, Strauss — who was later replaced by his brother, L. Z. Morris Strauss — Donald Brown, George Wheelwright, Land, and Julius Silver. Carlton Fuller, a former Bostonian who was the president of Schroder-Rockefeller, was also made a board member, became increasingly active in the financial affairs of the company, and ultimately became its chief financial officer. Three others, H. W. Chadbourne and a pair of employees, Sterling Pile and Allan Latham, Jr., an old schoolmate of Land's from Norwich Academy, completed the board. Land appointed himself Chairman of the Board, President, and Director of Research, the titles he felt had most significance in a science-based company. George Wheelwright was Vice President; Allan Latham, Treasurer; and Richard Kriebel was surprised and pleased to be named Secretary. The least comfortable in this corporate metamorphosis was Wheelwright.

The first priority the company faced after its reorganization was the headlight project, the idea that had particularly captured Wall Street's attention. The new funding allowed Polaroid to purchase in 1938 the opposing headlight patents from Short and Chubb. Lewis Chubb accepted Polaroid stock and the promise of a job on the headlight project for his son in exchange for his interest.

The second priority was the New York World's Fair. Land had hoped to persuade one of the major automobile makers to demonstrate the headlight system at the fair, but they all declined to make a commitment. The best that could be negotiated was an agreement with Chrysler for Polaroid to supply a three-dimensional film for its pavilion. Chrysler planned a four-hundred-seat theater as an adjunct to its main exhibit. The filmmaker was to be Jack Norling. Polaroid, one of America's newest corporations, a darling of Wall Street, the subject of a major article in the new *Fortune* magazine, the model of the scientific research-based enterprise that some were saying would lead the country out of the worst depression in its history into the technology economy of the future — this band of earnest technocrats set out to produce a film that they expected to be seen by millions of viewers over the next two years. The results were remarkably untainted by science or technology.

The finished film, in color and with sound, ran for twelve minutes. Its impact, of course, depended on sequences that demonstrated the dimensionality of the Polaroid system. Much experimentation had been done to find the most effective scenes. George Wheelwright's favorite was one he shot in his backyard, where his young son Mike swung a garden hose at the cameras, causing audiences to leap to their feet to escape the stream of water that seemed to gush out of the screen into their laps. The final film was quite different — to say the least — from anything Polaroid had attempted in the past. On May 7, 1939, the *New York Times,* misusing the company's trademark for the first, but not the last, time, reported on "the first full polaroid sound motion picture in three dimensions ever made."

Its title was *In Tune With Tomorrow,* and as the audience watched with fascination and sometimes alarm, parts of a Plymouth automobile danced onstage and began to assemble themselves. The illusion of fantastic reality was astonishing: the wheels and springs and pistons seemed to be moving in thin air, out beyond the screen, somewhere just out of reach of the bespectacled viewers. "All of the parts of a Plymouth car seem to possess human attributes," the *New York Post* reported. "They dance in, alone, in pairs, in groups, and fit themselves together, gradually forming an automobile. The picture projects itself in front of every spectator, and at times women scream, for a second of instinctive alarm, when it looks as if some metal part is coming right at them. When the chassis is assembled it sings, 'My body is in the plant somewhere. Oh, bring my own body to me.' "

Major Bowes, master of ceremonies of the popular radio amateur hour known for the gong that summarily ended a particularly bad performance, introduced the film. Spark plugs did a Rockette routine, but the gong did not sound. One hundred and fifty thousand people saw the show in the first two months, filling the little theater in which the film was shown all day, seven days a week. One reporter, responding to Dick Kriebel's prompting, wrote, "The daily supply of polaroid [*sic*] material contained in the souvenirs presented at the Chrysler Motors Exhibit exceeds the whole world's supply of this unique material five years ago. At that time, the polaroid material required to make a single viewer would have been valued at $500."

In another production in another pavilion at the New York World's Fair, George Wheelwright encouraged the stage manager to experiment with opaque skirts made of Polaroid on his real and spectacularly female chorus line. At the finale, a polarizing spotlight came on, making the skirts transparent. In such ways did technology salute The World of Tomorrow.

8

Main Street

Cambridge, 1940

On a raw day in January 1940, a small fleet of trucks and cars began shuttling from the Polaroid offices on Boston's Columbus Avenue across the Charles River on the Longfellow Bridge to a five-story concrete manufacturing building on Main Street in Cambridge between Kendall and Central squares. Some small measure of success, and Land's pressure to expand the headlight program, had forced yet another move. Orders for polarizer sheet increased slowly but with encouraging consistency. Eastman Kodak was still ordering small quantities for filters. Photographers were discovering that the polarizer produced dramatic contrast in black-and-white photographs that included clouds and sky. A photographic artist named Ansel Adams had recently begun to demonstrate the stunning impact of white clouds and black mountain crags against a black sky.

The largest of Polaroid's customers was still American Optical. Polaroid Day Glasses were becoming popular. They were successfully introduced at $2.95 a pair; later the price was reduced to $1.95. Polaroid sold more than a million pairs in 1939. They sold well not only because of their price but also because their superiority to ordinary tinted sunglasses could be demonstrated on the spot. The salesman and the customer had only to step outside on a sunny day and find an automobile or shop window that was suffused with the reflected glare of the sun. When the customer lifted the Polaroid glasses to his eyes, the blinding glare disappeared and the window became perfectly transparent. Ordinary sunglasses darkened the glare but did not eliminate it.

There was more than a trace of magic to this demonstration. It usually took several intent looks, with and without the glasses, to credit what the eyes were seeing. The invisible ribs of the polarizing lens blocked out the random rays of reflected glare and let through only the useful light of the scene. Whether customers perceived polarization as magic or as an achievement of science, Polaroid Day Glasses were clearly a bargain at $1.95. The Copley Plaza goldfish had inaugurated an enduring Polaroid marketing tradition. Demonstration proved so effective that within a year of the product's introduction dealers were asking the company for a lighted display so that customers could discover the benefits of polarizing lenses at the counter. Land obliged them with a cardboard peep show, which had a light bulb mounted inside to reflect glare off a picture of children crossing in front of an automobile, as seen through the windshield. Demonstration directly to the customer was a powerful selling tool. "Show me" was ingrained in many more Americans than lived in Missouri.

The J-machine had been disassembled and loaded into two trucks for the four-mile trip to Cambridge. The contraption was still cantankerous to operate and required constant attention from a team of baby-sitters. When it ran at all it had to continue operating for long periods without stopping, sometimes twenty-four hours a day, sometimes for several days at a time. Carlton Fuller, the Brahmin finance officer, watched this operation with curiosity tinged with awe. He thought that since the J-machine was doing something that had never been done before in industry, it was entitled to be treated tenderly. He, however, did not have to sleep on a cot beside it or answer the alarm bells that signaled breakdown. Its journey in the Shaughnessy & Ahern moving trucks was anything but tender as they navigated the icy ruts past the Salt and Pepper Bridge. Cambridge streets were rough at the best of times, even without the packed, iron-hard snow. The J-machine had disgorged miles of sheet before it was disassembled for the move. Now that it was to be reassembled in the new location it would be used as a backup. It had been displaced by a newly designed machine with more capacity and, it was hoped, less character. The L-machine would not require handmaidens in constant attendance. This new machine and Polaroid's burgeoning population had precipitated the move to 730 Main Street, where there was room for as much growth as could be imagined by anyone except Land. Polaroid had already become a large company; it had 240 employees.

The company engineers who supervised the move were very conscious of another tradition, that of inventing, designing, and constructing all the equipment the little company used. There had been no machine that could make sheet polarizer until Land, Wheelwright, Latham, and Wolf made one. Inventing the product meant inventing the manufacturing process, and that meant inventing the machinery. The engineers thought of themselves as a unique if not an elite group. "Invented Here" was deeply ingrained in the company from the beginning. No one else understood the process as they did. How could an outsider design a machine that had never existed before, even in the mind's eye, let alone on a drawing table? "NIH" elicited suspicions at Polaroid as deep and abiding as Detroit's.

The little convoy moved into a strangely malodorous neighborhood. Although it lay only twenty minutes' walk from Beacon Hill, the section of Cambridge near the river and adjacent to the campus of the Massachusetts Institute of Technology could only be characterized as an industrial slum. Once, when ships still entered the mouth of the Charles River, it had been called Cambridgeport, and canals reached from the Charles inland to factories and lumberyards. Schooners carrying timber and coal had given way to trains, and most of the canals filled in. Several of the candy factories that populated the neighborhood between the railroad tracks and the water had closed during the last years of the Depression, and a bankruptcy had brought 730 Main onto the rental market.

William J. McCune, Jr., had recently been hired by Polaroid. A twenty-four-year-old MIT graduate who was interested in automobiles, he felt that life had been extraordinarily good to him when he landed his first job with General Motors, which sent him to Bloomfield, New Jersey, to be trained for a posting to the Stuttgart headquarters of Opel, GM's German subsidiary. When war broke out in Europe in 1939, he was understandably reluctant to go to Germany. No other job offer materialized from General Motors, and late in 1939 McCune found himself on the train back to Boston, worried, anxious to leave GM, but uncertain where to go. Among the people he looked to was Professor Nat Sage, a friend on the MIT faculty. Sage knew of a small company in Boston that was doing interesting things. He showed McCune the article in *Fortune*. It needed a quality control engineer. Could he qualify? He would try. At his interview he felt he made a good impression on the young inventor-entrepreneur who ran out of the rabbit warren of laboratories for a quick introduction, charmed the shy young man from Glens Falls, New York, whose life's desire up to that moment had been to design automobiles, and abruptly disappeared.

McCune suspected he might be offered a position, but he wasn't sure. He went back to Nat Sage and they discussed his experience. "There were some things I liked, but it was a very *different* sort of place." He took the train back to Manhattan that night. When he arrived at his flat, a telegram from Sage was waiting: "Think twice before you turn down Polaroid." McCune went back to Boston. The first week on the job he was sent to Cambridge with Jack Latham to inspect a new building for Polaroid. The virtues of the totally characterless structure were discussed at length — space, light, high ceilings, proximity to the subway, which ran directly underneath, concrete construction. As they stepped out of the freight elevator into the frigid fifth floor, McCune was confronted with a dead pigeon half submerged in a lake of congealed chocolate. "They used to make candy bars here," Latham said as he closed an open window. McCune remembered his time in General Motors' glass and stainless steel offices. They were probably designing tanks there now, he thought, and at least he wasn't involved in war work. He stepped over the chocolate-covered pigeon, and they continued the tour.

The closest neighbor to 730 Main Street was the New England Confectionery Company, Necco. Several other surviving candy makers had plants nearby. In 1940, fumes emanating from factories were assumed to be a natural consequence of industry and were not decried as pollution. Candy factories had a smell that suggested candy gone alarmingly bad, just as dairies smelled of sour milk and breweries of stale beer. Two other large industrial plants occupied the neighborhood, the Cambridge Rubber Company, which melted down used tires collected in a black rubber mountain beside the plant, and Lever Brothers, whose soap refinery was just across the street. Foot traffic along that particular stretch of Main Street was brisk; cars and trucks drove by with their windows rolled up. Rents in the area were cheap, even by Depression standards; forty-two thousand square feet of space at 730 cost Polaroid fifty-four cents per square foot, or about $23,000 a month. Except for the aura, it seemed a far cry from the milk shed in Wellesley Hills.

Several other buildings nearby were empty or available. The crooked, narrow, four-story structure that had been the Kaplan Furniture Company across Osborn Street was even larger than 730 Main. This rambling old building had housed the laboratory of Alexander Graham Bell in 1876. If Polaroid should ever need more space, it certainly could be found in abundance. Its employees, moving the contents of desks, lockers, and labs from the noisy traffic of Columbus Avenue, were struck by the absence of life on Main Street. They wrinkled their noses as they carried cartons from cars and trucks into the new building. The Depression was almost tangible. "Does it always smell like this? What *is* it?" At first exposure no one could separate the melange of smells into their respective industrial components. The coal smoke of the freight trains that cut across Cambridge two blocks away was almost welcome; at least it was recognizable. Cambridge was a very different city from Boston. The only shred of elegance in view was the dome of the State House glimpsed through the mist across the Charles. "Main Street stinks," said a Shaughnessy & Ahern rigger. "You might as well be in a cow barn in the country."

9

The Copper King

Cambridge, Dearborn, New York, and Omaha, 1938–1940

The Wurlitzer catalogue for 1941, published late in 1940, offered chill comfort to struggling technologists. Its cover showed handsome men and women in evening clothes lounging around a sinister instrument of chrome and colored plastic whose selection-key teeth gleamed in a savage smile that seemed to promise bacchanalia for a dime. The obscene colors and convoluted design of the machine were in marked contrast to its elegant audience. The headline announced WURLITZER ADDS THE MAGIC OF POLAROID COLOR TO THE GLAMOUR LIGHTING ON THE MODEL 850. The war in Europe was a year old, and the United States was belatedly looking to its own defenses. The first numbers in the Selective Service draft had been drawn on October 29, 1940. Automatic phonographs were beginning to be called jukeboxes by teenagers and GIs, few of whom wore evening dress, but not by the leading manufacturer.

"Here, to Glamour Lighting on the grand scale, Wurlitzer adds the wonder of Polaroid Illumination to magically light its attention-arresting peacock panel." Nineteen forty had been the most difficult year in Polaroid's brief history. The winter move from Columbus Avenue had been more costly than anticipated and had drained everyone's energy. The new quarters at 730 Main Street seemed cavernous, cold, and empty, still disorganized by repair and construction. The young business effort had begun to falter, a continuing source of disappointment and frustration to the company and to Land. Expenses were on the increase; sales were not.

The headlight program had ground to a halt amid fencing matches with one Detroit spokesman after another. Polaroid, seeking friends and allies in the automotive industry, had found only critics and cynics. An antiglare headlight system could appeal to any motorist who had driven a car at night, but Lew Chubb, Jr., and the members of his team were discovering that interest and enthusiasm were not of the same density as persuasion and acceptance. The technical problems raised by the auto industry were symptoms more of indifference than of mere obstacles, which if overcome would open a way to making the sale. One by one the obstacles had fallen: heat generated at the headlight lens; the need for more power to overcome reduced light transmission; even the question of four headlamps had been answered, not by Polaroid, but by Detroit stylists who were looking more for novelty than safety. A more powerful alternator was on Detroit drawing boards to replace the generator if the war effort did not intervene. No technical road blocks remained. The reason for the industry's lack of interest was all too obvious: styling and horsepower sold cars; safety did not. People didn't want to be reminded that cars were dangerous. An increase in price to accommodate the system, estimated by Polaroid engineers at only $4.00 per car to the customer, could not justify itself to the marketing men of the industry in a period when automobile sales were slow and price reduction seemed to be the most effective sales strategy.

The unkindest cut of all came from Ford. After yet another presentation at the Dearborn testing grounds, Lew Chubb had felt cautiously optimistic. Night demonstrations on the test track had gone very well. Normally noncommittal executives and engineers had shown signs of enthusiasm. Charles E. Sorenson, Ford's chief executive, was said to be examining the proposal in person.

Sorenson's letter, when it came, brought 1940 to its nadir for Polaroid. Ford, it said, would try the program for twelve months if Polaroid would make an initial payment of $50,000 and supply all the materials free of charge. Mr. Sorenson obviously saw the headlight proposal primarily as a scheme to publicize Polaroid. Ford would cooperate, but Polaroid must pay the cost of the program. The tenth year of the Depression was no better time to sell safety to Detroit than the sixth. Land had begun to wonder if the time would ever come. Nothing was more frustrating than being dependent on someone else for the opportunity to succeed. It was Land's lesson of the mantel clock all over again.

Stereoscopic movies, 3-D as they were beginning to be called, had scored a hit at the World's Fair, but there were still no commercial takers.

Hollywood, like Detroit, was in no mood to experiment. Sound and color had exhausted the industry's appetite for technical innovation. Stars sold tickets, dogma stated, and the big studios kept firm control of the industry, as Orson Welles, then filming *Citizen Kane,* was learning. Land had staked high hopes on a demonstration of 3-D for Warner Brothers. Like the Ford visit, it seemed to promise a breakthrough. Colonel Jack Warner, who ruled one of Hollywood's most profitable studios with an iron hand in an iron glove, heard about Polaroid's 3-D film at the New York fair and agreed to a private showing in New York. Now it was the Polaroid movie team's turn to be optimistic. A Warner did indeed show up at the Museum of Science and Industry, but it was not the colonel, it was his brother Harry. He sat immobile through the demonstration, a series of the most spectacular sequences that had been filmed to date, including most of the Chrysler footage. Harry Warner watched stonily, the polarizing glasses perched on his nose. When it was over he rose to leave.

"How do you like it, Mr. Warner?"

"Not bad, but I don't get it. What's the big deal?"

"The depth, the impression of reality, three-D." The team did their best to explain the big deal as Warner donned his cashmere coat.

"I just don't get it," he said again as he clapped his homburg on his head and departed with his entourage. Not till several weeks later did a Hollywood friend tell George Wheelwright that Harry Warner had a glass eye. Three-D would never be a big deal for him.

"Glowing plastic pilasters! A gorgeously designed grille with tubes of gay champagne bubble illumination! A record changer background featuring the peacock motif. Add to this the ever-changing magic of Polaroid Illumination and you have an instrument that will be the center of all eyes in any location." Was this the embodiment of polarization that Land had contemplated? A jukebox? Even the "Most gorgeous phonograph ever built," as the catalogue put it? It was ludicrous. It was demeaning. But Wurlitzer was desperately needed. Nothing except Day Glasses had produced any significant revenue. A Polaroid study lamp, for all the energy and enthusiasm that had been poured into the project, had failed. A model designed by Walter Dorwin Teague had met with no more success than the earlier committee-designed efforts. People could see the benefits of polarization, but 1940 did not seem like the right year to part with $10 for a table lamp. The product that had been launched on the wings of Dick Kriebel's fulsome publicity fell to earth after an eighteen-month struggle.

•

One of Polaroid's earliest and most spectacular successes had in many ways been the most disappointing. The Copper King, one of the grand luxe conveyances of its day, had been built in 1938 as the most modern observation car on any American railroad. It was the jewel of the Union Pacific's crack seventeen-car City of Los Angeles, which, along with the Santa Fe's Chief, carried Hollywood royalty, the transcontinentals, the smart set, senators, and tycoons, as well as tourists and business travelers. The Copper King was featured in newsreels and in the science and mechanics magazines that in 1940 were telling the world that the future of zeppelins and autogiros had arrived. The yellow and red riveted outer shell of the City of Los Angeles gleamed, sleek and streamlined. The train had no rear platform: trains were now too fast for the porchlike appendages that had allowed an earlier generation of passengers to stand in the open air and smell the smoke and occasionally the pine trees as they receded down the track. Observation cars were fully enclosed. Passengers could relax, drink, smoke, or play cards in relatively silent comfort as they rocketed cross-country. Some trains even had a large speedometer on the club car bulkhead to give their patrons something to talk about when it touched eighty-five crossing the Nebraska plains.

The Copper King had a distinctive browlike roofline that curved over the back of the car, but its most striking characteristic had been devised by Land. Twenty-nine huge circular windows girdled the car, thirteen on each flank and three on the stern above the brilliant illuminated nameplate. Inside, passengers rode in a tastefully understated art deco parlor that suggested the best styling of Radio City Music Hall and avoided the worst of the Chrysler Building. The seats were soft, wide, and comfortable, upholstered in tan wool. They had no seat belts. The large tables were steady enough at speed to accommodate three long-stemmed roses in a slender crystal vase. The Copper King had room to spare: sitting room, leg room, head room, room enough for passengers and white-jacketed stewards to move up and down the aisle. Shock absorbers and the smooth western crushed-stone roadbed combined to produce a silken ride. But the most attractive feature of the Copper King was its view.

Land had invented a window the likes of which had never been seen before, or, indeed, since. His engineers designed an elegant installation, which was accomplished at the Union Pacific shops in Omaha in 1938.

The big round twenty-seven-inch windows were set flush to the skin of the interior, with a control knob at the edge of the circle. When a passenger turned the knob, the inner of two panes of polarizing glass rotated smoothly and silently. Here was a use of polarization that the public could understand. As the scenery raced past it was a temptation almost impossible to resist: each revolution of the knob made the window a little darker until it was completely black. Then each turn lightened the scene a shade as the polarizers uncrossed and moved to a parallel orientation again, the clouds, the mountains, the trees, fading in like a personally controlled movie scene.

This embodiment was worthy of the technology. People not only understood but enjoyed it. They could not, in fact, keep their hands off it. Most of the windows rotated constantly through the daylight hours back and forth across America. The practical benefits, control of reflected glare and direct sunlight, the enhancement of contrast, gave the view from the Copper King the spectacular contrasting tonality of an Ansel Adams landscape. But — better yet — variable-density windows were fun to play with. Dick Kriebel's brochure was a paean to the marriage of art and technology. "They are available not only for trains, but for planes, ships, busses, observation towers, and signal stations," it proclaimed. But, yet again, there were no further installations. Like the headlight system, windows that polarized were viewed as an interesting, even attractive, idea, but not as one that would sell seats on a railroad. The Copper King window was a succès d'estime, but it couldn't sustain a business.

"Ever alert to scoop the industry in spectacular lighting effects — to give Wurlitzer Music Merchants the newest and best, Wurlitzer engineers quickly sensed the startling contribution that Polaroid Illumination could make to Glamour Lighting on the 1941 Wurlitzer Model 850.

"Today this sensational development of science, mystical in its workings, magical in its effects, is Wurlitzer's and Wurlitzer's alone in the automatic phonograph field." Polaroid's sales in 1940 amounted to $72,000, about 5 percent below 1939, but, worse than that, 1939's modest profit before taxes of $35,000, most of it from Day Glasses sales, gave way to a loss of about $100,000 in 1940. Nothing told Land and Silver that they had yet built a business that could survive, let alone grow. They had a solid polarizer technology. They could manufacture the sheet reliably and in quantity. They had gathered a superbly talented group of scientists: Bill McCune, Jack Latham, Otto Wolf, Howie Rogers, Dave Grey, George Wheelwright, of course, and Martin Grabau with his Ph.D. and his glittering glasses. They had learned a lot about a lot of businesses — the automobile business, the movie business, the optical goods business, the lighting business, the school supply business. Yet Dick Kriebel knew, though Land would not admit it, that the only business they had mastered was the publicity business.

"Shining through two revolving discs of Polaroid Film — then through the peacock pattern built up of tiny pieces of colorless Cellophane in varying sizes and layers — and finally through a second Polaroid Film — pure white light is transformed into a myriad of gorgeous hues that give the Peacock Panel its spectacular color effects.

"Without exception or exaggeration, the Model 850 offers Wurlitzer Music Merchants the greatest opportunity they have ever faced to capture the cream of the locations in their territories — to hold them against all competition — to roll up new records for profits based on the spectacular contribution of Polaroid Colors to the eye and play appeal of this phenomenal phonograph." Must Polaroid now learn the coin-operated device businesses to survive? Would it be dealing with Wurlitzer Music Merchants? As it turned out, it did not. The Model 850 sold out and was discontinued. The 850s in service played on until the end of the war, their peacock panels glowing in a myriad of gorgeous hues if the Polaroid disks were still revolving. Wurlitzer turned its manufacturing, if not its marketing, talents to the war effort. It made radio transmitters, gliders, and rocket launchers until the war ended.

At the Polaroid Christmas party in 1940, Land called the group, 246 strong, together. Most of them had found a drink when Land climbed up on a chair. It was still an ordeal for him to speak to a crowd, even a crowd in which he knew every individual. However, he had improved with practice, and this evening's message was straightforward: they had endured a difficult year. In addition to business and manufacturing problems they had moved across the river with all the attendant expense and disruption. The world was engulfed in war. The United States was not in it yet, but — he spoke with chilling authority — it would be within a year. The Navy had offered Polaroid a research and development contract. George Wheelwright was leaving to join the Navy as a lieutenant. Polaroid would devote its principal energies to defense work. There was a collective intake of breath from the crowd. There would be a $25 bonus for each employee. Land wished his audience a Merry Christmas and stepped down. There was scattered applause and a babble of talk. What he did not tell them was that the United States Navy had saved the company.

10

Dove

Cambridge, North Africa, Guadalcanal, and Wellfleet, 1941–1944

Land had attracted the attention of the scientific community both in America and in England. In 1940 the National Association of Manufacturers gave him its National Modern Pioneer Award, a significant honor. The award committee, whose chairman was Dr. Karl T. Compton, president of MIT, was made up not of businessmen, but of scientists. In addition to spending twenty-hour days trying to solve the problems of manufacturing polarizing sheets and the seemingly endless, and still fruitless, search for a major business application for it, Land found time to make some provocative statements about industry and its relation to science. "Industry should stimulate basic science itself, not rely entirely on universities. This should shorten the transition time from pure to applied science by many years." "Industrial scientists should be encouraged to spend a substantial proportion of their time on problems not directly connected with their assigned tasks." Though most of American industry, if it had any interest in science at all, was primarily concerned with applied science, the thirties had been hailed as an era of progress. The New York World's Fair celebrated The World of Tomorrow, and the popular press loved inventions and inventors, but the concept of industrial scientists who might spend time on problems that engaged their personal curiosity sounded as radical to the business community as Marxism.

Land had assembled a brilliant scientific faculty at Polaroid. His ties with Harvard and MIT were even stronger now that the move had put

Polaroid on the Cambridge side of the river, close to MIT and a ten-minute subway ride from Harvard Square. It was not surprising that the Navy regarded Polaroid as a promising scientific problem solver. Polaroid had done no defense work, but Land's technologists had turned their hand to many tasks, had tried to create products that did not exist. Their very lack of commercial success had pushed them restlessly from one field to another. Land had not allowed them to settle into a routine. They were hungry for success.

A golden opportunity arrived early in 1941. Six companies, including Polaroid, were invited by the Navy to bid on a device for finding the elevation of an airplane above the horizon. The instrument was "to be suitable for use by not more than two men" and must be accommodated on the deck of a vessel. Land and his scientists pounced on it like cats on a piece of raw liver. Here was a chance to demonstrate how to shorten the transition time from pure to applied science. Even before the Navy received routine acknowledgments from the other five companies, Polaroid delivered a working model. The device was called a Position Angle Finder. Far from requiring two men to operate it, the optical instrument weighed less than twelve ounces and could be held in one hand. The Navy accepted it immediately, and it was used by all the services throughout the war. Polaroid had found a major customer at last.

One of Polaroid's peacetime products was in immediate demand by the armed forces. Goggles, a minor adjunct of the Day Glasses line, had been developed primarily for skiers. Polaroid soon began supplying them in large quantities for military purposes. The ski goggle had a soft rubber frame that fit tightly from the forehead around the eyes and over the bridge of the nose, into which snapped a flexible sheet of polarizer. An elastic strap held it tightly to the head. The goggle cut the blinding glare that bounced off snow and ice without significantly reducing transmission of useful light. Misting inside the shield presented a problem under heavy or sustained exertion, so Polaroid devised a rubber noselike attachment that let fresh air flow in and out behind the goggle to keep it clear. This was used not only by ski troops, but also as a safety goggle in factories where an eye shield was necessary.

Polaroid goggles proliferated throughout the military. Major General George S. Patton and his tankers wore "cavalry" goggles to protect their eyes against dust and glare. These had interchangeable lens elements, including one that intensified the glow of tracer bullets in daytime fighting. Polaroid also devised several types of aviation goggles: one with a second polarizing visor that could be flipped down in front of the clear shield; another for pilots who flew night missions, which they put on an hour before flight time to allow their eyes to adapt to the dark. Blind flying equipment for naval pilot training included an orange polarizing film that lined the inside of the two-seater trainer's windows. The student wore blue polarizing goggles, which allowed him to see his instrument panel, as well as anything else inside the cockpit, clearly. To the instructor, who wore no goggles at all, the plane's windows appeared transparent, while to the student they were completely opaque, unless he took off his goggles.

The Copper King window technology evolved into a special variable-density goggle whose two double circular lenses could be adjusted by a knob at the bridge of the nose. As the polarizers rotated to the crossed position, light was shut out. Naval lookouts used them, as did aircraft spotters who had to search for enemy planes, sometimes directly into the sun, the favored angle of attack. Polaroid even provided goggles for dogs, whose description noted sternly that "military dogs on the battlefield sometimes retreat against orders when flying pebbles and dirt get in their eyes. Polaroid designers have fashioned a canine goggle to protect the eyes of U.S. fighting dogs." The design was later adapted for fighting horses and fighting mules.

General Patton, whose family home was on Boston's North Shore, proved an early and urgent customer for Polaroid research. After his Sherman tanks were bloodied at the Kasserine Pass in Tunisia, he confronted a critical problem, both mechanical and psychological, that affected his gunners' ability to fire accurately in battle. In a terse report to the Office of Scientific Research and Development, he pointed out that the telescopic sight on the Sherman's three-inch cannon had an aperture so small that the gunner had to hold his eye to the eyepiece to effectively sight for direct fire. This was extremely dangerous because the gun had a recoil of about four inches, and the tanker risked his eye, if not his life, unless he jerked back before firing, making accuracy a matter of chance. A much larger aperture was needed so the gunner could hold his sighting eye at a safe distance. Patton wanted a solution by return flight from the States.

Howie Rogers had, in a remarkably short time, become one of Land's most creative scientists. He devoted a substantial portion of his time to a problem not directly connected with his assigned task, how to produce optical elements in large quantities. The casting of glass lenses and prisms and the subsequent polishing process to bring them to precise optical specifications consumed large amounts of time and money. The larger the elements, the more expensive they were to manufacture.

What Patton was asking for was, in effect, a large telescope for each tank. It would cost thousands of dollars and take months to create a glass prototype of the optical system involved. Rogers, however, felt sure that quality optics could be cast from plastic. If the molds were polished to the highest optical quality, he felt, the resultant castings could match the precision of glass, and their cost would run only a fraction of the price of conventional optics. Plastic lenses lent themselves to mass production; they could be made in any size; and they could be turned out fast. The OSRD authorized a crash program for Patton. Polaroid designed the gunsight with an oversized eye aperture as well as the necessary mirrors, lenses, and prisms to produce a large, clear image of the target of the M-5 gun. An accordion rubber boot allowed the gunner to hold his eye six and a half inches away from the deadly butt of the cannon. Plastic optics succeeded in spectacular fashion. Polaroid was later granted the rights to the process and used it to produce a myriad of military optical devices for fire control telescopes, signaling devices, and other instruments. The first production samples of the Polaroid tank scope were flown to Patton less than two months after he had made his request. Direct fire from his Shermans became more accurate overnight.

The new Polaroid building in Cambridge, which had seemed so large and empty in 1940, had filled up rapidly, and the company began renting space in adjacent buildings. Since the government had rationed sugar, Polaroid had plenty of empty candy factories to choose from. Land, McCune, and Wolf searched for scientists, engineers, model makers — all the people who might have been clamoring for jobs a year ago, but now turned up as rarely as palm trees on Main Street. Polaroid begged and borrowed from the faculties of Harvard and MIT, hired students and graduates from Smith College and grabbed 4-Fs. The company used women, since it had already learned, if good experience was not available, to put good minds to use. Land knew that, given the right ingredients, he could make a scientist in his own laboratory.

Contracts came flooding in: for an optical ringsight needed for aircraft and antiaircraft whose rings were transparent but visible, optical effects rather than the classic iron circle with the bead in the center; for a rangefinder operated by a single sailor that could feed electronic data to an antiaircraft battery; for a "snooper scope" with an infrared sensor that allowed a sniper to see at night when his target was illuminated by an infrared searchlight whose rays were invisible to the enemy. These projects, completed with the combination of speed, ingenuity, and original science that Land had made the company's hallmark, brought Polaroid the first of three Navy "E" pennants for excellence in 1941, several months before the Pearl Harbor attack. The company had sales of a million dollars in 1941, a goal that had seemed far beyond its grasp in the previous year. In 1942, a fourth Army-Navy E was run up the flagpole at 730 Main. Polaroid's people found themselves working more hours than they had ever imagined possible, hours of physical and mental exertion, sleeping on cots, eating sandwiches when someone remembered to fetch them, drinking cold coffee, and matching minds with the enemies of their country. Many factors would combine to win the war, but Land did not doubt that science would be the ultimate determinant. Science could overcome bravery, fanaticism, guile, and determination. The thought drove him, and he drove his people. Unless America could develop the best science, the Allies would not win. The equation was as simple as that. In 1942 the challenge consumed him.

Two years earlier, Land and Joseph Mahler had published a paper describing a new form of three-dimensional photography. Like the movie process, it depended on polarization to combine in the viewer's brain two images photographed by two cameras with an interocular distance between them. In this case, however, the combined image could not only be projected, it could also be viewed, through polarizing glasses, as a hand-held photographic print. Two transparent images were produced, one from each camera, the cameras spaced apart, as human eyes are, so that each saw the scene from a slightly different angle. The process produced pairs of images on transparent film, which were then laminated to a third clear sheet of film, one image on the top and the other on the bottom. An opaque reflective backing formed the last layer of the sandwich if it was not to be projected. Viewed normally, the two images appeared out of register, as though double exposed. Viewed, however, with a pair of Polaroid spectacles, the two images appeared as a single scene with the illusion of depth, shape, and amazing realism. Vectography, like many of the other polarizing applications, was a solution in search of a problem, and Polaroid's prewar files were filled with bland images of fruit, New England churches, and pretty lab assistants.

The war supplied the first great subject for the new medium. The Japanese occupation of Guadalcanal had struck as much panic among American strategists as anything the enemy did in their first triumphant year since Pearl Harbor. Guadalcanal, a dismal but strategically important complex of islands, became the target for the first American amphibious counterstroke of the Pacific war. The Marines were assigned to make the initial landing, the Army to follow. The choice of landing site was critical. Intelligence from the ground was nonexistent; the Japanese held the islands in an iron grip. Aerial photography had proved only marginally effective, so ingenious and extensive was the Japanese camouflage. The Navy's first wartime use of Vectography targeted the Japanese defenses on Guadalcanal. Shot from a PBY, the interocular, or distance between the two exposures, stretched to about three hundred yards — two seconds' flying time — to produce a maximum of depth in the combined image. The picture pairs were processed quickly back at the base with a field kit assembled by Polaroid in Cambridge and packed in a foot locker. The resulting three-dimensional photographs, viewed with Polaroid glasses, showed guns, bunkers, buildings, airplanes. The Vectographic images displayed depth and contour that camouflage could not hide. Three-D was vindicated. Even though the invasion of Guadalcanal was a bloody ordeal, the Americans went in with some idea of what they were facing. Vectography became a part of the planning for almost every subsequent invasion, including Normandy.

The early polarizer work used crystals of iodine and quinine to produce the light-filtering characteristics of Polaroid polarizing sheet. As early as 1937, Polaroid had become a large nonmedical user of quinine, made from the bark of the cinchona tree found in Java. By the time the Japanese invasion of the Indonesian archipelago shut off that single source of supply in January 1942, Land had already shifted from the crystalline structure of the J-sheet polarizer to the L-sheet, which oriented polyvinyl alcohol molecules in parallel chains that were then dyed with iodine. The result had proved more efficacious and more stable than the quinine crystals. However, since quinine was still the only effective treatment for malaria, an acute problem in the Pacific, the Allies needed a substitute for cinchona.

The synthesis of quinine had been attempted often enough to rank it among the classical problems. Quinine, an alkaloid, was well known to chemists and researchers, but it had steadfastly resisted every challenge for the previous ninety years. In 1856, William Perkin, then eighteen years old, spent his Easter vacation in a makeshift attic laboratory, trying to duplicate natural quinine made from tree bark. He failed, but in the process he discovered the first coal-tar derivative that would become the basis of the organic chemical industry. Herman Rabe had analyzed the complicated molecular structure of quinine, but failed to accomplish a synthesis. In 1944, Land brought together two brilliant young chemists who had worked for Polaroid as consultants: Dr. Robert B. Woodward had graduated from MIT at the age of twenty; now twenty-seven, he was one of the rising stars of American chemistry. Dr. William E. Doering, a colleague of Woodward's, was twenty-six. Land provided them with a Polaroid laboratory and assistants, his own insistent energy and ideas, and a challenge to solve the classical problem. It took exactly fourteen months, an achievement which exemplified what Land had been urging, that "industry should stimulate science itself, not rely entirely on universities." Synthetic quinine was hailed throughout the Allied world as a triumph. Polaroid gave the work to the U.S. government with no royalty or other commercial limitations. Woodward went on to synthesize cortisone in 1951 and in 1965 received a Nobel Prize.

Under the pressure of the war effort, Polaroid suddenly ballooned in 1942 to three times its size of the previous year. Most employees knew only the details of their own project. When tension began to override energies, tempers, and the ability to concentrate, Polaroid people would occasionally ask Otto Wolf if they could work out with the machine gun trainer.

It was the loudest room in Cambridge. Otto and a team of engineers had completed the prototype for the Navy and installed it in a room with twenty-foot ceilings, far removed from the laboratories. Five minutes with the machine gun trainer could energize the weary, cheer the jaded, and clear almost any mind of encumbering thought. In a darkened room, on a raised platform, stood a replica of a twenty-millimeter automatic cannon on a pedestal mount. A sling strapped around the combatant's waist pressed him against the curved arms of two shoulder braces. Shifting the weight of his body swung the gun, which was aimed at the sky since the purpose of the exercise was to kill airplanes. When the instructor threw a switch, three-dimensional enemy planes appeared, projected on a huge screen that leaned out over the room and extended to the ceiling. Two movie projectors behind the gun sent planes diving and banking across the field of vision with terrifying verisimilitude. Behind the screen loudspeakers bellowed the engine noise and the sound of the incoming machine gun fire of the attacking planes. The novice gunner twisted and turned to catch the planes in his optical ringsight. When he pressed down on the trigger, the gun shuddered and bucked, and chain-lightning detonations from a loudspeaker suspended six feet above his head threatened his eardrums. Realistic optical tracers projected from the muzzle lashed across the screen. An occasional oath, screamed above the din, punctuated the battle. After five minutes it was over. All hits were automatically recorded. The trainer produced no casualties and expended no live ammunition. It was the first, perhaps the ultimate, arcade game; only real war made more noise.

One morning in 1944, Land, Bill McCune, and Otto Wolf, standing in cold sea water, felt their bare feet sinking into the soft sand of Wellfleet's outer harbor. The contractor had just set a caisson, a piece of galvanized drainage pipe about four feet in diameter, into the sand and was attaching a pump hose to the lip. "How deep is this thing buried?" he asked.

"It's probably about three feet under the sand," said McCune, "but we can't dig it out. The water keeps filling it in. We've been out here since eight o'clock this morning." He had a sunburned nose, and his light brown hair was caked with salt and plastered to his head.

A naval lieutenant stood glumly behind them, glancing at his wristwatch. They were about one hundred yards from the road on a long, toast-colored sandbar. The water lapped lazily at the sand, soaking their trouser legs. They had left their shoes and wallets in a Jeep on the beach road. "You know, we only have this range until eleven," said the lieutenant. He was frowning at a damp piece of paper he had taken out of his breast pocket. "The Army has the range from eleven until four. Then we can come back and get this sucker dug up. But look, Doctor, it's ten-thirty now. I really think it's time to leave."

The contractor fastened the hose to a motor-driven pump set up beside the caisson. "What's the Army gonna do?" he asked, testing the connection. "I thought you guys owned this here."

"They're going to practice low-levels," said the Navy man.

The contractor stopped and looked up, holding the pipe wrench delicately between two fingers. "What say?"

"Bombing. Low-level. With hundred pounders."

"Din, let's get out of here," said Otto. "We'll come back and get Dove at four."

"The tide will be coming in then. We'll have to wait until tomorrow," said Land.

"Let's go," said McCune. The contractor was already splashing with giant strides toward the Jeep.

Land looked down inside the caisson. "I think we can empty this in a few minutes. Let's get it out now. I want to see the film tonight."

"Doctor, I'm leaving, sir. I think you all should come along, too," said the officer. He headed briskly after the contractor.

"Din, for God's sake come on. This is crazy."

"Otto, don't worry. After all, the safest place to be is the center of the target." McCune and Wolf each grabbed an arm and pulled Land away from the caisson. The three of them ran through the shallow water, laughing, splashing, and yelling like kids. When they reached the Jeep the lieutenant had the motor running. The wheels sprayed sand as they shot up the rise to the paved road.

"Dove" was to be the technological answer to a critical problem in naval air tactics. High-level bombing of enemy warships had proved largely futile. Once the bombs were released from high altitude, ships could take evasive action. The current alternatives were costly: dive-bombing, in which the pilot dove to within a few hundred feet of the target, released the bomb, and then climbed as fast and as steeply as possible to avoid antiaircraft fire, or torpedo attack, in which the plane came in slowly a few feet above the water to launch a heavy torpedo as close to the target as possible. Both methods exacted an almost prohibitive cost in men and planes. The Navy wanted a guided bomb that could be dropped from high altitude that would follow the maneuvers of a ship as it descended. The requirements of the project were deceptively simple: the bomb was to weigh one thousand pounds; the guidance mechanism must fit into the standard fuse cavity; the bomb itself must fit the existing release racks of a B-24 Liberator bomber. The Navy gave Polaroid a contract for $7 million, more money than the company had made in its entire history. The Navy also provided two B-24s, two single-engine bombers, support crews, and as many thousand-pound bombs as necessary. Polaroid filled the bombs with plaster for the development phase. The Navy named the project Dove.

Polaroid's design, pulled together with characteristic speed, mounted an infrared sensor in the bomb's nose, which was scanned by a rotary mirror. Ships radiated a heat pattern from their steam turbines onto which the sensor could lock. As the ship moved, the sensor tracked it, and servo motors in Dove's nose continuously flexed control surfaces, small retractable spoilers mounted forward on the bomb, to deflect its flight toward the target. The control unit, a metal cube about ten inches on a side, was studded with vacuum tubes. A wet cell powered the unit; a gyroscope kept it on course. This crude bird, designed before the era of microelectronics, actually worked. The first guided missile, its motive power was gravity.

The fuse cavity of a thousand-pound bomb was large enough to accommodate a small movie camera to record test drops. Otto Wolf discovered that the Keystone Camera Company before the war had made a compact 16 mm camera that was ideal for the purpose. Land asked for a list of customers from Keystone and sent them a letter offering a war bond to anyone who would contribute the camera to the Navy. About a thousand came back, and plaster-filled Doves with movie cameras in the nose began raining on Maine, New Hampshire, and Massachusetts. Since they usually disappeared into the woods of Maine or New Hampshire, Cape Cod, where they could be retrieved out of the sand, became the target of choice. The Navy offered Polaroid access to a bombing range off Wellfleet, to be shared with other users, most of whom had live ammunition to expend.

At four in the afternoon, the group returned to the beach. They had a rubber raft on the back of their Jeep. The water had risen, and the caisson was not visible. Guided by their previous tire tracks they launched the raft, and McCune rowed it out to their site. They looked in the water for the caisson, the pump, any traces of Dove. All they found was a series of craters gently filling up with sand below the surface of the water. "Otto," said McCune, "always remember where the safest spot is."

"You bet. It's right in the center of the target, no question about it."

"They just forgot to tell those Army pilots that."

"Dove doesn't know it either," said Land thoughtfully. "The only place it's going is the center of the target." They paddled back to their Jeep.

Dove was never dropped in anger. Two bombs developed by another group of scientists fell on Japan first. The Navy later adapted the heat-seeking technology to rocket-propelled missiles, and Dove became Sparrow and Sidewinder.

11

The Compound

Santa Fe, 1943

Sarah McComb's house, one of the largest east of town on Canyon Road, two full stories of umber adobe with burnt brick coping atop the parapet of the flat roof, stood on the banks of the Santa Fe River just above the ford that gave access to the Alameda on the other side. When she had built the house in 1920, she added, almost as an afterthought, three smaller guest houses to form a compound surrounded by a high stucco wall of the same earth-rose tint as the houses. Her building materials were inexpensive: adobe brick, pine beams, local flagstone, Mexican tile. Labor was cheap as well. To build four houses in the Spanish Pueblo style cost less than half that of a single new house in Philadelphia. The wall kept out strangers, the dust of Santa Fe's dirt streets, and the noise of the occasional automobile. It held within the two-acre Compound a romantic play city of mud architecture, furnished with New England antiques mixed with the traditional wooden and leather furniture of New Mexican craftsmen. In the center of the shady garden a Spanish fountain was surrounded by lilac, hollyhock, grape hyacinth, snowball bush, bridal wreath, and Boston ivy. In the spring bulbs pushed up jonquils and daffodils. Poplar, elm, ponderosa pine, and cedar overhung the walls. Spindly cottonwoods lined the banks of the little river, which was dry ten months of the year until the snowmelt from the Sangre de Cristo range above town flooded down to clear the stream bed of its winter refuse, green the banks with tall grass, and fill the acequias, the irrigation ditches that angled from the river to the gardens of the town, with bubbling brown water.

Sarah McComb came from one of the Philadelphia and Boston families that had recently adopted the little northern New Mexico trail town, seven thousand feet above sea level in the paws of the Sangres. Since the seventeenth century, Santa Fe had been fought over by Plains and Pueblo Indians, Spanish, Mexicans, and Americans. It was a capital city ten years before the Pilgrims saw Plymouth Rock. After the First World War it was invaded by artists. A thin artistic gloss washed unevenly over the patina of poverty, racial rivalry, and religious fervor that encrusted the town. The Cinco Pintores, the five painters who codified the town's artistic pretensions in the twenties, quickly became a local industry. Fifty artists followed and then a hundred. D. H. Lawrence, Paul Strand, Willa Cather, and Edward Weston added to Santa Fe's reputation as an outpost of art in the Southwest. Their images of the three indigenous cultures, the savage architecture of the land, the majestic weather, and the pellucid, horizontal, crystalline light echoed what the Indian artists of the Seven Pueblos of the Rio Grande basin had expressed with passion and delicacy for a thousand years. The Atchison Topeka & Santa Fe Railroad never came closer than the railhead of Lamy, twenty-six miles away, but in 1910 Fred Harvey built La Fonda near the square in Santa Fe on the foundation of a two-hundred-year-old adobe inn. The town became accessible year round to jaded city folk with sufficient taste and imagination to see beyond the dust and the mud, a fashionable place to escape eastern realities.

In 1943, a new reality was being developed forty miles across the Rio Grande in the foothills of the Jemez. The lights of Los Alamos burned all night, faintly visible in Santa Fe. During the war, Sarah McComb began to let her three guest houses for rent to suitable tenants by the week or the month. Dinner was served in the spacious dining room of the main house, an attractive mélange of Navajo rugs, Acoma pottery, Spanish Colonial *santos,* and Chippendale furniture. Piñon and juniper logs were stacked near the conical adobe fireplace before which tea or sherry was served in the afternoon. Land and his three-year-old daughter, Jennifer, had returned in the December twilight from a walk around the town, carrying his Rolleiflex.

Land had been feeling the pangs of late-night guilt about taking a few days off before Christmas. He had worked through Christmas before, but this time Terre had forbidden it — or so she thought. Jennifer had been directing their photography. They had taken pictures of a burro delivering firewood, the cathedral with its two truncated towers, the Indian women selling jewelry and pots under the portal of the Palace of the Governors, the ancient capitol building on the square, and more than one picture of Jennifer herself. As they sat down in front of the aromatic fire, Land grateful for the time with his daughter and the week's respite from the pressures of Cambridge, both a little breathless from the unaccustomed altitude, she asked, "Why can't I see them now?"

Land had no answer to the question. Their teatime was cut short as he rose abruptly. He asked her to look for her mother, and he set out walking again, alone in the December afternoon. His head was full of chaotic notions tumbling one over another. Polaroid had skirted the field of photography repeatedly since its inception as Land-Wheelwright Laboratories in 1932. Land had learned much about the properties of films and how to alter and rearrange them. The movie field had extended his education in photographing three-dimensional movies, printing the almost-matching reels of film, and mastering the difficult art of projecting them perfectly synchronized and in focus, frame by paired frame. Vectography had taken him further into photographic chemistry as Polaroid designed and produced field kits for developing Vectographs at airfields all over the world. Land had assimilated the technology of photography in the course of these projects, read everything, all the literature, old and contemporary. Polaroid had even begun to experiment with the manufacture of color movie film for the Navy, a film he secretly wanted to call Polacolor if the opportunity ever presented itself to sell the material to civilian customers.

Now his mind was awhirl. Jennifer's innocent query was the epitome of a Landian question, which took nothing for granted, accepted no common knowledge, tested the cliché, and treated conventional wisdom as an oxymoron. His first thought was to wonder why he had not asked the question himself, but he quickly gave himself over to building a mental structure, which rose as the construction of a building, photographed one frame a day from the same spot, might look if played at normal speed by a movie projector. The foundation was scooped out, quick as lightning. The steel shot up, stick by stick and story by story, as if it were flying together. The walls and windows clapped into place as swiftly as water filling a glass. Land, as he walked the darkening empty streets of Santa Fe, under cottonwood and aspen, the first pungent piñon smoke in his nostrils from a thousand fires in a thousand adobe fireplaces, was experiencing the intuitive scientific vision of a lifetime. As he later described it, "A field will emerge conceptually so full blown in the creator's mind that the words can scarcely come from his mouth fast enough to describe the new field in its full implication and elaborateness." For it was full; it was elaborate; it was not a hint or a teasing, provocative idea to file away for later analysis and experimentation. It was everything.

"This domain, which neither he nor the world had known until some magic moment, now is for him so vividly real and well populated with ideas and structures that he will lead you around through it like a guide in a European city." Land began to yearn urgently for someone to talk to. He remembered, with a shock of joy that stopped him for a moment in his tracks, that Donald Brown was also in Santa Fe, staying at La Fonda. What a thrilling, marvelous coincidence! He turned his steps in the direction of San Francisco Street and headed for the square, three blocks away. Not until a chilly wind lifted his jacket collar did he realize he had come out without a coat.

"Then it appears to him that all that is left to do is to parallel that intricate 'reality' which came into being in his mind with a corresponding reality in the world outside of his mind. Sometimes this process of creating the outside reality may take five years, sometimes five hours. For the creative person this process of establishing the correspondence between the outside reality and the one within his mind is a timeless undertaking, reminiscent of the relativistic trips through space in which people return to earth only a little older, while the rest of mankind has aged.

"As I walked around that charming town I undertook the task of solving the puzzle [Jennifer] had set me. Within the hour, the camera, the film, and the physical chemistry became so clear to me that with a great sense of excitement I hurried over to the place where Donald Brown . . . was staying, to describe to him in great detail a dry camera which would give a picture immediately after exposure."

Jennifer and Terre ate dinner together in the dining room of the Compound, close to the fragrant fire. They talked about the day's innocent adventures and wondered at Land's sudden disappearance. Land and Brown ate no dinner at all. Land had found his friend in the noisy lobby of La Fonda, waiting to be admitted to the dining room. Brown's protests fell on deaf ears as Land hurried him upstairs to his room.

"In my mind it was so nearly complete and so real that I spent several hours describing it, after which it was perhaps more real to him than even the ultimate reality." Land wanted to get on the telephone and start someone — start half a dozen, a dozen — to work. As he poured forth the details to Brown, he began thinking on another level. Every one of Polaroid's best engineers and scientists, almost without exception, was immersed in Project Dove. How could he start work on something else, something totally unrelated to the war?

As the flood of ideas subsided and Brown began to review the notes he had been scribbling for the past three hours, he asked Land where it had all come from. Land did not answer the question directly, but told him with utmost confidence that he could do it — he could do it all. Three years of work lay ahead of him, but he knew, he was *sure* he knew, what had to be done. Some years later, he elaborated more fully. "What is hard to convey, in anything short of a thick book, is the years of rich experience that were compressed into those three years. It was as if all that we had done in learning to make polarizers, the knowledge of plastics, and the properties of viscous liquids, the preparation of microscopic crystals smaller than the wavelength of light, the laminating of plastic sheets, living in the world of colloids in supersaturated solutions, had been a school and a preparation both for that first day in which I suddenly knew how to make a one-step dry photographic process and for the following three years in which we made the very vivid dream into a solid reality. . . .

"The transfer from the field of polarized light to the field of photography was for us all a miraculous experience, as if we had entered a new country with a different language and different customs, only to find that we could speak the language at once. . . . The kind of training we had given ourselves in the field of polarized light had endowed us with a competence we had not sought and did not know we had, namely, a competence to transfer what must be a common denominator in *all* honestly pursued research, from one field to an entirely different one."

Land and Brown talked into the evening until they were both exhausted. Brown organized his notes and planned to call his New York office the next morning at seven to catch his partner when he walked through the door at 9:00 A.M. New York time. Land walked slowly home through dark streets, drained, tired, but elated at the realization that he had found what he had been searching for. As he crossed from the Alameda over the dry riverbed, his footsteps quickened. He wanted to see his wife and say good night to Jennifer.

12

The Camera

Cambridge, 1943–1948

The first research report on the photography project, dated December 18, 1943, bore the cryptic heading "Podak." It opened the SX-70 file, a new folder for the new project. SX-68 and SX-69, two military files, remained thin, their brief lives measured by a few reports of unpromising experiments. SX-70 began robustly with several reports a week, then several a day. Even before 1943 was over, it was apparent that SX-70 would grow to be a fat file. In fact, it grew to be the company. Podak vanished early. Presumably whoever thought a Polaroid-Kodak would result from the rapidly accelerating photographic project was persuaded to revert to the simple folder designation as a code name for the activity. Each day Doxie Muller's telephone rang at 6:30 A.M. sharp. Land gave her his critique of the previous day's work and outlined her tasks for the current day so she could think about them as she walked from her apartment to Osborn Street. She saw him at the end of the day, often late in the evening, when Land would trot briskly down the corridor past the wooden and glass cubicles to ask questions about the day's experiments. She began with a simple regimen, exposing film and dunking it into single-bath developer solutions. Before she went home she wrote up her day's report for the SX-70 research file and carried it with stained fingers to be signed by her lab supervisor. Land expected it on his desk that evening, with any sample pictures clipped to it. The images themselves, usually grayscales shot against a wall or a blank card, were murky, unrevealing. Land lay in his reclining chair, alone at midnight, studying each one like the fragment of a treasure map.

He was still almost completely consumed by the Dove project. Land and McCune were pressing as hard on the men and women of the team, the best of Polaroid's scientists, as it was possible to do without breaking them. As 1944 began, Allied airpower hammered Germany, preparations for the Normandy invasion were under way, and the war in the Pacific flamed as dangerously high as it ever had. Dove was deemed critical by the Navy for the ultimate defeat of the Japanese fleet. The heat-homing bomb moved closer each day to a working prototype. The two essential subsystems, the heat seeker and the guidance system, which would let Dove not simply follow a target but cut across its evasive arc and seize it in an explosive embrace, were fully functional. In the brief intervals between late-night conferences or tests or experiments, Land and McCune found a few moments to talk about the photographic project. It served as therapy for the unremitting struggle with the obstacles still facing Dove. In addition, they both knew that the Navy's love affair with Polaroid could cool rapidly when the war was over. Whether that was a year in the future or five, Land planned to be ready.

He had already decided an important issue: there would be no "black box." The self-developing camera must be self-contained. It should not require a separate development chamber into which the exposed film was fed. The camera would include its own development chamber, and Land thought he knew how to accomplish this. He had considered the concept of a tank or reservoir of developing liquid inside the camera that could impregnate each negative sheet. Two problems argued against a reservoir. As its contents were used to develop each picture, the remaining developer would be exposed to air in the container, become oxidized, and lose strength. If a day or a week or a month elapsed between pictures, the developer would become degraded, possibly useless. The issue of containment appeared equally critical. The caustic developer solution could corrode a reservoir. Leaks from rough handling would be messy and even dangerous.

One evening, as they sat wearily on the green cement stairs of 730 Main between the basement and the first floor, trying to gather the energy to stand up and go home, Land described to McCune his idea for an envelope-like container, which would hold the developer solution. He called it a pod. One pod would be affixed to each sheet of film. Precisely enough developer to cover that sheet would be sealed inside, always fresh and untainted by the oxygen of the air, ready to be released when the pod was opened at the moment the picture was to be developed. The idea struck Bill with its simplicity and its elegance. An airtight container would not be hard to devise. There would be no tank half full of liquid inside the camera. Segregated in small batches, the caustic developer would be less likely to leak onto the fingers of the photographer. Land described the size and shape of the pod, its construction, and its material. The stairs grew colder, but the two men stayed on, too absorbed to move. All the time they talked that night Dove was still flying in the back of their minds.

In the cubicle next door to where Doxie Muller performed her damp chemical experiments, a lab technician, Fred Binda, began to cut and fold and seal a series of pods, in various sizes and shapes, made of every possible material Land could conjure up. In the research shop, Maxfield Parrish, son of the famous artist whose confectionery landscapes had enjoyed such popularity in the twenties, constructed bars, jaws, rollers, and other devices to open the pod. A bewildering array of forces and factors came to bear on the spread system, as it was called: the compressive force needed to break open the envelope; the speed at which the film should move through the spreading device; the viscosity of the developer; the width of the gap between the jaws or rollers; even the temperature of the air, which affected the spreadability of the jellied reagent.

Land knew that the spread system was the key to the success of a self-developing camera. If developer did not coat the entire surface of the negative, the image would be flawed. He focused the energies of all the members of the still tiny, still secret SX-70 team on the problem. Doxie Muller experimented with the contents, Fred Binda with the container, Max Parrish with the applicator. They toiled in different cubicles in the bowels of Osborn Street, three sorcerer's apprentices whose activities would eventually be enclosed in a single dark chamber. The alchemist darted in and out to peer over their shoulders, to poke, to fiddle, to adjust, to correct. He smiled, joked, encouraged, sometimes frowned, his brow black with frustration. Then he bolted. Dove still had priority, which it held for eighteen months longer.

On V-J Day, August 15, 1945, Land walked into Bill McCune's cluttered office at 730 Main. Bill stared out the window, a smile on his lean visage, listening to the bedlam of the crowd in Times Square echoing from a little black plastic Emerson radio on his desk.

"Let's find someone else to finish Dove," Land said without preamble.

Bill turned down the radio. "Great!" he said. "I want to get on SX-70. I've got a lot of ideas about it."

"I want you on it. I want all of our best people on SX-70, full time. But we have to find someone to take over Dove."

"You know it's taking a hell of a chance. We don't have any of the answers yet."

"Of course we do. We have all the answers. We just haven't asked ourselves all the questions yet. And we won't know what *they* are until we get you, and Dave Grey, and Otto, and Murray Fairbank, and Bob Casselman off Dove and working on the camera. It *is* taking a big chance," Land said quietly, "but there's the possibility that Dove and the other Navy contracts will be canceled. In any case, now that the war is over we have to develop another business as fast as we can. It will be a race. A close race. If we win, we survive. A race to finish the camera before we run out of money."

The radio squawked quietly on Bill's metal desk as a yellow afternoon sun tried to penetrate the sooty panes of the window. "Eastman could finish Dove," he said. "They did some brilliant work on the proximity fuse."

"Why don't you call them tomorrow morning? No. Call them tonight. I'll talk to Washington. I think the Navy will agree. We need to get moving. We haven't much time."

The war has been over for fifteen minutes, thought Bill, and already we're out of time. "It's great, isn't it?" he said.

"What's great?"

"The surrender!"

"Oh, I expected that a week ago," said Land.

Early in 1946, Land studied an array of brown-and-white images spread across his worktable. Some were sharp and crisp, with satisfactory tonal gradation; a few glowed; several were hopeless. None had been developed in a camera. All had emerged from a black box, a bench-mounted system carefully manipulated by lab technicians. Land swept the pictures into a tray, stood wearily, and began pacing. He and a team that included Doxie Muller and another young woman, Elizabeth Friedman, continued to concentrate on the diffusion transfer process, the method by which Land intended to create the image on the positive sheet. He had divided the former Dove scientists into two groups, both headed by Bill McCune.

One grappled with the system: the method of exposure; the configuration of the film and camera; the spread system. The second, including Otto Wolf, had begun to visualize how the film would be manufactured. Their job was maddeningly frustrating since the specifications of both camera and film changed almost every week. As the system group experimented with packs of sheet film and a nonrotating spreader, the manufacturing group sketched a process. When the system team reversed their field and reconsidered a roll film format with rotating steel rollers, the process plans were shoved behind the drawing table with the previous rejects and a new set begun.

One by one, the Navy and Army orders were indeed being canceled. Dove had flown to Rochester, freeing the best of Polaroid's engineers and technologists for the SX-70 program, but also drying up the principal stream of revenue. As a result, people were being let go every week. By 1946 the company's population had fallen from twelve hundred fifty to a few over five hundred. The sunglass group mounted a valiant effort to build a civilian business, but Army and Navy stores were filled with inexpensive surplus sunglasses and goggles, many manufactured by Polaroid.

Everything seemed to Land to be moving with maddening slowness. He decided to light a fire that in fact he might not be able eventually to control. The winter meeting of the Optical Society of America had been announced for February 21, 1947. Land told Dick Kriebel and Bill McCune that Polaroid would disclose the camera system in New York. The two were appalled by the audacity of even considering a date for a public demonstration, let alone committing to the society. Land calmed their apprehension by describing it as an occasion to present a scientific paper. They would simply outline the principles of the one-step photographic system, principles that were now even more clear and unassailable to Land than they had seemed in Santa Fe. His associates did not believe that he would limit the presentation to just a paper, and he knew it.

In truth, Land's plan extended well beyond the scientific paper. He knew how daunting were the hundreds of interlocking problems Polaroid faced. The survival imperative was clear and present to them all. They had no alternative but to succeed with the camera. Everyone left at Polaroid knew that, at the present rate of decline, the business, the company, and their jobs might not survive 1947 or the first half of 1948. Nonetheless, Land held on to February 21, 1947, as a weapon available for use against his own people, including himself, when their efforts slowed, as he knew they would. In the face of the implacability of nature, even committed men and women flagged. They needed an additional stimulus. Sometimes survival wasn't a sharp enough goad. Public exposure could be compelling, even terrifying. His people were all capable of more than they knew. Land would prepare the paper, but there would be much more going on the night of the twenty-first. They *would* succeed. They *would* overcome nature. They *would* be ready. And ready, to the inventor, meant ready to walk upon a broader stage.

The spread systems in the Deardorff 8 x 10 camera and the smaller Speed Graphic that Land ultimately used for the demonstration in New York were still laboratory compromises. They worked, but they did not have the simplicity and reliability needed in a product that might be manufactured by the hundreds, even thousands, as Land and McCune had speculated. In the tumult of publicity after the Optical Society meeting, that speculation no longer seemed farfetched. A seed of fear began to grow. They had aroused an interest, a curiosity, a *desire,* the intensity of which had surprised all of them, perhaps Land as well. A feeling of almost desperate urgency animated 730 Main and Osborn Street. The anxiety to produce a working prototype that could be manufactured and sold to the public had become almost palpable. That now-famous picture haunted the SX-70 team. McCune thought of it every morning as he drove to work: Land peeling apart the picture of Land. Both faces staring out at the world, challenging and promising at the same time. Now they had to deliver on the promise. Bill felt it as a very personal responsibility. Promises had to be met. But Land actually seemed to be enjoying the crisis. McCune decided that crisis was Land's normal habitat. He wondered if he had always known that about his boss.

It was a relief to shift his thoughts to a young woman he had hired in 1942. Elizabeth Friedman had been trained as a chemist at Connecticut College. She was not one of the Smith girls learning their science in Land's lab. She had already made a contribution to the film effort. And she was a knockout as well, a real beauty. He decided to ask her to dinner if he could ever find an evening free. Bob Woodward, the Harvard professor who served as one of their consulting problem solvers, was courting Doxie Muller. I guess we're all so busy, Bill thought, that we have to invent our social lives in the lab as well. As it turned out, both romances resulted in marriage.

It was obvious, as a prototype system evolved, that the camera would have to be manufactured by an outside supplier. Assembly of the film would be more than enough to tax Polaroid's meager resources. Land had consulted Eastman Kodak on several key questions. Eastman had agreed to supply the negative, coated on a unique paper base. The film configuration had finally been determined: two rolls, one of negative, one of positive receiving sheet, joined at a common pull tab. Kodak also came up with a good suggestion for a company to manufacture the camera. Samson United made small household appliances such as irons and toasters. Located in Rochester, the company was willing to finance the tooling for the camera itself, so eager was its management to develop a new product line. The recommendation from Eastman, by far the Rochester region's largest employer, was enough for Samson United to undertake the gamble. None of its officers had a very clear vision of the future of this strange process called instant photography, but if Kodak was involved, they would go along gladly.

The camera group had made great strides since the Optical Society meeting. David Grey produced a mathematical tour de force in which he modeled all the variables of the spread system, without benefit of that new device called a computer that was being played with down the street at MIT. As the pieces of the spread system began to fall into place, Murray Fairbank devised a simple but reliable shutter mechanism that guaranteed precision with a minimum of moving parts. Land nagged them: this was to be a camera "for the mothers of America."

In 1947, despite their superb efforts in aircraft factories and shipyards, the mothers of America were not deemed to have much manipulative skill. Hence the camera must be kept simple, mother-proof. The camera team examined one at a time the problems inherent in making a picture. At the top of the list stood the choice of shutter speed and lens aperture. The Kodak camera set the industry's standard. Every Kodak except the Box Brownie offered a choice of f-stops to be selected with a lever and shutter speeds to be chosen by turning the lens bezel. The size of the lens opening determined the sharpness of focus in the picture. "Depth of field," in photographic jargon, described how much of a subject would be seen sharply by the camera lens. The smaller the lens opening, the greater the zone of sharpness. Depth of field increased at the expense of light entering the camera to expose the film. Shutter speed also affected both sharpness and the amount of light admitted. A shutter that opened and closed quickly limited the motion of the subject, as well as any movement of the camera in the hands of the photographer. Motion at either end of the picture-taking axis robbed the image of sharpness. But fast shutter speeds let only a brief flash of light into the camera.

Much of the craft of photography concerned itself with the choice of appropriate apertures and shutter speeds. The mothers of America needed help, as did the fathers. The children of America would usually make the right choices if they could get their hands on the camera long enough to learn the controls. Polaroid's camera design team devised an ingenious simplification of the basic photographic choices. Settings for aperture and shutter speed were linked together and expressed by a single Exposure Value number from one to ten. The team approached General Electric, which agreed to design an inexpensive exposure meter to read the light of the scene expressed in the same EV numbers, rather than footcandles. With the meter clipped to the camera a mother need only glance at the number on the meter dial, then set the same number by turning a knurled wheel on the brow of the Polaroid camera shutter board to achieve an optimum combination of shutter speed and aperture.

This simplification eliminated a few artful combinations of f-stops and shutter settings that a skilled photographer might have used in a particular situation, but it offered stunning simplicity that served well in 90 percent of picture-taking situations. Within a few years the EV system would be adopted, with some modifications, as the standard of the amateur photographic industry. Like Samson United, GE agreed to tool and manufacture the exposure meter with no investment on Polaroid's part. The pace quickened. The camera hastened toward its rendezvous with the mothers of America. Meanwhile, the design team and the manufacturing team still called to each other down the hall late at night, asking questions that had to be answered before morning.

Otto Wolf built his film factory on two large tabletops, one in a lighted room, one in a darkroom. While the first automatic machinery was being designed and built, he opted for hand assembly for the introduction of the system. Twelve women sat around the square, green baize–covered table in the lighted room, carefully cutting and rolling the strips of positive sheet, gluing the pods precisely in place. Those who worked in the darkroom had a more taxing job. Spooling the rolls of negative proved difficult at best; when done by touch in a black, airless room, it became arduous, eventually disturbing and disorienting. The darkroom girls had to be released every half hour to escape the blackness. Some could not endure it at all. Within the first year of manufacturing, Polaroid would begin searching Boston for blind people who experienced no such oppression when they worked in the darkrooms.

Bill Hooker had been given the assignment of organizing film manufacturing. He admitted to being distantly related to the Union general whose equestrian statue stands stoically in front of the Massachusetts State House. General Hooker, an effective if somewhat slow-moving field commander during the Civil War, towed a long baggage train in the wake of his army. Among this entourage were scattered a battalion, if not a regiment, of camp followers. As they straggled through a town, the question might be asked, "Whose are those?" The answer, "Hooker's," outlived the general's other exploits. The Polaroid film girls were not amused by jokes about their supervisor's name. Neither was Land. He knew that his fate rested in their hands.

Otto and Bill Hooker prowled around the film room for hours, watching the process of cutting, gluing, spooling, assembling, sealing the film in bags, and inserting it in boxes. They analyzed the movements of the women's hands and planned the machinery of the future. No one knew quite what to expect. The euphoria of the weeks following the Optical Society meeting had evaporated, and eighteen months passed in a haze of struggle. Julie Silver cautioned Land over and over again not to overspend or overbuild. "Try it out," he urged. "Let's see if it sells. Then we can build some more." Ro Messina, the stolid Polaroid engineer who shuttled back and forth to Samson United in late 1947, supervising the camera manufacturing start-up there, had an initial purchase order for only sixty cameras in his pocket. Land had heeded Julie's conservative counsel. His own confidence was in no way diminished, but he saw the wisdom of starting small. They had so little money. They had so much to learn. Film manufacturing was only part of it. The developer, the "goo," as they called it, changed whenever Eastman sent them a new batch of paper-based negative. Each variation in the negative required a new goo recipe. They still experimented with the tension between the rollers in the camera. Half a dozen big questions occupied the mind of each of the team leaders, not necessarily the same questions. Nevertheless, for all the tension and uncertainty, the weeks in which the camera and the film finally came together had moments of joy as well.

Land and McCune stood together in the workroom, watching the deft movements of the women's hands as they rolled films like socks and tucked them into foil bags. Large lights hanging from the maze of pipes in the ceiling cast a bright aura over the table. It floated in the gloom of the room, an island of light, the green felt surface covered with piles of white film rolls. The sure, flashing fingers built stacks and shoved them forward, croupiers moving chips in a game that had become more exciting than the players had ever anticipated. Land was thinking about the shoppers at Jordan Marsh, the Boston department store where the camera would go on sale the next day. He wondered if the people would be wearing hats. A group of people in hats and overcoats would make a dark picture. McCune worried about Ro Messina, who was bringing down sixty cameras from Rochester that night. Would they be finished in time? Would they have been tested in all the ways McCune had specified? Would the quality be there? A loose screw or a leaky bellows would shame him deeply. He had lectured about quality until his associates could finish his sentences for him. Now all he could do was wait.

"How many cameras are going to Jordan's tomorrow?" asked Land.

"Fifty-six, but obviously they won't need that many. They'll leave some in stock at the end of the day and bring the rest back here. I want to run another quality check. We really haven't had time to do enough checking."

"The salesmen may need them all."

"Well, I think the camera will sell well in time. They'll need them all eventually. They may sell them out by Christmas."

"How many cameras do you think we'll need for next year?"

"I don't have any idea. We'll have to get Casselman to give us a better estimate after we have a few weeks' experience at Jordan's," Bill said. "How many do you think, Din?"

"I think we can sell fifty thousand cameras in a year's time," said Land.

The grandeur of that statement sent them both off into their thoughts again. That would surprise Julie, thought Land.

Polaroid has only three hundred sixty people left, thought Bill with a twinge of panic. How many would we need to make film for fifty thousand cameras?

Then the two men just stood together, enjoying the sight of the pretty hands flying over the green table.

13

Demonstration

Boston, 1948

Jordan Marsh, Boston's oldest department store, sat at the intersection of Washington and Summer streets, glaring at its archrival Filene's on the opposite corner. In 1948 the two defined the Boston downtown shopping district. Such other landmarks as R. H. Stearns, S. S. Pierce, Bailey's ice cream parlor, and Locke-Ober were usually described in relation to them: "One block up from Jordan's on Winteh, then turn left into Winteh Place; you can't miss it." Jordan's combined a venerable assemblage of adjacent buildings, wings, and an annex connected by a covered bridge over the street. Its departments were periodically rearranged, enlarged, shut down, or reopened with appropriate fanfare as the tides of commerce ebbed and public taste changed. The photographic department was one of its smallest. Although it had a good location on the ground floor of the Hovey Building, with its own entrance on Washington Street, most customers used it as a convenient passageway to the larger and busier jewelry department. Jordan's photo department did not carry a wide variety of merchandise. Eastman Kodak supplied most of what was offered. At the top of the line was the Kodak Reflex, a rather prosaic twin-lens reflex camera. There were folding Kodaks with collapsible bellows and prism viewfinders, and Baby Brownies which sold for only $2.75 but took very acceptable black-and-white snapshots. The Brownie was the first aim-and-shoot camera. "You press the button, we do the rest," reiterated Kodak.

There were almost no German or Japanese cameras available at Jordan Marsh. Agfa, Leica, Rollei, and Voightlander still struggled to lift themselves out of the rubble of the bombing raids. The few Japanese cameras on the market were cheap copies sold in the toy department. Before the war, Eastman Kodak had been overshadowed only by Agfa in Germany and Konishiroku in Japan. Now it reigned supreme, its share of the American market more than 90 percent. No corporation — neither General Motors nor General Electric — dominated its industry as did Kodak. Kodak not only made and sold most of the cameras and film in the United States, it controlled film processing and printing as well. The lion's share of this lucrative business, handled by Kodak itself, emanated from Rochester. Those processors who sought to compete had little choice but to buy equipment, chemicals, and paper from Kodak. Eastman supplied film, equipment, and processing to Hollywood, portrait studios, the X-ray field, aerial photography, virtually every facet of industrial and professional photography. Technical advances came quickly in the professional field, but cameras for amateur use evolved at a more leisurely pace. Kodak did not worry much about competition, and margins were lucrative.

The rapid expansion of Eastman did not pass unnoticed by the New Deal trustbusters. Kodak had faced a series of antitrust actions in the thirties and forties, the latest of which had forced the divestiture in 1948 of the Eastman Kodak chain of camera stores. Even with this setback, however, Eastman's products enjoyed broad distribution across America. Kodak was the predominant line in every camera store, every photo finishing outlet, most drugstores, and every department store that carried photo products. Dealers were dependent on Eastman Kodak for almost all their volume. Although Kodak could not control retail prices without violating the letter of the Robinson-Patman Act, it literally controlled the market, which achieved much the same end.

Industry trade associations were largely staffed with Kodak executives and appointees. Dealers made 30 to 40 percent margins on sales of cameras and film and much more on photo finishing. Kodak itself made margins of 80 to 90 percent on film. Discounting was virtually unknown in the retail marketplace at this time. Land's presentation to the Optical Society had attracted a great deal of attention in the industry, having been widely reported in the photographic trade journals and fan magazines; but many people, including some at Eastman Kodak, regarded the new process of instant photography benignly as a novelty, a scientific curiosity, not as potential competition. A new word coming into the language, *gimmick,* was often used to describe Land's invention. The gimmick was a cloud much smaller than a man's hand on Kodak's horizon.

The first Polaroid Land Camera, christened the Model 95 because it was designed to be sold for $95, followed contemporary camera design in many ways. It looked like a very large Kodak with its flat shutter board, small lens, accordion bellows, simple folding viewfinder, and hand strap. Not only larger than a Kodak, it was also much heavier. The two precisely machined steel rollers inside the development chamber contributed to the avoirdupois; the 95 weighed five pounds with a roll of film loaded.

Although the exterior looked familiar, the interior of the camera resembled nothing ever seen. The roll of film was composed of three elements, a strip of negative in one coil, a strip of positive sheet in another, and eight pods of the viscous development reagent. The roll of film — really two connected rolls — was an origami of precision paper die cutting and assembly. The dual rolls fit into chambers at each end of the camera. When the camera was closed and the leader pulled through the slot, the first frame of negative moved into position behind the lens. After the exposure, the end of the film roll was pulled again and two events occurred: the rollers ruptured the lead foil envelope of the first pod, and the matching positive sheet was drawn between them, facing the exposed negative. The reagent in the pod spread evenly ahead of the pressure of the rollers between positive and negative, which came to rest, a sandwich with an even layer of reagent coated like mustard between the two sheets, behind the back door of the camera.

The development process began as soon as the reagent touched the negative. The cycle of diffusion transfer, first demonstrated by Land at the Hotel Pennsylvania, began moving developed grains of silver from the negative and depositing them on the positive sheet to form the image. After one minute, the photographer halted the development process by opening the large back door of the camera and peeling the die-cut positive out of its frame away from the negative and the still-active reagent. After removing the picture, he latched the door, and the camera was ready to take another picture with a new negative frame positioned in the focal plane. If the picture was peeled away too soon, it would be underdeveloped, without much contrast and lacking detail; if it was left too long, it would come out dense, dark, and overdeveloped.

In addition to care in the timing, it took strong hands and arms to manipulate the Model 95. Women often had to rest its weight on a shoulder when aiming it. Although the external design of the camera had been executed by Walter Dorwin Teague, the respected industrial designer who had tried in vain to rescue the ill-fated study lamp, the Polaroid camera was not an object of beauty. It had, however, the unmistakable appearance of a device that did something unique. Like a machine gun or a pair of scissors, it could not be mistaken for something else. Like the Coca-Cola bottle and the Model T, the Polaroid Model 95 camera was absorbed directly into the American consciousness, forever and immediately recognizable.

When the Polaroid crew arrived at Jordan Marsh the day after Thanksgiving to set up the first public demonstration of the new camera, they were given a spot behind one of the counters that lined the room on both sides. The three men surveyed the narrow, unprepossessing space. One man was there to work the camera, another to handle a set of large placards, which would describe the demonstration. Ro Messina helped them unload cameras and film in clean new cartons from Samson United, then drove his DeSoto back to Cambridge. "Call and tell us what happens," he said as he left, not quite able to mask the concern in his voice. Even though Christmas was only a month away, Jordan Marsh's photographic department was not very busy. A few desultory decorations hung from the ceiling; a Salvation Army bell clanked intermittently outside the street door.

The two demonstrators piled the Polaroid cartons behind the counter and in the stock room. A single carload looked as though it might suffice for a long time — months perhaps. A late-night crisis of marketing confidence at Polaroid had lowered the camera's price to $89.75. The price of a roll of film stayed pegged at $1.75 for eight exposures. The Polaroid pair endured a few good-natured gibes as they completed their final preparations, but the Jordan's clerks were curious to see what this intrusion was about. When he had fitted the flashgun, the man with the camera invited the staff over to his counter. A few shoppers drifted in to watch as well. Since it was late November, men and women were indeed wearing hats against the New England chill.

A fedora in 1948 was unusual only by its absence, especially in Boston. The hats created a problem because the people in the back could not see what was going on. The two salesmen conferred briefly, then climbed up on top of the counter. The man with the cards held up the first one: "The new Polaroid Land Camera." The man with the Model 95 leaned over his audience, whose eyes were at the level of his kneecaps. Sighting through the viewfinder, he chose a face about three and a half feet away and pressed the camera's workmanlike trigger. The flashbulb erupted with a loud pop. The crowd flinched. More people drifted over to see what was afoot. The man with the cards held up the next one: "The picture is taken." This redundancy was not lost on the growing audience. "We can see that, you dummy," came a voice from Southie. The photographer pulled the film tab and glanced at his watch. The crowd speculated on what might or might not happen next. The seconds crept slowly by. The two salesmen began to learn how long a minute can be in front of an expectant and skeptical crowd, a lesson Land had endured at the Optical Society almost two years earlier.

"We should have something to say while we're waiting."

"We need a PA system so they can all hear. Where did everybody come from?"

"I don't know. The place was damn near empty before we climbed up here."

"Is it done?"

The man with the camera checked his wrist again. "Not yet. Almost. Should I let it cook a little longer?" They had unconsciously assumed the vocabulary of the kitchen to describe the process Land felt would revolutionize photography and art. A man in the audience began to clap rhythmically. "Here goes," said the demonstrator as he lifted his camera and presented its back to the crowd. He opened the trap door and inserted a fingernail under the tab of the deckle-edged print. Slowly he lifted the point of the tab. The crowd fell silent. Then he stripped the print from the womb of the negative and with a gesture of perfect confidence, without glancing at it, thrust it in front of his rapt audience. They saw a clear, sharp, brown-and-white image of gaping faces and dark hats.

The salesman with the cards presented his next-to-last offering: "Finished, dry pictures in 60 seconds." Applause was heard. He lifted his last message: "Next demonstration in five minutes." The two men looked around. The narrow room was full. People pressed against the counter, talking to them.

"Wait a minute, I couldn't see the picture!"

"How much does it cost?"

"Does it work on water?" The salesmen looked at each other blankly.

"Oh, I get it — 'Land,' " the placard man said.

"Take another one."

Instant pictures were an instant success. The crowd pressed against the counter. They not only wanted to see the camera, they wanted it.

"We need someone here to sell while we demonstrate," said the man with the camera. A woman was gripping his foot.

"Look, you go ahead and work the camera. I'll write up orders. We don't need the cards. They can see what's happening anyway." The complementary functions of sales and advertising thus allocated under fire, the team went back to work. It was a long day; they continued until two events forced them to stop. "I'm out of cameras; give me the demonstrator. I've got a guy who'll pay list for it," said the salesman as the manager of the jewelry department pushed his way through the crowd, the assistant manager of the store in tow.

"Look at this." The jewelry manager had to raise his voice above the tumult. "It's some kind of medicine show! I haven't had ten people in my department all day. They can't get through this jam, for Christ's sake."

The assistant store manager looked around the room. He moved to the cash register and punched the drawer out. "How much did you sell?" he asked, counting rapidly.

"Fifty-six cameras including the one we were demonstrating with and all the film."

"They told me this was some kind of gimmick."

"Well, we are plumb sold out of gimmicks for today. We thought we had more than enough."

"When are you coming back?"

"Tomorrow at two o'clock."

"Can't you come in when we open at ten?"

"The cameras won't be delivered from the factory until noon."

"You mean you're selling them as you make them?"

"Right, but we called the office an hour ago and we're increasing production."

"Lord. Look, get in here as early as you can tomorrow," said the assistant manager. "We'll open up some more space in the department next door."

14

Stan

Cambridge, 1958

I walked up Main Street, wondering about the smell. I had taken the Red Line from Park Street in Boston to Kendall Square, the first subway stop on the Cambridge side of the Charles. As always, the T was loud, chill, fetid, slow to arrive, quick to start, and enigmatic as to routes and names of stations. Kendall was a minor stop. Most of the passengers stayed on, swaying in unison in the rocking cars, heading for Harvard Square, two stations beyond. When I climbed from the bowels of the station up the steep stairs, the noise of the train fading away quickly beneath me, ankle-deep in trash and a few forlorn maple leaves, the rusty black portals of the MTA opened on an aggressively nondescript view: the streets were virtually devoid of people; a few cars and trucks moved rapidly past; a sudden gust drove grit down the sidewalk; students hurried by, heading for the MIT campus three blocks away. The square contained a printing plant, some small offices, a branch bank, the Kendall Square post office, a drugstore marked CLOSED, and the F & T diner. The street furniture of signs, lights, mailboxes, and utility poles leaned awry, dirty and hopeless of repair. Some stores stood empty; others looked as though they would soon follow. An eating place beside the subway exit identified itself as the Terminal Lunch. It did not look enticing. I pulled up the collar of my coat against the gray chill of the afternoon and started north, looking for 730 Main Street.

An odor — a complex odor — kept intruding on my thoughts. It was a medley of smells: a barber shop quartet, a sextet, an olfactory octet. It contained a certain harmony, although the individual parts were not immediately recognizable. Something sickly sweet in the tenor range almost overpowered the rest, but right behind it sang the sharp, acrid, high-pitched stench of hot rubber. A chemical theme wove itself into the whole and was supported by an underlying bass of coal smoke from a freight train crossing Main Street a few blocks ahead. There must be an industrial fire somewhere, I thought. Maybe a slaughterhouse is burning, or something at the town dump. I assumed that when the wind changed, this unusual smell would disappear and the shopkeepers and laborers of Cambridge could breathe again. I had no intention of becoming a laborer of Cambridge. I was here out of curiosity, responding to a challenge. An artist friend of mine, Paul Giambarba, had urged me to come. A clever cartoonist and an excellent designer, he had done several illustration jobs for me at the publishing house where I worked, and we had become friends. Polaroid was another of his clients. "You have to go over and see them," he said.

"Why?"

"Well, what do you like about the publishing business?"

"I like the people, I like books, I like the variety, all the new titles every season."

"Bullshit. What do you really like?"

"Well, I like doing the advertising and the promotion. I like selling things. I like adding up the score," I said with mild surprise. That was what I liked, although I had never articulated it before.

"Then go over to Polaroid. It's a funny place. They do things differently there. It's not a Boston kind of place. They're growing and it's exciting. You may think publishing is fun, but it's a sleepy business. This is the big time. I'll set up an appointment for you with a guy I work with over there."

Before I took the subway ride to Cambridge I did some homework. Polaroid was a huge company in my eyes, with annual sales of $65 million in the photography business and the sunglass business. The two didn't seem very closely related, except that they were both consumer products. The company was run by a genius named Land. I talked to two people who said they had known Ed Land when he was first getting started. They both told me they could have bought Polaroid stock when it was first offered. Neither did. Both regretted it and said the stock was overpriced now. It seemed odd to me that the initial frame of reference for this company seemed to be the stock. No one I talked to knew much else about Polaroid except Land, the stock price, and the camera. Land, I learned, was a Boston celebrity, not so well known as Ted Williams or Arthur Fiedler, but surely better known than President Pusey of Harvard or Stratton of MIT.

I had allowed my lunch hour plus an extra hour to visit Polaroid. I was due at the personnel office first, then at an office on Windsor Street to visit the man Giambarba knew. I passed a row of dirty brick buildings and a concern that sold industrial belting. A leather belt turned an endless figure eight on two big iron wheels that protruded from the ancient façade. A sour wind whipped sand in my face and, as I turned away, I saw the entrance to 730 Main Street. It faced a brick building across Osborn Street, which had a curious fence of yellow pipe along the curb between its front entrance and the narrow street. I spoke to the guard at 730 and established my identity. He directed me down a drab hallway to a bench. I was impressed by the presence of the guard, which suggested industrial secrets. There were no guards in a publishing house. Beyond that I was nonplussed.

If this was the big time I had badly misjudged it. I certainly had not known what to expect. Polaroid resembled nothing so little as the antique elegance of publishers' offices on Beacon Hill. Nor did it look much like my Hollywood conception of a $65 million corporation. It looked like the back of a post office: linoleum floors, institutional buff walls, dirty windows looking out on a parking lot where a red Porsche sat forlorn amid a motley collection of sedans. I left my waiting-room bench and wandered down the hall. Odorous laboratories and dark supply rooms opened off the passage, but on turning a corner I was taken aback. Ahead of me was a library: a large, open, well-lit, shelf-lined room, rows of stacks behind its counter, a magnificent photographic mural of waves breaking against a rocky shore mounted on one wall. Men and women sat in walnut chairs at walnut tables, studying. This quiet, busy, beautifully appointed room contrasted so with its surroundings that I could only stare. I fancied myself a connoisseur of libraries. In eight years in publishing, I had spent time in many of the great public libraries in America: Baltimore, New York, Boston, Chicago; many university libraries; the Boston Athenaeum on Beacon Street, one of the most beautiful private libraries in the world. To find such a handsome example in this odoriferous neighborhood was a shock. I walked back to the bench where a short, stocky, dark-haired young man was looking concerned. "I thought I had lost you," he said, glancing at me curiously.

"I was looking at the library."

"It's the company library. Land has a thing about libraries. We've always had a company library as long as there's been a company. He has a collection of photographic books in his own office, all catalogued through the central card file. There are two full-time librarians here. Our scientists give it the most use, I suppose. We have all the current scholarly journals on chemistry, physics, and optics. And the book collection is pretty extensive. Whatever they don't have, they can get from Harvard or MIT. Come on in." The young man said his name was Robert Palmer, and he wanted to talk for a few minutes before I went over to Windsor Street. We sat down in his cubicle of an office. "You're looking for a job." It was not a question.

"No, I don't think so. I talked on the phone with Stanford Calderwood. He knows a designer friend of mine who told me to call. I'm going to see him today just to get acquainted."

"Yes, well, Calderwood had me check you out. Your references are excellent. You have a good credit rating."

"They are? I do?" I thought of the stack of bills on my desk at home. "What references? I didn't give him any."

He smiled disingenuously. "Well, I know a lot of people around town. It wasn't hard to find a couple who know you. I hope you don't mind filling out this application."

"I'm not applying for anything."

"Fill it out anyway. It'll save us all time in the long run." We seemed to be operating with differing sets of assumptions. When I finished the form, I asked him just how it would save time in the long run. "Well, if Calderwood wants to hire you he'll do it. He's like that. You won't know what hit you. He'll blow you out of your socks. Polaroid is the most exciting place to work in Boston, maybe in America. I've been here two years. I can't think of anyplace I'd rather be. You'll feel the same. I can tell."

"Where is Land's office?"

"On the top floor of this building: his lab is in the brick building across Osborn Street."

"What's the yellow fence for?"

"That's to catch Dr. Land when he runs from one building to the other. We almost lost him under a cab last month. I'd better send you up the street. Calderwood is waiting for you."

The Windsor Street office, three blocks away, was smaller and, if anything, grimmer than 730 Main. An ancient factory building, it lurked behind an abandoned school, a defunct grocery store, and a cluster of the tenement houses, peculiar to Boston and Cambridge, called triple deckers. The street was crowded with dirty cars that looked as though they rarely if ever left the curb. A cluster of maple trees, their lower limbs broken, stood defiantly in front of a large housing project across the street. I guessed that this must be a temporary location for Polaroid. I knew the company had built a new film factory on Route 128 in Waltham. I had driven by it, a rather ordinary façade surrounded by trees and lawn. They must be planning to relocate out there as soon as the other facilities were ready. Another guard passed me on to the receptionist. "Alice, show this fella to Mr. Calderwood's office." Alice sent me down another linoleum corridor.

The building had no transparent windows, but Calderwood's office suggested executive privilege with its panel of glass brick that admitted a feeble glow of outdoor light. The room was dominated by a deprived philodendron that leaned, tall and stooped as an old man, in one corner. The room contained a desk, a large tank of fish swimming in turgid water, magazines and newspapers in a big pile on a table. A chair stood behind the desk, but the room held nothing else. A balding, pink man in shirt sleeves and a polka-dot bow tie bounced into the room.

"Hello, young man," he cried. "See that plant? I told Land that if that plant ever dies, I'm gone too. People keep dumping coffee on it, but it's still alive." I noticed that someone had emptied an ashtray over its roots. "Sorry I can't offer you a chair." He leaped into his desk chair, propped his feet on the mess of papers on the desk, and stared up at me. "Tell me about yourself. Giambarba says you should be working here."

An interesting office. No guest chair. I smiled at him and told my story standing up. It didn't take long: born in Nebraska; went to Knox College in Galesburg, Illinois; family relocated to Seattle; graduated from the University of Washington; first job as a college textbook salesman, a "traveler," for Harcourt, Brace and Company; fired after a year; hired by Arthur Thornhill at Little, Brown and Company; college sales again for a couple of years in the Midwest; then moved to Boston to do sales promotion and advertising for trade books. He listened attentively. "I'm from Nebraska, too," he said. "It's a good place to be from. Why do you want to work in a nutty place like this?"

"I don't."

"Yes, you do. Otherwise you wouldn't be here. I like your stuff, by the way." He pulled out a folder of promotional pieces, mailings and displays I had turned out over the past year or two. "No, don't say it, I know you didn't send them to me. I got them from Giambarba. They're good. They don't have anything to do with the camera business, but I can see how they'd attract some attention in the book business. You need something more important to work with than this stuff." He held up a mailing for *Expectant Motherhood,* a staple of Little, Brown's backlist.

"We sold a hundred and twenty thousand copies of that last year," I said. "What's more important than motherhood?"

"Photography is more important than motherhood, and I've got a book we're about to put out that's going to sell twice that," said Calderwood, jumping to his feet. "It's called *Pictures in a Minute.* People are going to pay two bucks to buy an instruction book for their cameras. It's written by a photo magazine editor, and I'm going to teach him how to sell it." He pulled a dummy book off the shelf behind him and handed it to me. The author's name was John Wolbarst.

"Don't you have an instruction book for the camera?"

"Yes, but it's lousy. That's another thing you can do. We need a writer around here. We need all the instruction materials done over."

"Who wrote them?"

"I did, but I'm a newspaper hack. I worked for United Press for three years after I got out of the Navy. I wrote murder trials and two-headed calves and elections and airplane crashes, but I'm damned if I have the patience to write a decent instruction book."

"Why is Polaroid a nutty place?"

"To start with, it's run by a man who has more brains than anyone has a right to. He doesn't believe anything until he's discovered it and proved it for himself. Because of that, he never looks at things the way you and I do. He has no small talk. He has no preconceived notions. He starts from the beginning with everything. That's why we have a camera that takes pictures and develops them right away. Isn't that what a camera is supposed to do?"

"I don't know."

"Of course it is. It's obvious. But Land was the first person to think about it that way. The rest of us always assumed you had to send the negatives to a photo finisher. I've been a photographer all my life and I'm a smart guy, but I didn't think of it. It never even occurred to me." The bow tie bobbed up and down as he talked, the words squirting like water out of a high-pressure hose. "Let alone *how* to do it! That's a whole other story. The chemistry in the film is so complex, we can't make people understand what a miracle they're buying in a roll of Polaroid film. That's something else you can do. We need somebody to write the story of the film."

"Look, Mr. Calderwood —"

"Call me Stan, young man. I like you. I think we'll work well together. But I'm not going to pay you any more than you're earning at What's Its Name. You have to prove you're worth it first. Je-sus Kee-rist! Look at the time. I've got to run up the street." He climbed out of the chair and began hurrying around the room picking up things, the fluorescent lights shining on the patch of pink skin on the top of his head. I understood that he was heading for Land's office. "Come to see me tomorrow at four. There's some other people I want you to meet. There's the good guys and the bad guys here, like in any company, the Navy, UP, anyplace. It won't take you long to meet the good guys. Here's an envelope of stuff I want you to read. Tell me what's wrong with it. And here's a camera and some film. Learn to use it. I want to see all the pictures, even the bad ones. Especially the bad ones, understand? How much do you make?" His jacket was half on, but he paused and stared at me with innocent brown eyes.

"Ten thousand a year."

"And how old are you?"

"Thirty."

"I guess there's still time to teach you something. Kee-rist! I've got to get going. I'll see you tomorrow." He was gone, an oversized artist's portfolio clutched under his arm, his blue coat half on, an Irish tweed hat stuck precariously on his pink head. I heard his feet clattering down the linoleum. The room was quiet except for the hum of the aerator struggling in the fish tank. My arms were loaded with a camera, six boxes of film, a brown envelope of printed material, and a flashgun. I wondered if the guard would let me walk out with it all, but he did.

15

U-2

Washington, Cambridge, Burbank, and Sverdlovsk, 1954–1960

The U-2 was a strange-looking bird. Its designer, Kelly Johnson of Lockheed, said that he could add wings "like a tent" to one of his earlier creations, the F-104, the fastest plane in the world when it was introduced in 1953, and produce an aircraft that could fly higher than any conventional airplane had ever flown, above seventy thousand feet. Furthermore, he promised to do it in eight months. A promise like that might provoke laughter, or at least polite disbelief, coming from someone else, but Johnson, an authentic legend in American aviation, had built the F-80, our first tactical jet fighter, in 141 days back in 1943.

The U-2 came together at Lockheed's sprawling Burbank complex in a remote hangar reserved for "black programs" called the Skunk Works. Security was so extreme that no janitor was allowed past the high chain-link fence topped with barbed wire that surrounded the building. The U-2 was designed and built in a welter of cigarette butts and soiled paper plates.

The plane that rolled slowly out of the Skunk Works in July 1955 looked like nothing so much as a giant glider. The Pratt and Whitney jet engine was almost invisible; the two intakes faired smoothly into the lean fuselage. Its titanium wings extended twice the length of the plane's body and drooped noticeably. They would have scraped the tarmac if not supported by a wheel on a stilt attached to each wing tip. No insignia or markings of any kind relieved the dull black skin of the bird. As it was towed out to the runway it suggested the awkward elegance of a swan poised for flight, the tiny single-seat cockpit over the nose an empty, sightless eye.

The real eye of the U-2 existed in its belly. There a set of powerful Hycon cameras could survey a swath of the earth's surface 750 feet wide. The twelve thousand feet of Mylar film contained in their magazines could record a photographic path from Washington, D.C., to Phoenix on one flight. But the most remarkable feature of the U-2's camera system was the eye itself, a lens of unprecedented power and resolution. From seventy thousand feet, on a clear day, it could delineate people walking on the earth. Every detail of buildings, industrial equipment, military bases, vehicles, airfields, and missile sites was seen with stunning clarity. So airworthy that it almost leaped from the runway, the U-2 climbed at tremendous speed in a steep upward arc to more than thirteen miles, its distinctive scream dissipated in the silence of the stratosphere. It could fly thousands of feet higher than any interceptor on earth, beyond the reach of current antiaircraft guns or missiles, with a range of almost five thousand miles on one thousand gallons of jet fuel. The black airplane was the most perfect intelligence-gathering device ever conceived.

In 1954, memories of Pearl Harbor still haunted America's leaders. Dwight D. Eisenhower had been given a Rand Corporation report which warned that a Soviet strike might destroy 85 percent of the Strategic Air Command's bomber force at one blow. The president was determined that a Pearl Harbor never happen again, but hard information about Russian capabilities was virtually nonexistent. Much of what the West knew about Soviet arms and aircraft was shown to them by the Russians themselves at their May Day celebration at which troops, tanks, missiles, and planes were paraded past a reviewing stand in Red Square that contained, in addition to the Soviet leadership, observers from most of the countries of the world. On one memorable occasion a flight of ten new Bison bombers thundered overhead, to be followed by a second flight of nine, and then nine more, roughly three times the number Western analysts believed the USSR had built. Only later did speculation surface that the same flight may have overflown Red Square three times.

Paranoia about the "bomber gap" and the "missile gap" racked the United States in the fifties. Nikita Khrushchev, an unpredictable bombast, had come to power in Russia. Eisenhower was under great pressure from Democrats like Henry Jackson and Republicans of the stripe of

William Knowland to "close the gap." But the president, who had seen as much war as most men on earth, was reluctant to begin a new arms race. Still, the specter of the burning ships off Diamond Head would not leave his mind.

Harry Truman had established a science advisory committee to keep him apprised of developments in technology that could affect national security. Eisenhower continued to use the group, headed in 1954 by Lee DuBridge, president of Cal Tech. DuBridge was surprised one evening to be challenged by an acquaintance, Trevor Gardner, assistant to the secretary of the Air Force for research and development. Gardner told DuBridge that the advisory committee wasn't doing its job, wasn't focusing on the critical issue of how to prevent a surprise attack. Profane and blunt, Gardner shocked DuBridge, who promptly invited him to address the committee, which then took Gardner's message to the president. Eisenhower confessed his own fears on the subject. DuBridge eventually recommended that a special group be formed with the specific assignment of studying methods of protecting the country against another Pearl Harbor. James Killian, the president of MIT, was chosen to head the technological capabilities panel. He quickly assembled a blue-ribbon group of scientists and engineers, although resentment against the Eisenhower administration's treatment of J. Robert Oppenheimer still rankled the scientific community. The intelligence committee of this panel was headed by Edwin Land.

Killian had made a logical choice. Land was well acquainted in Washington. He knew much of the country's scientific establishment personally. He was a visiting lecturer at MIT and would later persuade Killian to join Polaroid's board. Killian had no hesitation about describing his Cambridge friend as "an authentic genius." Land quickly assumed a leading role in the events that began to unfold in the old Executive Office Building next to the White House. His trips between Boston and Washington became more frequent, his stays longer.

The Killian group began an intensive analysis of the means of gathering intelligence that could reveal both the Russians' capabilities and their intentions. The panel shared a scientific distaste for the traditional methods of espionage using agents and diplomats. They sought a new way to look at the Cold War enemy. In 1951, Land had attended an MIT seminar on Beacon Hill where he had heard General James Doolittle talk about the potential of aerial reconnaissance. Land had also heard other

Air Force officers express the opinion that the technology for deep penetration of Russian airspace with impunity lay ten years in the future. Land felt he knew something about speeding up the process of technological development. Then he met Kelly Johnson.

Land and Killian went to see Eisenhower in November of 1954. They recommended an aerial intelligence-gathering program of breathtaking scope. They expected their audience to be a brief one, followed by a period of study and discussion. Eisenhower surprised them by approving the idea in principle with the stipulation that the program be run by civilians rather than by the military. Later that month Allen Dulles of the CIA got approval from the president to proceed with Lockheed. They tentatively planned to build thirty planes for $35 million. No one quite believed that Kelly Johnson could have the first plane flying in eight months, except perhaps Land, who recognized in him a kindred spirit.

James Baker, a brilliant Harvard optical designer, was given a task that rivaled the airframe designer's. But by the time the U-2, as it had been designated, began its test flights from a remote dry lake in Nevada, the first camera system was ready. Baker's lens was a marvel of resolving power. Eastman Kodak created the 70 mm film on a light, tough Mylar base. By July 1956, the U-2 was ready, awaiting only the president's signal to begin the overflights of the Russian land mass for which it had been designed.

From the first flight on July 4, 1956, to the day Gary Powers was shot down on May 1, 1960, the U-2 changed the course of history. The amount of information gained in the overflights almost swamped the Western intelligence community. It was said that the U-2's photography was to intelligence of the fifties what code breaking had been in the forties; suddenly a hidden world was totally revealed. It quickly became apparent that the bomber gap and the missile gap were misapprehensions. The United States and the Western powers had overestimated Soviet strength. The Russians followed every U-2 flight on radar, but could not touch the planes at seventy thousand feet. The U-2 program remained one of the best-kept secrets of the Cold War, kept secret by the Russians as well as the Americans, since Soviet officialdom could not admit that their air defenses were being breached on a regular basis.

The first U-2 flight brought back detailed pictures of the Kremlin in Moscow and the Winter Palace in Leningrad. Richard Bissell, the CIA officer who directed U-2 operations, wanted a conclusive demonstration of what his bird could produce. Subsequent flights totally revised American and NATO thinking about Russian capabilities. Michael R. Beschloss, author of *Mayday,* the definitive account of the U-2, wrote: "The U-2 brought a measure of stability to the nervous relations between the United States and the Soviet Union. By providing intelligence that helped to reassure Eisenhower that Moscow was planning neither a surprise attack nor a crash missile program, the U-2 allowed him to resist enormous post-*Sputnik* pressures from the Pentagon, Congress and the public to escalate the arms race."

Then, on May Day, fifteen days before Eisenhower and Khrushchev were to meet at the summit in Paris, Gary Powers took off from Peshawar in West Pakistan, headed across Russia for Bodø, Norway, 3,788 miles away. Soon after he crossed the Soviet border sixty thousand feet above the Urals, he began to experience trouble with his autopilot. Over the city of Sverdlovsk, where Czar Nicholas II and his family were killed in the revolution, Powers's plane was hit and disabled. Powers fought his way out of the cockpit and parachuted without hitting the "destruct" switches that would have exploded the plane. He landed on a state farm and was captured. Most of the U-2 technology literally fell into the hands of the Russians. A new phase of the Cold War had begun.

Land continued to serve presidents. He was a member of science advisory panels for Kennedy, Johnson, and Nixon. Johnson awarded him the Presidential Medal of Freedom in 1963. Land resigned his advisory post in Nixon's administration during the Watergate scandal.

16

Demonstration

New York, 1960

Stan Calderwood, Neil Schreckinger of Doyle Dane Bernbach, our account man, and I were sitting in the faded plush seats of the Ziegfeld Theatre on Sixth Avenue and Fifty-fourth Street, two blocks, although I didn't know it then, from Land's old apartment. The Ziegfeld had been one of the most beautiful theaters in New York in its heyday and for fifty years had given shelter to plays and musicals, the great and not-so-great of Broadway. Now it was a television theater, bought by CBS and converted to a strange show business hybrid, half theater and half studio. The balcony and boxes had been stripped of seats and held hundreds of lights, big storm trooper spots, smaller fixed lights with barn doors adjusted to dump light precisely on the stage below, key lights, floodlights, baby spots. The television cameras of 1960 devoured light, could hardly get enough of it. Air-conditioning vents to suck out the heat of the lights had been chopped through the intricate plaster ceilings and arches so lovingly adorned by the original architect. Six large monitors in black boxes were suspended from a bar that ran the width of the house at balcony height. They showed the edited television image that was being fed to the CBS studios and from there broadcast to the country. The theater seats were dusty and the floor not very clean. The Ziegfeld reminded me of the Dundee Theatre in Omaha, Nebraska, on a Saturday afternoon, but there was no smell of popcorn, rather an odd combination of sweat, perfume, and hot metal.

Stan had a camera case on his lap and was holding a brand new Model 800 camera. He had just checked the rollers inside the camera for the sixth time to make sure they were spotless, no speck sullying the shiny steel. A little bump of dried matter could poke through the layer of developer, spreading only one ten-thousandth of an inch thick between positive and negative, and leave a white spot on a finished picture, sometimes repeated as the roller turned, producing a line of phantom bullet holes across the image. Stan was not looking at the camera, however; he was staring at the stage.

"Jee-sus," I heard him whisper. "Pull the tab." He was not speaking to me; his eyes were on Durward Kirby, the announcer who was standing onstage, talking to and partially obscured by the television cameras. One camera shifted stealthily to the left, moving without effort on silent wheels in response to the tug of the cameraman, revealing Kirby, who stood four inches over six feet. He had huge hands and a long fleshy face with the permanent half smile of one of the larger breeds of dog. Next to him, seen in the gap between the hovering cameras, stood Garry Moore, the star of the show, looking up at Durward, an expectant grin on his elfin face, his crew cut level with Durward's necktie.

"Now, I just snapped the picture of Garry here with his Christmas list," said Kirby. Moore mugged at the television camera whose red light was glowing to show it was the camera of the director's choice for the close-up, holding next to his face a big sheet of paper with a list of names and presents. "And that picture will be ready in just sixty seconds." Durward was holding a Polaroid camera in one paw. The advertising agency had chosen him as a television demonstrator because he was one of the few available performers who made the camera look easy to handle. He had the biggest hands of any man I had ever seen. The image repeated on the six monitors above our heads shifted from the close-up of Garry to a two-shot of them standing together.

"No it won't," said Stan in a loud voice edged with panic, "not unless you pull the tab." Durward talked on, working his way through the commercial, which was being broadcast live to an evening audience of about eight million people. The *Garry Moore Show* was second only to Ed Sullivan's as the most popular variety program on the air. It dominated the ten to eleven o'clock period on Tuesday nights. Polaroid had been one of its sponsors since September. We were the only advertiser besides Timex watches with the hubris to integrate live commercials into the format of a network show. Some simple prop or piece of stage business, in this case the Christmas list, served as a lead-in, and the audience was often unaware that it was watching a commercial until it was half over.

The live Polaroid spots had become a feature of the *Garry Moore Show,* provoking occasional ad libs by the principals and regular applause from the studio audience. The director was reluctant to blink his applause sign for a commercial, but he seldom needed to. If the audience didn't respond immediately to the climax of the spot, a close-up of the picture just taken, the three of us would lead the applause from our seats, the studio audience obediently following. I was checking Durward's lines on a script, a stopwatch in my hand, to be sure he did not miss any of the important points in the commercial. The stopwatch was not actually necessary, since the show management had adopted a lenient attitude toward our timing. We were supposed to complete the spot in sixty seconds, for which we were paying the network a little over $35,000. To do that we shortened the picture development time to fifty seconds, allowing the first ten seconds for introduction and picture taking. The pitch for the camera came during the fifty seconds of development, and the finale was always a quick look at the picture itself, followed by a reaction shot of the pleased subject and the photographer. The television camera added enough contrast to make the slightly underdeveloped picture look finished.

Some of our commercials had run a few seconds overtime, some as much as ten or fifteen, but since they seemed to add to the excitement of the show, the director simply let it pass and made up the overage later in the hour. Live television shows were loosely scripted with room for delays and ad libs. The control booth, where the director confronted a battery of monitors, switching the feed from one camera or another to the broadcast signal, talking over an open channel to the headsets of all the cameramen, the floor director, and the stagehands, presented a scene of quiet, almost eerie, manipulation. The first time I watched over his shoulder I marveled at the director's nerves. With a minimum of rehearsal a live, hour-long show would come together each week as smooth as butter. I recognized these as very professional people. They knew the alternative to perfect timing would be visible coast to coast. Live was *live* in 1960.

Stan leaped up in his seat and shouted at the top of his voice, "Pull the tab!" Everyone in the theater-studio jumped. Startled faces in the control booth turned our way. An usher in a CBS uniform ran toward us, making

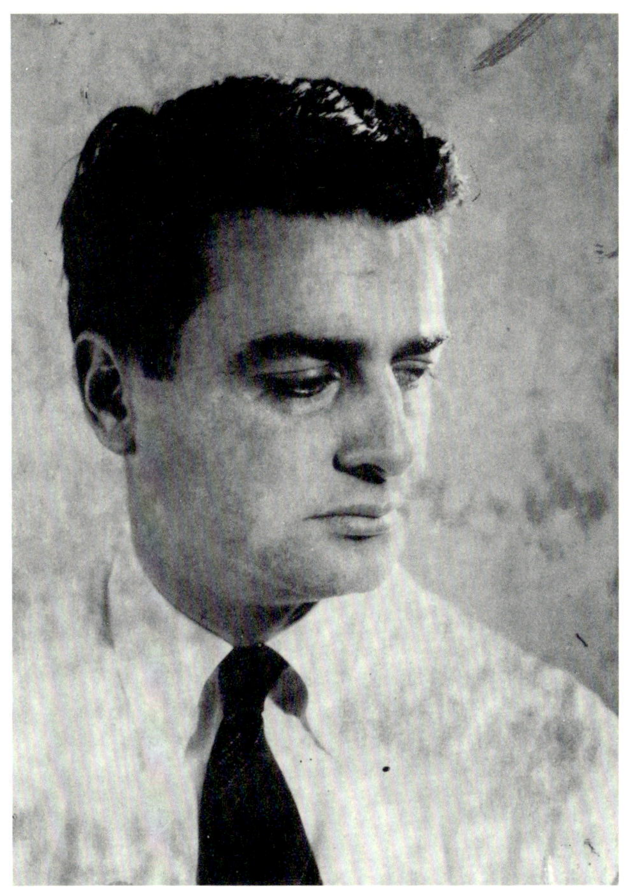

Edwin Land in a 1946 laboratory test photograph.

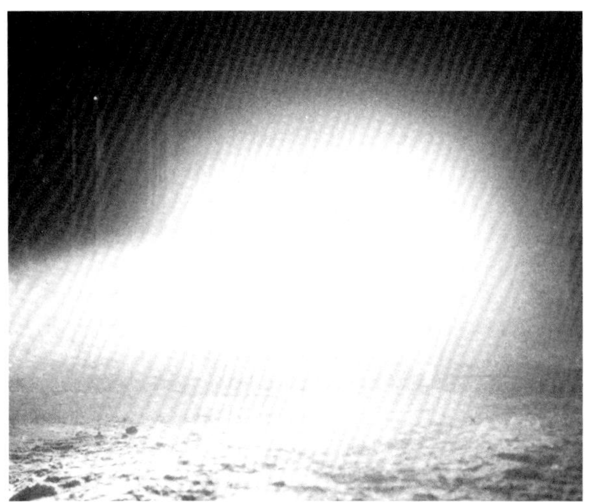

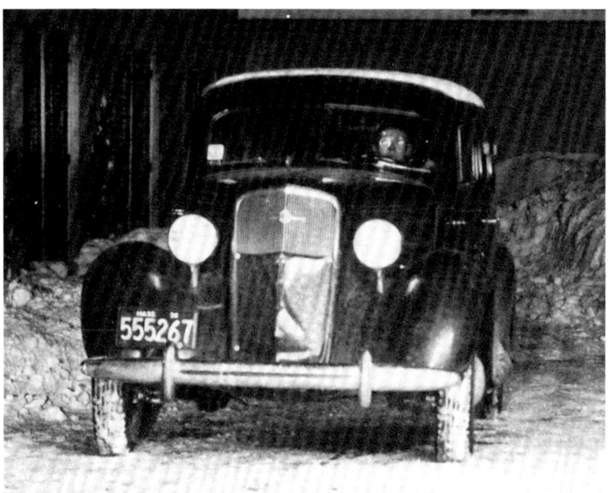

Eliminating headlight glare: a 1936 test in Harvard Yard of the system around which the company was organized. The same car is shown in both photographs—top, through an ordinary windshield, and bottom, through a polarizing windshield.

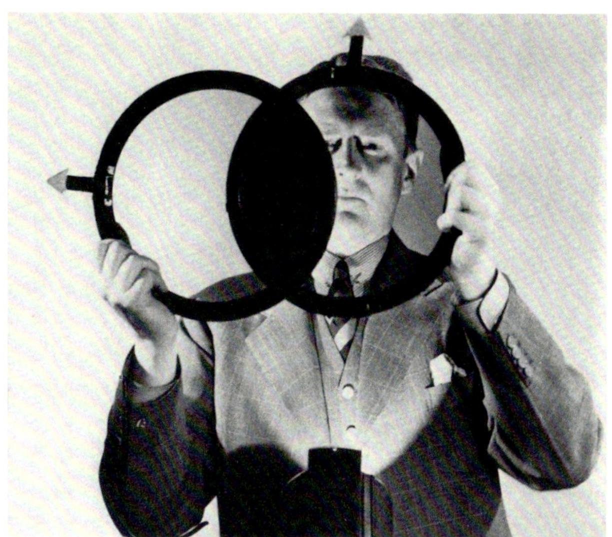

George Wheelwright holding two disks of polarizer. When the polarizers are crossed, light cannot penetrate. The intersecting circles became Polaroid's trademark.

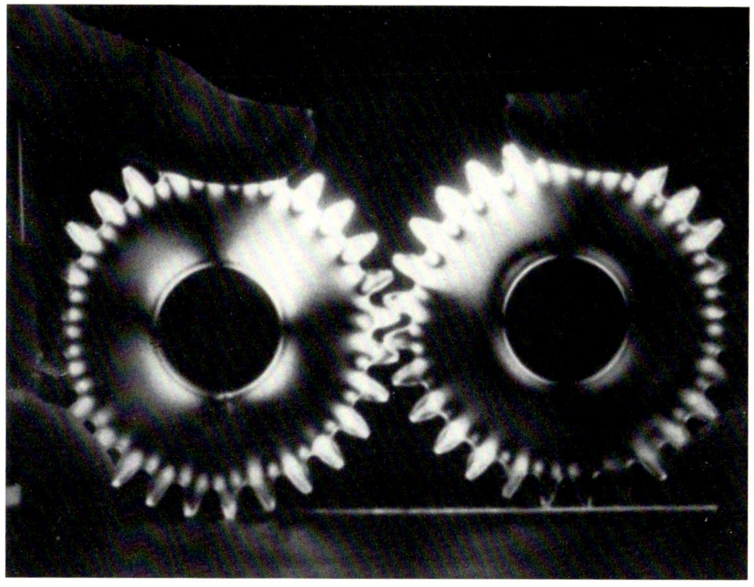

Plastic gear wheel models, showing points of stress when illuminated by polarized light.

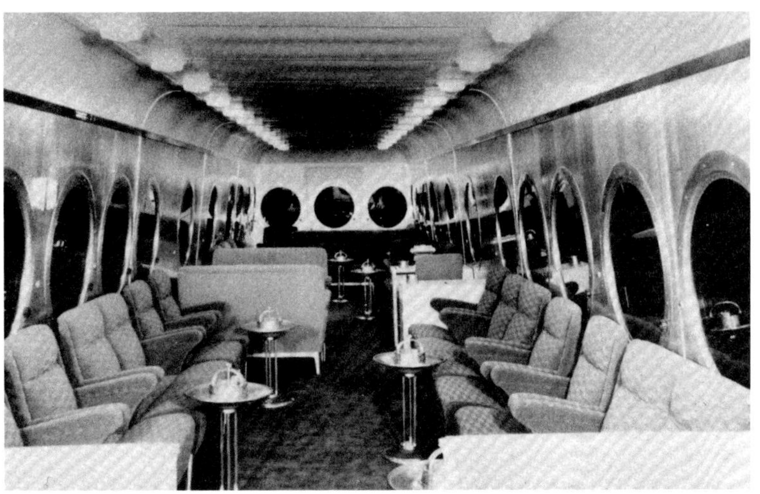

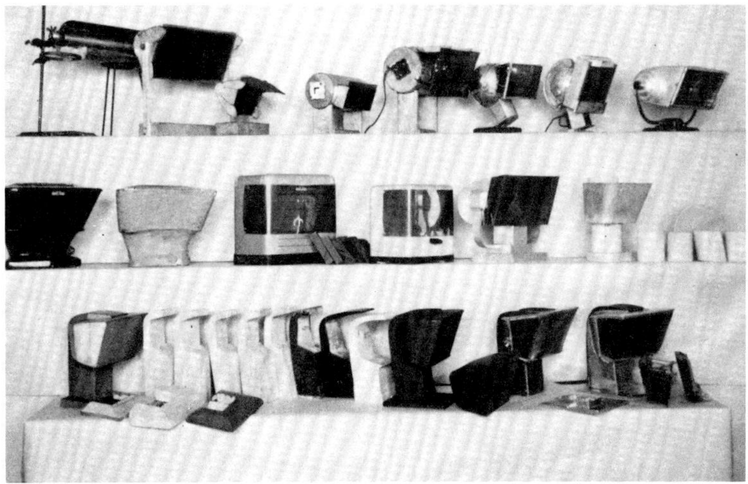

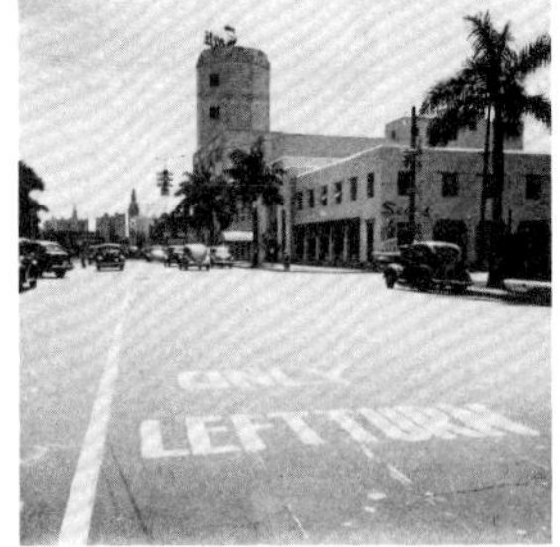

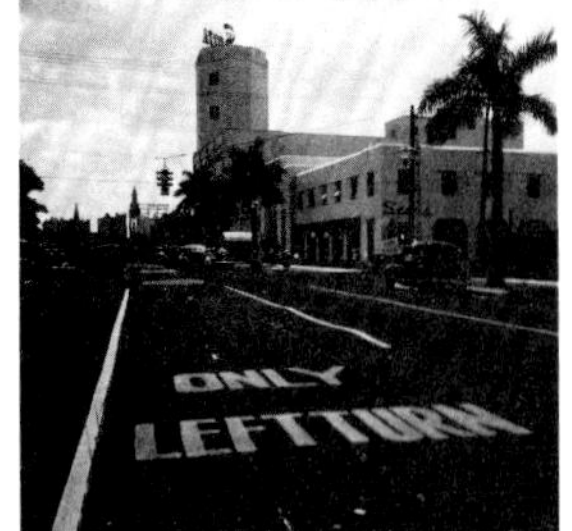

Top: The Copper King, the observation car of the streamliner City of Los Angeles, with its magic windows. *Middle:* The Polaroid study lamp was unsuccessful in all its configurations. *Right:* Polaroid Day Glasses eliminated glare from streets, beaches, snow — and bowls of goldfish.

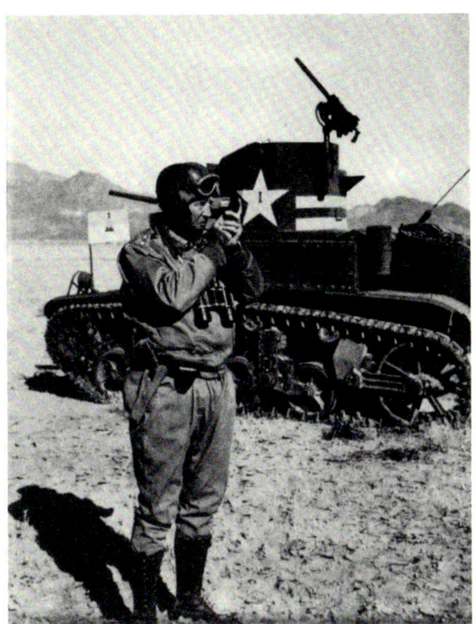

Polaroid responded to Major General George S. Patton's urgent requirement for a new tank gunsight.

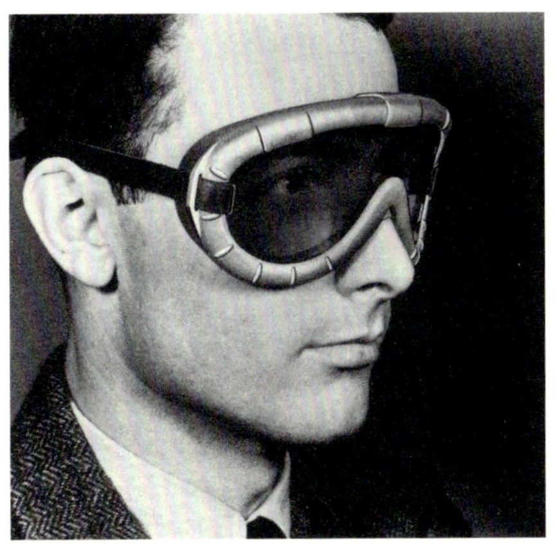

William McCune modeling wartime goggles.

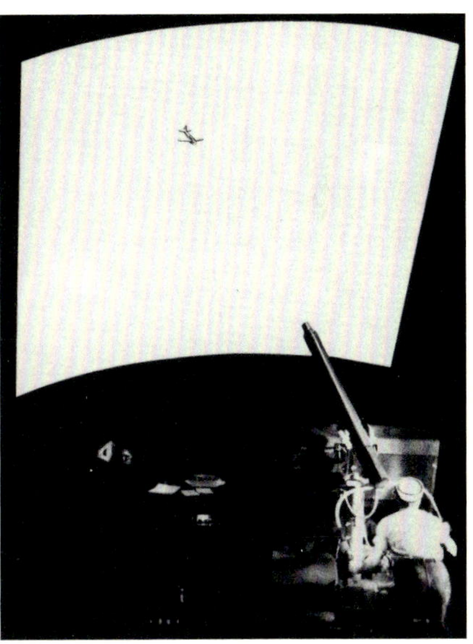

The Polaroid Machine Gun Trainer, which used no live ammunition, was a forerunner of the arcade game.

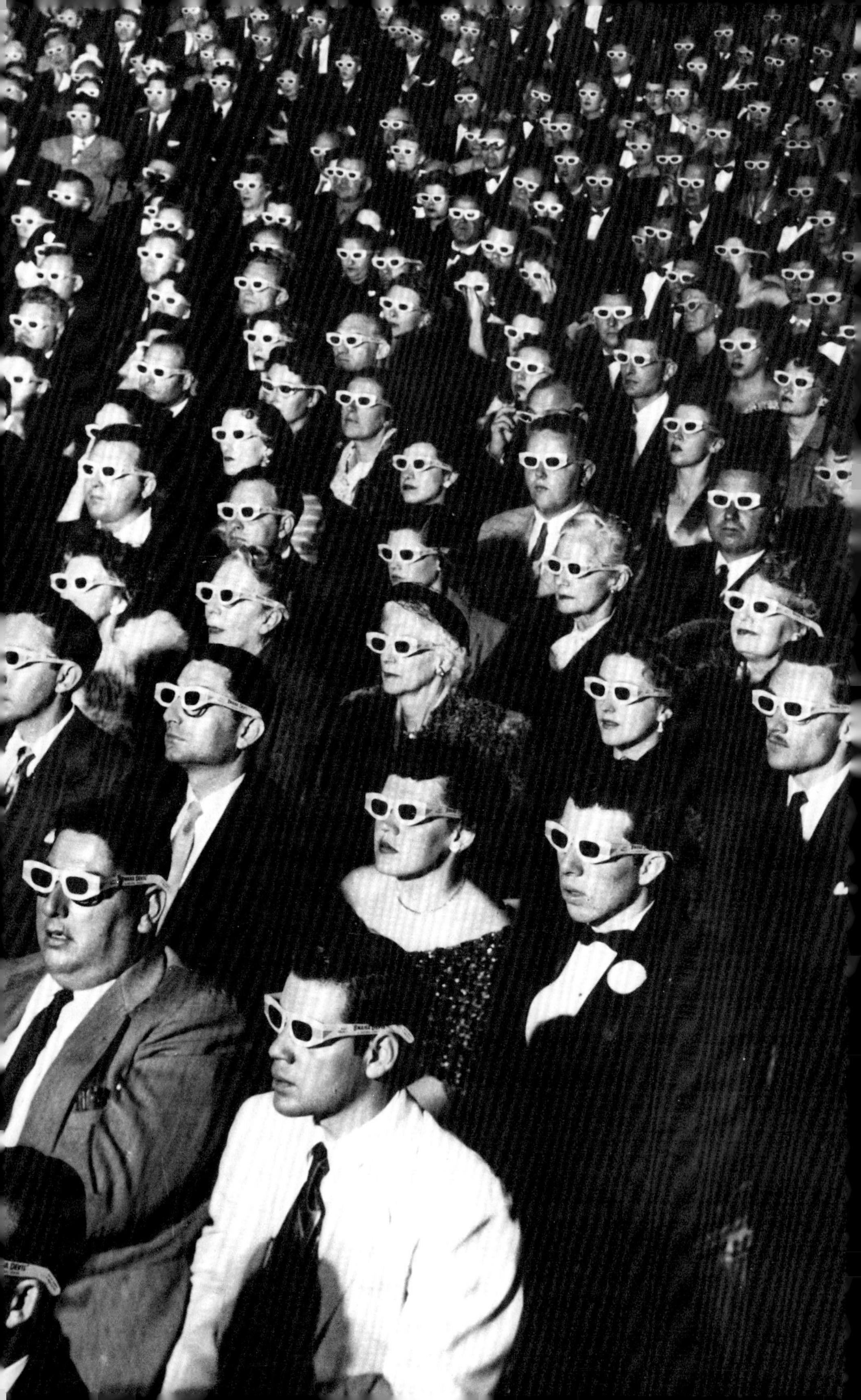

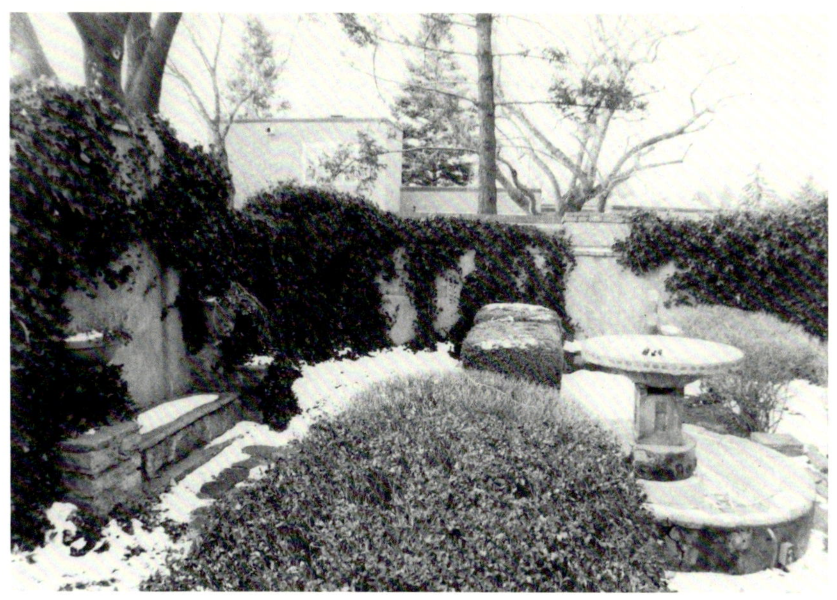

The Compound in Santa Fe, much as it looked in 1943. (*William Field*) *Right:* Land's daughter Jennifer in an early laboratory test picture—which she could see right away.

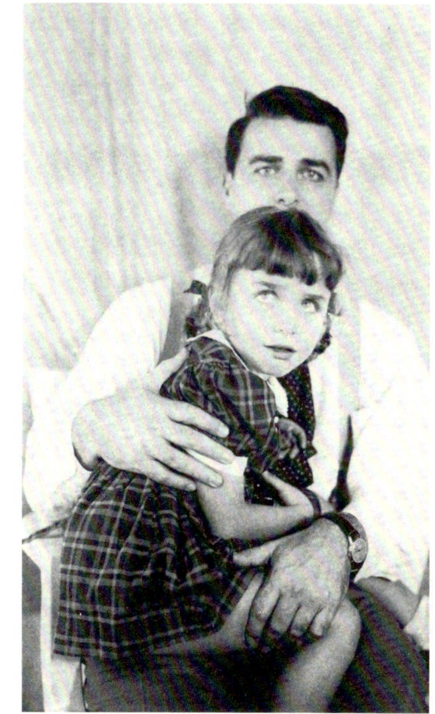

OPPOSITE PAGE

Postwar audiences gawked at 3-D movies like Warner's *House of Wax*. (J. R. Eyerman, *Life* magazine. © Time Inc.)

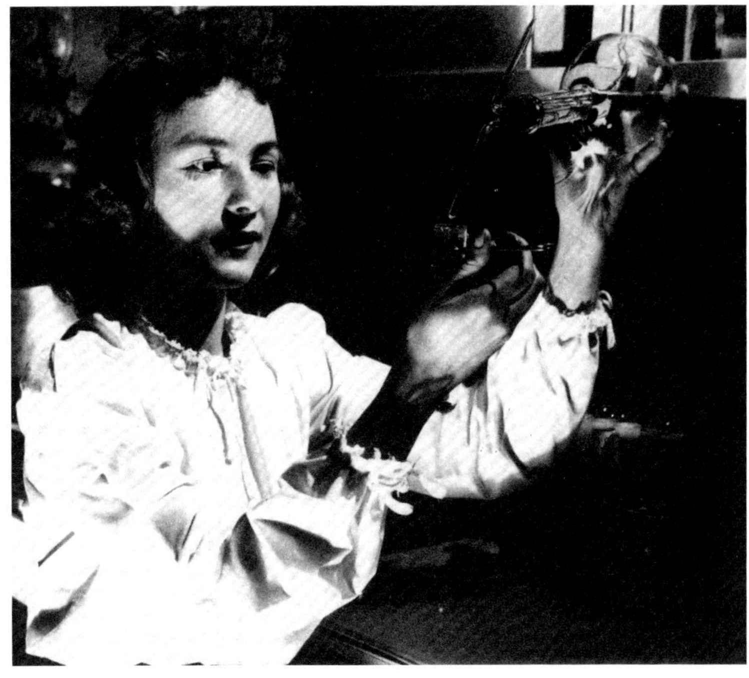

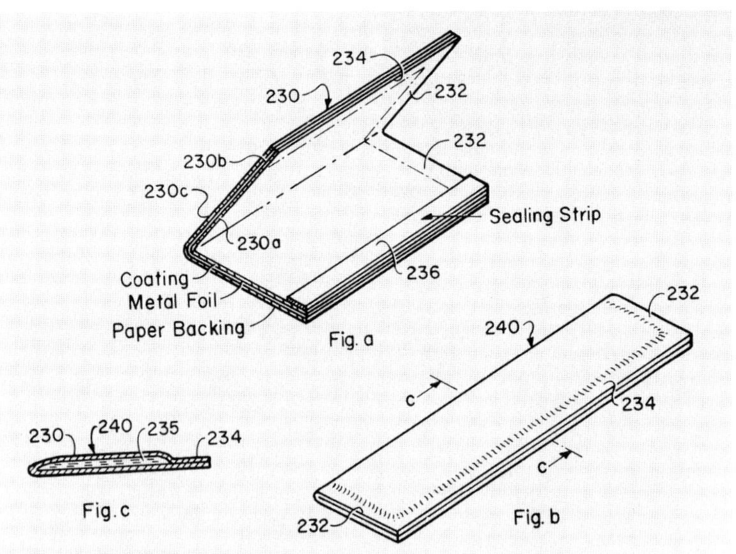

Top: Eudoxia Muller performed the first photographic experiments under Land's direction. *Bottom:* Diagrams from the patent application for the pod, Land's critical invention for the one-step photographic system.

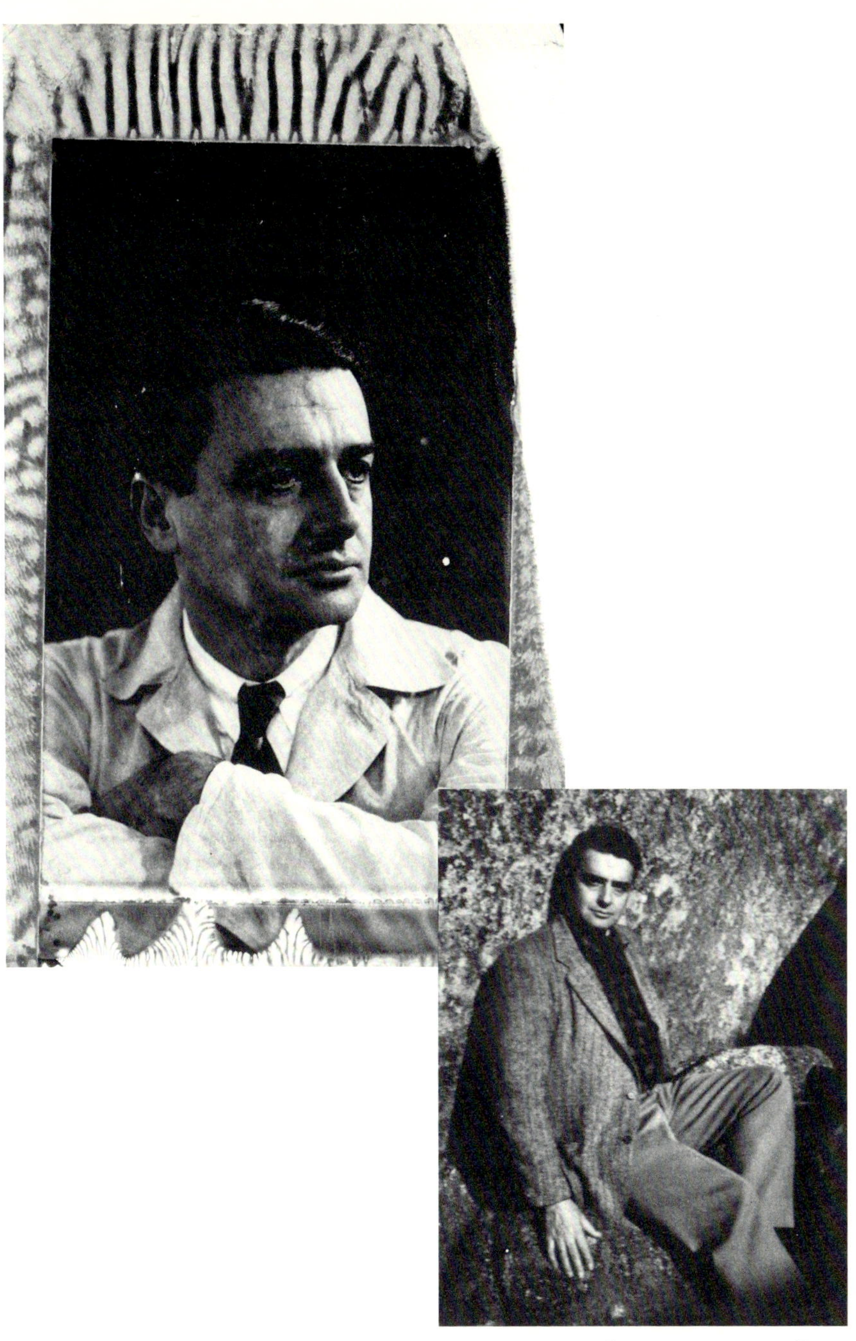

When secrecy was still important, the subject of test photographs was frequently the inventor of the process.

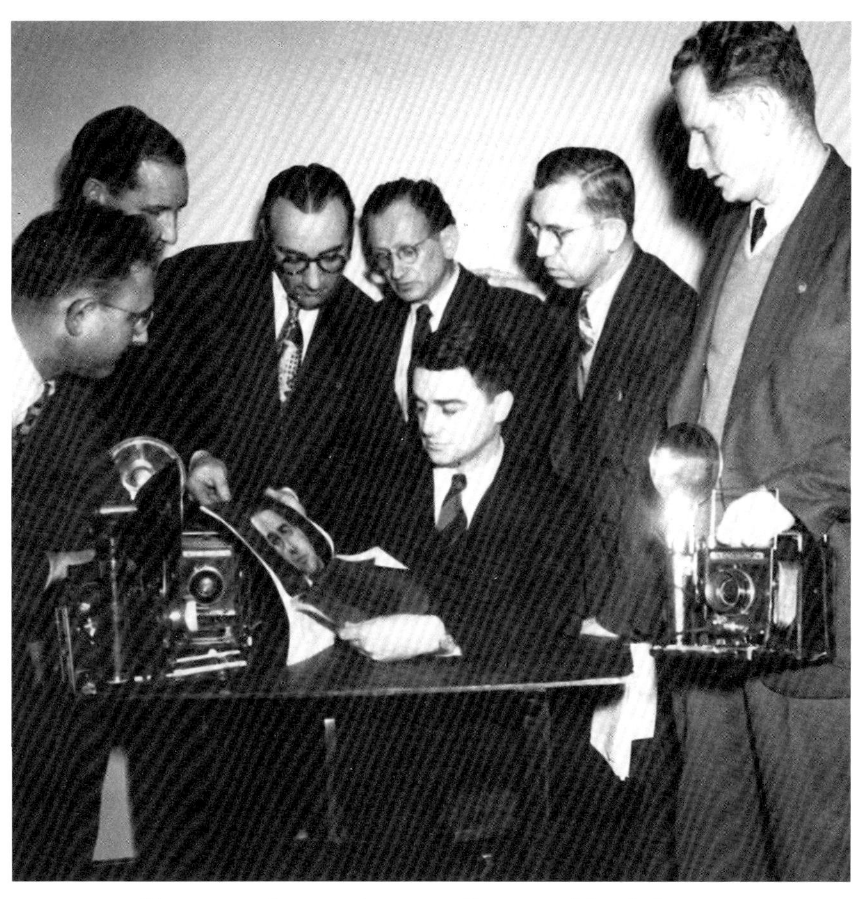

Newspaper photographers crowding around Land after his demonstration at the February 21, 1947, meeting of the Optical Society of America.

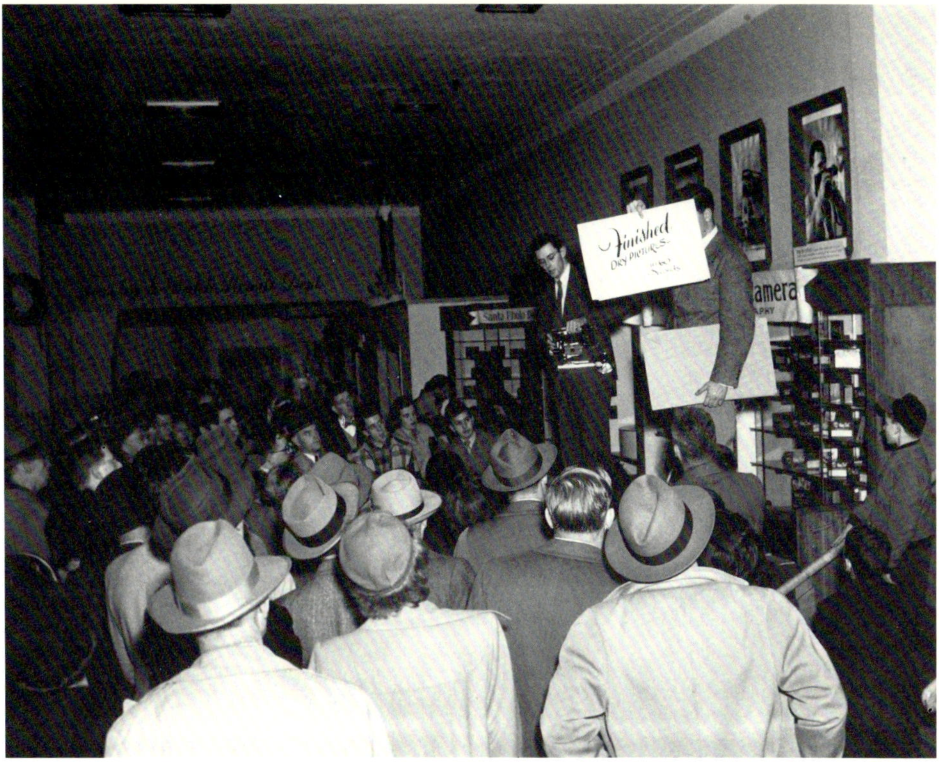

The first Polaroid Land Camera caused pandemonium when it went on sale at Jordan Marsh in Boston on November 26, 1948.

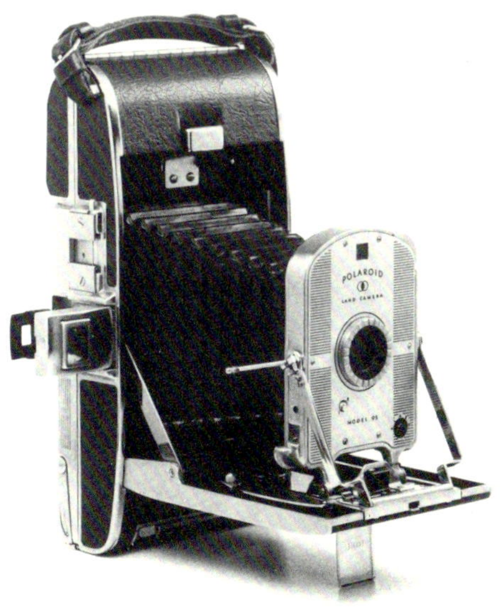

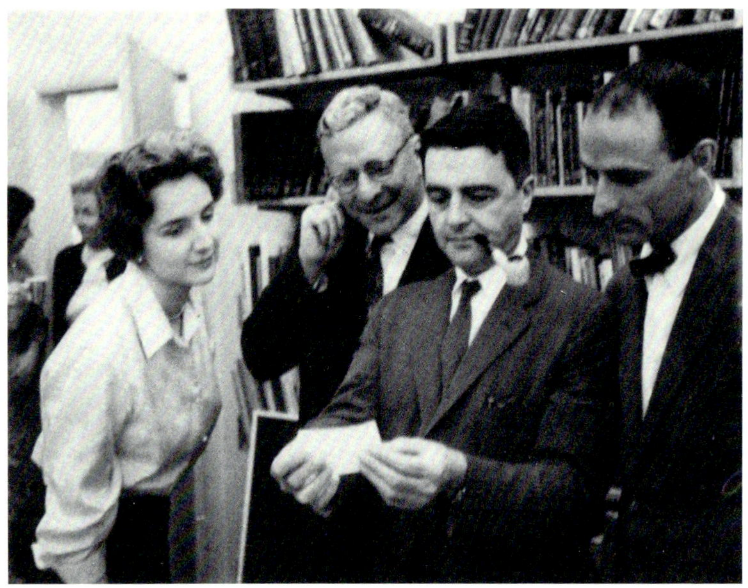

Polaroid people were always looking at pictures. Land shows a sepia print to Meroë Morse, general manager David Skinner, and Bill McCune. *Below:* Instant pictures became an overnight sensation.

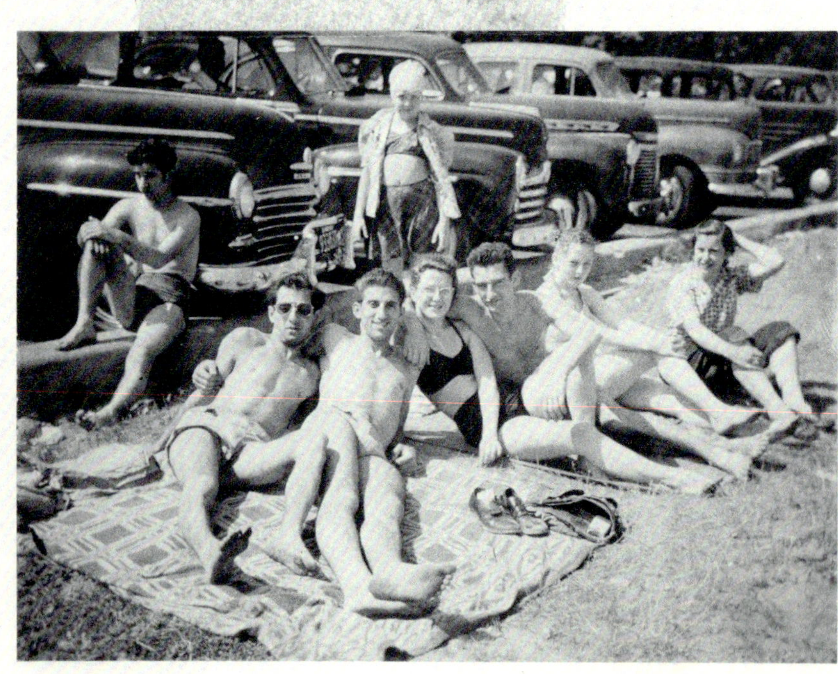

shushing gestures. Durward looked slightly puzzled. "Pull the tab," Stan cried again, a pleading note in his voice. People on both sides of us were hissing imprecations. The usher reached over and began to grapple with my boss. Neil Schreckinger, our debonair account executive, had pulled a copy of the *New York Times* over his head to blot out the scene. "Pull the tab!" The stirring admonition rang out yet another time across the orchestra pit.

Durward's face broke into an apologetic smile. "Oh, yes," he said, "of course. I have to pull the tab before the picture can start developing." He flipped the release button on the back of the camera with a thumb like a cucumber. I glanced at my watch. We were forty-five seconds into the commercial. I was very conscious of the studio audience of about three hundred souls. They were watching Durward intently. It occurred to me that eight million more were watching him at home. Durward grasped the end of the film and gave it a mighty pull. We watched in awe as he tore the film past the stop pins and succeeded, as much by his vigor as by the extraordinary length of his arms, in pulling the entire roll, seven exposures in all, since one had been used as a test before the show, out of the camera, where it dangled from his extended fist like a dying snake. A hush fell over the house. Stan dropped into his seat with a strangled cry. Neil seemed to disappear.

Live television held no terrors for Garry Moore, a trouper trained in small-town radio and barnstorming stage companies. He smiled sweetly at Kirby, who was surveying his accomplishment with surprise. "Well, Durward, you've outdone yourself. Folks, this camera is practically foolproof, but that doesn't count Durward. Now I know that my picture is in there somewhere, if we can find it." He picked up the tail of the five-foot strip of film and, as he held one end and Kirby the other, began plucking out pictures. The audience snickered as Garry peeled first one — "No, not that one" — then another. The laughter increased and the director cut to Durward's expression of anguish as the search moved fruitlessly up the line.

Because the exposed picture had been the first one pulled out of the camera and hence remained closest to Durward's hand, it was the last to be peeled away from the strip. The laughter rose to a roar as Garry said, "It had better be this one or I'm back in daytime radio." Then he lifted off a perfectly exposed picture of himself and his shopping list and held it steady for the close-up. There was silence for a moment, followed by a rush of applause from the audience. We did not join in. "You see," said Garry, "even Durward can't spoil a Polaroid Land picture. See the camera at your dealer's tomorrow. It makes a great Christmas gift. But we've got to get you the heavy-duty model, Durward," he said.

"Jee-sus Kee-rist," said Stan in a whisper.

"I don't believe this," said Neil.

The audience went on applauding as I glanced at my stopwatch. We had run a little over three minutes. The show director was facing major surgery. "What a disaster," I said. Stan leaped to his feet and ran up the aisle, Neil and I following as soon as we could gather up briefcases, film, and the rest of our gear. I found Stan pacing back and forth, glancing occasionally at the stage as the show raced through the final quarter hour in thirteen minutes. "What a disaster," I said again because I couldn't think of anything else.

"Disaster?" said Stan, grabbing me by the shoulders. "Disaster? It's a triumph! It's a blockbuster! It's the best live commercial ever done on television. What happened, for Christ's sake? Durward pulled the whole roll of film out of the camera. The whole goddamned roll! It looked like about the worst thing anyone could possibly imagine doing to a camera. And there he stood looking like he had just dropped his trousers!"

"He probably wished he'd been so lucky," said Neil.

"And then what? Then Garry, that beautiful little man, how I love him, the fast-thinking, ad-libbing little son of a bitch, he starts looking through that mess for a picture. Ed Sullivan would have thrown it all offstage and brought in the Hungarian acrobats, but not Garry, not my little sweetheart. He peels one, and then another, and then another."

"Didn't I hear him say 'yuck' when he got developer on his fingers?" asked Neil.

"Never mind. It was real. *Real!* That's what's important. You couldn't see that on the air and ever believe that a Polaroid commercial was faked. It gives us credibility for the next ten years. And then, and *then.*" Stan was yelling again, and we both had to quiet him down. The last musical number was finishing, Andy Williams was singing "Moon River," and the Garry Moore dancers were trying to get offstage as fast as they could in response to violent wave-offs from the floor director. "And then," Stan whispered fiercely, *"he finds the picture!* Oh, it's beautiful! In that mess he finds the picture, and it's the last one so it's had time to develop, and it's perfect. You can pull an entire roll of film out of a Polaroid camera and still get a good picture. Is that a great commercial or what?" He slumped into an usher's chair and leaned his glistening head against the dusty red damask of the barrier. We heard applause, and the audience began to file past us, heading out to the cold New York evening. "Go get the picture from the floor manager," Stan said hoarsely. "We need this one. I want to be able to prove that it really happened the way it looked. And collect the cameras and film. We've got to get out of here."

"I'm sure I heard Garry say yuck when he was peeling the pictures."

"Neil, of course you heard him say yuck. I heard him say yuck. Everyone in the country probably heard him say yuck. I could have done without the yuck."

"I hear they're going to tape this show next year," I said. "If we had been live on tape, we could just edit the yuck out of the audio before it goes on the air."

"In fact," said Neil, "if they go to tape we can probably shoot the commercial before the show and just drop it in."

"Yeah," said Stan. The adrenaline was beginning to dissipate. "We probably can. That'll be the end of live television."

"Well, we'll probably all live longer. And we'll know what's going on the air before it goes out."

"That's what I'll miss. No more three-minute commercials."

"And no more yuck," said Neil.

"Hell, I'll miss that, too," said Stan.

I went to collect the show picture and the rest of our equipment, and then we left by the alley exit before the director found us.

17

Bounce Flash

Cambridge, 1961

The Original Bar and Cafe on Main Street, one block north of 730, around the corner from Windsor Street, was a cavern of dark varnished booths with broken brass coat hooks sprouting from the stanchions to back-stab the unwary. It was an uncompromising eating and drinking establishment. The bar, which opened off the big restaurant, served draft Narragansett for fifteen cents; the foreign import was Carling's Black Label. In 1961 the Original offered Polaroid customers the same beef stew at the same price that had been dished out to the candy makers in 1931. Its manager preferred to lurk in the noisy little kitchen or out in the alley rather than actually to face the clientele in the restaurant or the bar. He was Greek, as was most of his menu.

Two waitresses tended the double line of booths, took orders, delivered food, collected money, ignored complaints, cashed Polaroid checks. The stout blonde was May, the slender dark one with the mouth was Flo. They knew every Cambridge employee of the company, including Land, whose bottle of Tanqueray sat on the shelf behind the bar with his name on it. The company maintained two Cambridge cafeterias, but the institutional food drove its employees to the Original at least once and often five times a week, no matter how vile the weather. It was a place where we could eat economically, talk to pretty secretaries and lab techs, brood alone on the vagaries of company politics, read, get an edge on to face the afternoon, or actually work with our associates during lunch if the prospect pleased us.

Polaroid's growth had not changed the Original; if it did not expand or redecorate, it was nonetheless always crowded. The pressed tin ceiling was frescoed in animal fat. The booths, historic relics polished by overalls, lab coats, blue serge, and rayon dresses, shone with a patina that was simultaneously shiny and sticky all year round, but stickier in the summer. May and Flo, sometimes called Ebb and Flo on busy days, sometimes called May and May Not, did not change their uniforms or their repartee. The bartender rarely spoke at all, except at closing. The invisible Greek was content to extract the same revenue from his customers year after year, for he was not troubled by the ambitions that drove corporate managers on the treadmill of growth. If he sent his son to Princeton he was going to do it on his own program, which included serving stuffed vine leaves every Wednesday and fried all-purpose fish on Friday. If his customers did not like the food they could eat elsewhere.

We often speculated that there was something sinister about the fact that the next nearest restaurant was six blocks away in Central Square. No Chinese or Italian entrepreneur dared cross the invisible circle drawn with the Original at its center. No hamburger fryer or pizza baker ventured within its circumference, only a doughnut shop next door — also owned, it was rumored, by the Greek — which opened early to serve coffee to the Cambridge cabbies. Polaroid was growing at the rate of 20 percent a year, but the Greek did not care. He knew the value of a monopoly, and he spent his energies maintaining it. His food was consistent. As Flo reminded us, "It may be cheap but it's not very tasty," and she boasted that no one had ever died from eating at the Original. But that could not be proved, and many did not believe her.

On Tuesdays the specialty was baked chicken and pilaf. As we were gingerly exploring it, Bill Field, Polaroid's art director, expounded on bounce flash: "A professional will bounce his strobes out of an umbrella or off a reflector to get a nice soft, diffused light without harsh shadows. The idea is to use the ceiling of your living room in the same way. With high-speed film you can bounce flash off a white ceiling and get a daylight look to flash pictures. Land wants a way to do this without flashbulbs, so the engineers have put together this, ah, *thing* that looks like a floor lamp with the reflector aimed at the ceiling, only it has a strobe in it instead of a regular bulb. You set it behind the piano or somewhere and it just stays there. The other half of the thing is a little radio transmitter that you insert in the flashgun of the camera instead of a bulb. It's about the size of my thumb, and when you want to take a picture anywhere in the room you just press the shutter; the transmitter sends a signal to the strobe and it goes 'blap' and floods so much light on the ceiling that you get good bounce anywhere in the room. You can walk around the room and shoot wherever you want. The lamp recharges itself in about a minute."

"What will it sell for?" I asked, trying to guess what appendage of the chicken was on my plate, fearing I knew all too well.

"We'll never know. Casselman took one home for the weekend to try it out. It worked fine for a roll of film; then he was eating dinner with his family when an oil truck drove by and the strobe went off by itself and scared them out of their chairs. It blapped again when their neighbors used their electronic garage door opener, and it blapped every time the furnace went on. It kept them awake all night. I don't think it will survive. The engineers aren't saying much about it."

"Where do these products *come* from?"

"Land figures out how to do something, and he assumes we can sell it."

"Who's going to buy a floor lamp that bounces strobe light off your ceiling?"

"No one, but how many times has he been wrong?"

"The Doctor is a smart cookie," said Flo, taking the wings and necks away and leaving coffee. "You kids stick with him and we'll all be rich."

"Are you a stockholder, Flo?"

"I was gonna, but it's too high. I'm waiting till it comes down."

"What if it doesn't come down, just keeps going up?"

"Whatever goes up comes down. Just ask my ex-husband," said Flo.

The stock was a frequent topic of discussion at the Original. Bill, who had preceded me at Polaroid by two years, had bought ten shares when he came to work in Cambridge from the offices of the New Haven Railroad. The stock promptly split two for one in 1956 and three for one in 1957, when it was first listed on the New York Stock Exchange. Bill's sixty shares were currently priced at $182 a share, so his original investment of $725 was worth $10,920. He couldn't believe his luck. We agreed that the stock was ridiculously overpriced. He planned to sell before the bottom dropped out. I asked what he would do with the money.

"I don't know, invest it I guess. In something that will grow, maybe more slowly, but for real. Something solid."

"A steel company?"

"Right. Something for the long term, something basic, like farm machinery."

"Isn't photography basic?"

"This isn't photography, this is show business. Have you bought any stock?"

"I have two kids. I can't afford to make money."

Land's stock and that of his wife and daughters had risen to a paper value of $143 million. Land's name was beginning to appear on lists of America's richest men. Land did not sell any shares. The circumstances of his life evinced little more luxury than at the end of the war, when he and his wife had purchased a big Georgian house on Brattle Street in the Harvard end of Cambridge. He traveled regularly to Washington, where it was rumored that he did something important in the Eisenhower administration that never got mentioned in the press. A member of the Harvard University visiting committees for astronomy, chemistry, and physics, a Visiting Institute Professor at MIT and a fellow at MIT's School for Advanced Study, Land had been recognized. He had achieved his stated goal of creating the kind of science-based company that might lead industry into the promised land of technological commerce, a company whose products would fulfill needs, or at least wants, not hitherto perceived by the public. He had received six honorary degrees, five science doctorates and a doctor of laws, making him Doctor enough for everyone in the world but the editor of the *Wall Street Journal.* Harvard's doctorate had been awarded in 1957, twenty-five years after the colloquium on "A New Polarizer for Light in the Form of an Extensive Synthetic Sheet" and five months before Polaroid's stock was listed on the New York exchange. Land had served as president of the American Academy of Arts and Sciences for two years and been named a fellow of every photographic society in the world worth mentioning. Nor had he spurned any medal.

But mostly Land worked; the habits of twenty-hour days and month-long nonstop projects, formed at Dartmouth Street and continued during the hectic years of the war, were unbreakable. Though the issue for Land, to say nothing of his company, was no longer survival, his intensity of effort had not lessened. On the contrary, the development of an instant color film absorbed him at least as urgently as had Patton's tank sight. At fifty-one, he knew only one way to work.

Time for the week of March 17, 1961, called him "a scholarly New Englander who had completely changed photography" and who "presided over his company like a physics professor engaged with his students in a great adventure." That phrase had a suspiciously Landian ring. Land had instructed Dick Kriebel to be cautious about requests for interviews with the Chairman of Polaroid. Each request was examined with care, discussed from every aspect, postponed, and pondered upon. But then, most often, granted. The reporter, after being held so long at bay, arrived in Cambridge in a state of frustration, grateful that he had not blown the assignment, persuaded by insiders both in and outside the company that Land almost never saw the press, armed with a list of tough questions, ready to pry information out of a clam. Instead of a clam he found a tabby cat.

Land had just moved his office from the top floor of 730 Main to a suite on the ground floor of Osborn Street, adjacent to his personal laboratory. One approached the office from a tiny entrance hall that led to an impossibly steep flight of stairs, up and down which clattered the lab technicians, engineers, and photographers who inhabited the upper reaches of the old Kaplan Furniture Company building. Outside on the curb, the yellow pipe fence, reinforced several times over the years, prevented Land from running across the street unless, as he did on occasion, he vaulted over it — to the delight of passing employees and the consternation of the security guards in both buildings. Land's office door on the hallway stayed locked. Security precautions, tight during the war years, had never been relaxed, even though Polaroid no longer had government contracts. His deeply ingrained suspicions made Land more comfortable with a locked door. Later on, closed-circuit television kept an eye on his hallway. One of three secretaries answered the bell, or perhaps someone waiting to see Land, apparatus or lab notes in hand. Despite the lock, Land was accessible to almost anyone, of no matter what rank in the hierarchy, who was doing something interesting. Some, such as Howie Rogers or Elkan Blout, always had access. Others, like Bob Casselman or Dick Kriebel, got in whenever Land felt the need for reassurance that the world outside his office was behaving, responding as it should. George Wheelwright, who had returned from the war to a company he hardly recognized, departing soon after with his shares of stock, did not often call. A reporter, standing in the brightly lit anterooms of Land's suite, would be bewildered by the confusion, the lack of formality, the clutter.

Three secretary's desks were equipped for typing, filing, and other conventional office activities, but only one looked used. It belonged to Natalie Fultz, a former Women's Army Corps colonel who was in command of Land's calendar and of his correspondence, which in fact flowed mostly in. Natalie was competent, forceful, and, within the limits of her ability to get Land's attention and cooperation, very efficient. She had favorites, and her list did not necessarily coincide with that of her boss. She enjoyed company when she walked up and down the stairs of the Polaroid buildings, since claustrophobia kept her from using the elevators. The other two secretarial desks were piled with miscellaneous objects. So were the tables, shelves, chairs, and any other empty surface. Optical instruments, telephones, reference books, television sets, Japanese cameras, radios, microscopes, clocks, toys, and apparatus that defied description lay scattered everywhere, brought in for or by Land to examine, play with, and dissect. A low table groaned with periodicals spilling onto the floor. Phones rang incessantly. Three cubicles opened off the large room. One had been converted into a pantry-kitchen with a small refrigerator, a hot plate, a sink, and a yellow Formica counter that held a tea tray. The other two housed the paraphernalia of projects that were being carried out under the eye of the Director of Research. The visitor's impressions were of confusion, harsh fluorescent light, a strange dissonance of objects and people.

Natalie's desk protected the door to Land's sanctum. It opened, and Land stepped out to greet the reporter warmly, formally, a little shyly. The visitor was ushered from noise and light into a dark cave whose high walls were lined with books. This library contained several thousand photographic and scientific books, including such rarities as a complete bound set of *Camera Work,* Alfred Stieglitz's superb photographic magazine published between 1902 and 1917. The lighting of the room, cunningly distributed among recessed ceiling fixtures, spots, floor and table lamps, was governed by a rheostat dialed so aggressively low that the artifacts of this extraordinary chamber could barely be discerned.

Land offered his visitor a chair facing the large desk, but then began pacing about the room, disappearing and appearing between pools of yellow light as his guest swiveled to follow his progress. Everywhere the visitor's eye found mysteries and questions: a transparent clock with no visible works, a large model of a molecule perched on the desk like a particularly unattractive insect, an art deco floor lamp, an antique optical instrument, arcane color charts. Pulling himself together, the reporter extracted his notebook and mentally reviewed the questions he had planned: difficult questions about sales and the price/earnings ratio of Polaroid stock. As the reporter opened his notebook, Land picked up a camera. As the reporter framed his first question, he found himself framed in the viewfinder. Distracted by the silent gaze of the camera's eye, he nevertheless persevered. "Mr. Land, how do you explain your failure to interest Detroit in the headlight scheme you —"

"Blap!" An eruption of white light scalded the ceiling, causing the reporter to leap to his feet. Land smiled and pulled the end of the film from the camera with practiced ease.

"This is something new we're testing," he said quietly. "It's an interesting concept which our engineers have embodied in this" — he glanced at the ungainly lamp — "ah, unit with which we've been experimenting. Have you ever heard of bounce flash?" The lecture flowed, inexorably. The reporter was instructed in how to hold the camera correctly and in its use. He took a picture of Land behind his desk. He was shown how to pull the tab in the approved way, the picture timed precisely, using the sweep-second hand of his watch. He learned how to peel the print from the back of the camera when it was just ready, and as they examined it together, the reporter leaning over Land's shoulder, Land pointed out ways it might be improved. "Try moving a little closer to include the top of the desk here. Perhaps you might frame my head a little higher."

"Blap." The strobe erupted again, the process repeated. The morning wore on and the reporter became proficient.

"Here, you have produced," said Land, holding it up to the light on his desk, "the picture to illustrate the story." It was indeed an excellent portrait of Land, hands clasped in his lap, looking thoughtfully at the camera, books in the background, the somber black circles under his eyes the only part of the picture untouched by the flattery of bounce flash. "It's quite professorial," said Land, smiling, "but I sometimes think of myself as a physics professor engaged with my students in a great adventure." The reporter set aside the picture and made a hasty note. Lunch — tenderloin of beef and a tossed salad — was brought in, not from the Original, and the interview proceeded as they ate. "Discoveries are made," said the professor, "by some individual who has freed himself from a way of thinking that is held by friends and associates who may be more intelligent, better educated, better disciplined, but who have not mastered the art of the fresh, clean look at the old, old knowledge."

"Yes," said the reporter, "yes, indeed," writing so rapidly he did not stop to consider whether the passage contained meaning.

"Did you get it all?"

"Ah, let me read it back."

"Yes, please do. No, 'mastered,' not 'mustered.' Yes, that's correct. Did you enjoy lunch? This is an excellent photograph. Notice the sharpness, the subtle delineation of the tones in the shadow areas. Let me coat it for you. This new 3,000 ASA film is not only the fastest amateur material available, but its tonal gradations are superb. Ansel Adams has been using it in the 4 x 5 format and getting some astonishing results. I think it will make a fine picture for the story. You never thought of yourself as a photographer? The Polaroid camera is a great teaching device. Of course you may keep all the pictures, except, I think, these two. Have I coated all of them? Yes, I'll sign it here on the tab; you don't want to write on the image area by the way; it damages the surface. Anything you want to check in your notes? If you have any questions later on just call me. Natalie will put you through right away. You may want to read the story to me on the phone. We can work on it together." Land stood at the open door of his study, pools of light behind him like the sun slanting through jungle growth. He smiled warmly at his departing guest, whose hands were filled with pictures, which he fluttered in drying motions. "I don't often meet reporters," Land said. "This has been most pleasant. Most pleasant indeed. I'll look forward to your call."

18

Progress Report

Cambridge, 1962

Land was sleeping in his mechanical lounge chair, his feet elevated, an old plaid blanket pulled up under his chin, when I opened the door to his office. He had been working until a few hours earlier in the laboratory behind his office, called the Back Lab. He and a team of twelve had put in some eighteen hours, interrupted only for tea, cookies, and lamb chops delivered from the Athens Olympia in Boston, seedless grapes, and, later, roast beef sandwiches from Elsie's in Harvard Square. Land believed in feeding the brain. A lab technician might occasionally faint from exhaustion, but never from hunger. Land hated to stop working. Once begun on a course of action, he wanted to experiment until the hypothesis was proved. He would not entertain the assumption that his hypothesis might be disprovable until and unless it was actually disproved. He worked like a predator, stalking a solution, a proof, with perpetual patience and perpetual energy. His intuitive leaps had landed him on the neck of his prey too often for him not to believe that he could do it the next time and the time after that.

Although his assistants were sometimes more than twenty years younger than Land, he regularly worked them to exhaustion and continued with fresh replacements for hours longer. Many of them had graduated from Smith, some with no scientific background. Land proved many times over that a bright young liberal arts student could learn the routines of the laboratory and the structure of a scientific discipline as rapidly as applicants with technical experience. He liked the fact that his students had little to unlearn, but he did not tolerate corner-cutting or sloppiness. Land's Back Lab was a teaching institution whose graduates might succeed to senior research positions at Polaroid, but usually did not go on to laboratories where academic criteria counted more heavily. Its first alumna was Meroë Morse, who in 1962 was director of Polaroid's prestigious black-and-white laboratory. Brilliant, Smith, beautiful, she set the standard.

Land conducted work in the Back Lab on the academic lines of hypothesis, experiment, proof. Time and time again, he set a patently impossible goal and led his young troops into unknown territory, out beyond established boundaries, sustained only with occasional lamb chops and cookies. They started in pursuit of the hypothesis, experimented until they could go no further, then twisted and turned, looking for a new trail that would lead them somewhere. They could wander for days, weeks, even years. Sometimes they found a trail that took them quickly to a solution. The variables were so numerous as to defy prediction, yet Land usually cornered his prey. "Science is an awkward, disorganized, inefficient activity," he said. "It is simply more efficient than any other human activity." He might or might not bow in Churchill's direction when he said this. Once on the trek, he sent back no dispatches. How could you report when you didn't know where the trail led? He did not want to discuss a "problem" — he hated the word — until he had an answer. Then it did not exist. Land lived in a world that did not recognize problems. The larger Polaroid laboratories, staffed with Ph.D.s and equipped with the ultimate in equipment, developed finished products; Land's Back Lab was a pilot facility dedicated to erasing problems.

I knew that Land did not like to give progress reports, but on this particular day I had come to ask for one: was Polaroid's color film going to require the user to apply a protective coating to the picture the way black-and-white film did? Coating a print was a sticky chore, difficult for all but the most dexterous picture taker. A vagrant bug could inhabit an image to eternity, truly a fly in amber, should it happen to alight on the surface before the liquid plastic dried. The marketing group cared intensely about whether this obnoxious step would be part of the new color process. Coating aroused strong emotions within the company. It reminded people that an uncaring nature always stood close at hand and disaster lurked not far away.

In 1950, two years after the introduction of the Polaroid camera system, Land, working with the black-and-white lab, reconstituted the chemistry of the film to produce black-and-gray tones rather than the brown-and-sepia of the original pictures. The public reacted enthusiastically to black-and-white. Polaroid had gained a reputation as a company capable of significant scientific achievements. The Army-Navy E flags were folded away in a filing cabinet in the basement of 730 Main, but people remembered that Polaroid had done secret scientific work during the war. Now, only forty-eight months after the introduction of magic pictures, Land had progressed from sepia images, which harked back to the early days of photography, to instant black-and-white. Sales, which had risen from $1.5 million in 1948 to over $6 million in 1950, jumped to $9 million in 1951 and $13 million in 1952. Polaroid was growing at the rate of 50 percent a year, one of the great postwar success stories. Profits, nonexistent in 1948, were $1.5 million before taxes in 1951, more than the total earnings the company had managed in the years before the war.

The difference between brown-and-white pictures made on the original Type 40 film and the crisp black-and-white images made on Type 41 was more than aesthetic. Polaroid became less of a novelty and moved into the photographic mainstream. Land sought out Ansel Adams as a film and camera consultant, a post Adams held for the rest of his life. When Type 44 PolaPan film was developed, with Ansel providing advice and spectacular test images from the field, even the most skeptical professionals acknowledged its beautiful tonal qualities.

Land and Adams formed the habit of photographing together every year either in New England or the Southwest. Once, when Land returned to Santa Fe and met Ansel at the Compound, they set out around the town with the latest camera from Cambridge, which boasted an improved rangefinder and a superb new lens. They noticed a courtyard with a Spanish gate whose rough hardware and silvered pine planks appealed to Adams. The owner stood in her front door watching them. Ansel stepped forward to speak to her while Land hung back, the new camera concealed behind him. "Good morning, madam." Ansel swept off his Stetson, the bearded face split by its most ingratiating smile. "We were admiring your gate and wondered if you would mind if we photographed it?"

"Oh, not at all," she cried, charmed by Ansel's courtly manner. "You and your son just make yourselves at home."

Six months after the introduction of Type 41 all hell broke loose. The telephone at 730 began to ring and did not stop. Polaroid pictures were fading, turning flat and gray, losing detail, sometimes even the entire image. Hell hath no fury like the lover whose favorite picture has disappeared, or the bereaved whose last photograph of the departed laid out in the casket has also gone beyond. Overnight, Land found his new field in the direst jeopardy. Cameras and film were being returned by customers to dealers and by dealers to Polaroid. The crisis blew up like a summer squall, the clouds getting blacker by the hour, the chorus of telephone bells rising to a crescendo. Land, Howie, and Meroë quickly determined what was happening. Unlike the sepia film, whose development stopped when the print was stripped from the negative, the new black-and-white film carried with it enough emulsion after being separated from the negative to allow the development process to continue. The image kept developing until it began to disappear, the silver halide grains turning from black to white until, in the most extreme cases, all detail evaporated from the shiny surface of the print.

No worse disaster could have been imagined. The lights in the lab blazed all night. A dozen solutions were discarded. Land, haggard and gray-faced, worked with a frenetic energy. The sepia image had been superbly stable. His statement at the Optical Society meeting in 1947 had been no exaggeration; the sepia pictures exhibited as good, if not better stability characteristics than conventional prints. But to retreat to the sepia process was now unthinkable. Polaroid had to find a solution to the decay of the black-and-white image. The clamor in the marketplace had become a roar of anger.

There were in fact two problems. One was to stabilize the development process and stop it as soon as the print was peeled from the camera. The second was to protect the surface of the print, which turned out to be more vulnerable than the relatively scratchproof sepia image. No combination of additional layers or new compounds seemed capable of producing these complex results. By eliminating the darkroom from the photographic equation, Land had no choice but to rely on internal chemistry alone. Nature, however, was intractable.

In a moment of fatigue and despair, Land dropped into a battered desk chair in a corner of the lab and fished a cookie from an open tin box. The room was filled with exhausted people working singly or in small groups, checking sensitometry, pulling test spreads, analyzing the latest failure. Land began to think about the lab technician in the darkroom who would wash and fix each conventional negative and print after development. Polaroid had no one to rely on but the photographer. An untrained person could not perform such sensitive tasks. Or could he? What if it was a simple one-step operation? No tanks or drying racks? No need for experience or skill? Land jumped up, shooting the chair on its casters into the corner, and grabbed the arm of the nearest lab coat. "Let's start over," he said.

The Coater was a plastic vial that contained an applicator whose spongy surface was impregnated with a liquid polymer and an acidic solution. The applicator was three inches long, the width of the picture. After the print was extracted from the camera, the photographer, now recruited to perform what a photo finisher had been doing with more skill and equipment in the darkroom, would stroke the swab over the surface of the picture until it was covered with the solution. The acid stopped further development, and the liquid plastic, after drying for about a minute, formed a tough, flexible coating over the image. Land had solved the two problems, alleviated the crisis, and perhaps saved the company, all in the space of less than four weeks. He had accomplished this, however, by degrading his original invention. Instant photography was no longer a one-step process. Coating was not at all easy to do, and difficult to do well. Magic pictures had lost some of their magic. Nevertheless, disaster had been averted, and sales of the system continued to grow. Land knew the coater was an inelegant compromise. He vowed to find a way to eliminate it, but he would not succeed for thirteen years.

In the fall of 1962, the final stages of instant color product development were completed. Kodak had begun production of the prototype color negative in Rochester and shipped initial quantities to Waltham, where film assembly was about to begin. The commercial introduction was only two months away. Color was going to be Polaroid's greatest new product since the introduction of instant photography itself fourteen years earlier. Planning for the introduction had been extensive and elaborate. Several reasons dictated that it should take place in Miami: it was only a few hours by air from Boston; it was a tourist mecca with a steady stream of visitors heading home to all parts of the country; the winter weather was good there, with warm days and plenty of sun, both conditions necessary for the production of good instant color pictures in the current state of the art, for in cold weather development of the color image slowed almost to a halt. Plenty of light was needed to produce a good color picture. The speed — sensitivity to light — of the film at this time hovered around 25 ASA, a fraction of that of the Polaroid black-and-white film. But under the right conditions results with the new material were nothing short of miraculous. To see a black-and-white picture taken, pulled, timed, peeled, and presented — that had been done millions of times since 1948. People had seen this miracle at weddings, picnics, beaches, funerals, in bedrooms, and live on television. But to see that image flower into color would be a totally new experience. It would produce a shock of pleasure and recognition: color was truly magic. Land was about to release that magic to an audience which, his marketing group believed, would stand in line, fight for, pay almost any price to own.

But would that magic have to be swabbed with a sticky, malodorous coater? It was a reasonable question, and I desperately desired an answer. We had reached an impasse on a dozen aspects of the color introduction — brochures, posters, the packaging for the film itself, instruction folders, magazine ads, television scripts. Artists, copywriters, photographers, and printers were waiting impatiently for an answer. Time was rushing past, deadlines piling up like logs in a jam. Money — an enormous amount of money — was being spent.

Land opened one eye. "Oh, yes," he said. "You've come for lunch. Have you been here long?"

"Yes, Dr. Land. I mean, no. Just five minutes or so."

"Please call me Din. We've known each other too long for formality. Do you like Chinese food?"

"Yes, Dr. Land."

"Good. It's coming from Joyce Chen's. They'll set up in a moment. What's on your mind?" Like a passenger settling himself on the deck chair of a liner, he pulled the plaid up under his chin.

"I was wondering if color film is going to require a coater."

"Color. Yes, color. How are you with color?"

"I don't know, Dr. Land. What do you mean?"

The door to the outer office opened, and one of Land's office assistants came in to set a small luncheon table beside the bookshelves. Land jumped up, slung his tartan over his shoulder, took a large volume down, set it on his spacious worktable, and leafed through it until he found the right page. "Do you know these plates?" he asked, inviting me to examine them.

"I think so. I was tested with them when I joined the Naval Air Reserve."

"What did you do in the Naval Air Reserve?"

"I pumped gas into Corsair fighters and picked up trash around the hangars."

"Indeed? Did they ever tell you how the color test turned out?"

"No."

"Perhaps we can discover why you were assigned those particular duties." He motioned me to the lunch table and we sat down. Several bowls of Chinese food were brought in, but Land pushed them to one side. Even though the room was warm, he kept the blanket over his shoulders like a shawl. The food smelled delicious. He indicated the open book. Each color plate was a large circle composed of many small circles of different colors varying in size from a dime to a small dot. At first glance, the pattern of colors was completely random. "This, of course, is a standard test. The military have been using it for years. We have more sophisticated tests now. Do you see a letter or a number formed by the dots in the plate?"

I studied the page. A tenuous pattern of pumpkin-colored circles seemed to emerge. "Ah, yes. A seven."

Land turned the page. "And this one?"

"I think I see a Q."

"And this one?"

"I see nothing. That is, nothing like a letter or a number."

"And this one?"

"A two." There were twenty-six plates. When we were finished, Land looked at me thoughtfully. The food was rapidly approaching room temperature.

"How long were you in the Naval Air Reserve?"

"About six months."

"You are the first person I have encountered who misread every plate. Have some vegetables chow yoke?"

"Ah, thank you. What does that *mean*?"

"I believe it means stir-fried vegetables with water chestnuts."

"No, I mean about the plates."

"Oh, yes. It suggests that within the conventional definition you are color blind."

"What does color blind mean, exactly?"

"There is no comprehensive answer. As you know, I've been working in the field of color perception for a number of years. Have you read my Retinex papers?"

"No, Dr. Land. That is, I couldn't understand much of it."

"I'll ask Natalie to give you the complete set. Some beef and pea pods?" Land ate swiftly and with relish, using his chopsticks efficiently. He eyed my efforts with a fork. "It tastes so much better with chopsticks," he murmured, almost to himself. "When did you decide that advertising was to be your chosen field? Was it long after you left the Naval Air Reserve?"

"Well, yes. Several years."

"I suppose you look at engraver's proofs and press proofs and that sort of thing?" He proffered the rice bowl.

"Yes. No, thank you, I guess I'm not as hungry as I thought."

"And film clips of television commercials? What do they call them?"

"Rushes or dailies, yes."

"Interesting that you should have missed every single plate. What color is this?" he asked, presenting a pea pod between his chopsticks.

"Green."

"Of course. And what is green?"

"Ah, like grass, leaves."

"You see, the problem is as much philological as it is physiological or psychological. You can describe a color only in terms of other manifestations of the color in the world. Red is like fire, yellow like the sun, and so on. You cannot articulate green. Hence, I cannot know, at least from you, what you see when you see what I believe to be green. Any dessert?"

"No, thank you, Dr. Land."

"It is quite fascinating that the advertising manager of the company whose destiny is totally, inextricably bound to color should misread every one of these plates. I think, by the way, that the current campaign is delightful."

"Thank you."

"What is the name of our advertising agency?"

"Doyle Dane Bernbach."

"How long have we had them?"

"Eight years, Dr. Land."

"Oh, yes. Of course. Well, I credit your good taste. Most advertising is the most god-awful tripe. No, I don't see your little . . . singularity . . . as a handicap in your profession. Almost anyone can recognize colors. Taste is as rare as the unicorn. Please be in the Back Room tomorrow morning, what shall we say, about seven-thirty? Would that be all right?" I was shaking my head, vainly trying to indicate that it would take more than an hour to drive in from Hingham at that time of the morning. Land lived fifteen minutes from his office. "I have another test I want you to take. It is far more specific than these plates. I think you may become a valuable control in the color research." Land stood up and tossed the blanket back on the lounge chair. He walked to the door of the Back Lab. His eyes sparkled. He looked refreshed, impatient to plunge back into unknown territory.

The control moved unhappily to the door. "I'm sure I can see colors, Dr. Land," I said.

"I'm sure you see *something*. We'll try to find out what it is. And please call me Din." He disappeared, as if in a puff of smoke.

Land's dissatisfaction with the coater had not diminished. Nature had defeated him before; rather, since nature did not care, he and his lab group had simply failed to find an elegant solution. Now he had retired to the Back Lab to rethink the problem from the beginning for the thousandth time. The chemistry of color film was of course far more sophisticated than black-and-white. It had taken sixteen years to develop: two years while Howie Rogers sat thinking about it in a chair in the black-and-white lab; eight years of molecular construction and reconstruction in the color laboratory; and six years of intensive work, with Kodak's assistance, to prepare the prototype for production. Land was sure a way could be devised to lower the pH within the layers of the negative to stop development at the appropriate time. A chemical timing mechanism was required; perhaps another layer of the film sandwich, perhaps more than one. Land worried the problem like a lion gnawing a bone, searching for some trace of nourishment. The complex chemistry of the color negative became even more intricate as he played with it, but in three months he and Rogers had demonstrated the solution to their own satisfaction in the laboratory. The new layers were incorporated into production in Rochester at the cost of thirty days. The introduction of the color system was delayed two months, but color no longer relied on a coater. "If you can state a problem — any problem — and if it is important enough," Land said, "then the problem can be solved." The problem had proved itself manifestly important enough to deserve solution in 1950, but it took thirteen years to state it correctly.

19

The Swinger

Abaco and Cambridge, 1965

Polaroid seemed a world unto itself in the early sixties. Its managers struggled to comprehend, let alone control, the growth that was lifting it rapidly to the threshold of the *Fortune* 500 list. Sales increased by 25 to 30 percent a year every year from 1961 to 1965. New foreign subsidiaries were established as instant photography outstripped the abilities of distributors to keep pace with the vibrant amateur business as well as the newly emerging industrial and scientific photographic markets. New products tumbled out of Polaroid's labs: variations on the pack camera design, new film types, a camera that made a photographic driver's license including the applicant's statistical information on the same piece of film as his face in uncounterfeitable color. The momentum of Land's idea had made Polaroid the darling of the go-go stock market. The price of the stock soared on thermals of anticipation of even higher sales and earnings. Xerox seemed the only other company in America that combined growth, new technology, and a monopoly in the same glamorous mix. Kodak, indeed most of the photographic industry, was growing as well, but the spotlight shone on Polaroid.

I rarely had time or occasion to wonder if the "big time" was as fulfilling as I had anticipated. After a six-month assignment in Europe to help organize the advertising and promotion efforts of our new German subsidiary, with side trips to our companies in Holland, France, and the United Kingdom, I was propelled into television production. Stan had become increasingly occupied with management battles within Polaroid's harried executive suite. It was apparent to us both that the faster I learned, the more rapid would be his progress as well as mine. I had little or no training for selling cameras on television, but I decided that my value to Land, McCune, Calderwood, and the others who gripped the tiger's tail lay in my point of view. I knew as little about the science of photography as did Polaroid's audience. But I understood that while the magic might to some extent be explained, it should never be explained away. It was clear to me that Polaroid's ideal medium was television. Every night we demonstrated magic pictures to a larger and larger audience. I felt, however, that the emotions that were inspired by the act of making a picture — joy, embarrassment, love, envy, and fear among them — should not be ignored in favor of the technology.

Commercial filming always disappointed. Planning a commercial, briefing the agency, debating storyboards, and reviewing Polaroid pictures of the cast and the location aroused the anticipation of doing exciting creative work with cameras and actors away from the corporate routine and the gray environment of Cambridge. The reality often turned out to be tedious and repetitive even if the surroundings were not. Live television had begun to disappear, and live commercials were broadcast only during time-outs at football games or on the sidewalk at the Macy's Thanksgiving Day parade. Filmed commercials were shot at California picnic spots in February, next to Christmas trees in dusty Manhattan studios in July, at June weddings in whatever part of Florida looked most like Connecticut in December, but most often at a beach. Since our first color commercials appeared on television in 1963, Joan Wolf, the Doyle Dane Bernbach producer who worked with Bob Gage and Phyllis Robinson finding cast, locations, props, and costumes, had searched widely for beautiful beaches.

Polaroid spots had been filmed up and down both coasts, from Leo Carrillo Beach in Malibu to Hollywood Beach in Florida. Joan's difficulties stemmed from matching production schedules that had lead times of three or four months to air date with the realities of the tourist season. Several resort hotels, anticipating fun and excitement provided by a film shoot on the premises at the height of the winter season, had discovered that nothing was more selfish and preemptive than a production crew, moving unerringly to the best spot, monopolizing it for days, scattering motor homes, noisy electric generators, and miles of cable across lawns and walks. The guests were lucky if they saw the actors at all. They could not avoid the grips and the gaffers, whose arrogance was at least of star quality.

I had received the assignment of producing an introductory campaign for a new camera due in the summer of 1965, and Joan Wolf had succeeded in arousing that anticipatory excitement again. She had discovered the most beautiful beach in the world, one which had never been seen in a commercial. It was pristine because the hotel was newly built and not yet fashionable. A curve of unmarked pink pearl sand with the requisite palm trees and trade winds, it lay closer than California and would cost less than Florida. It was, in short, Treasure Cay on Abaco Island in the Bahamas. Bob Gage and Phyllis Robinson produced a set of exciting storyboards, simple and, in a daring departure from Polaroid television style, sexy. The new camera needed sex, or something.

Everyone agreed that the small white plastic box was the ugliest object to be christened a Land camera since the Model 95, for it had evolved from a series of concerns and compromises. Since the color introduction in 1963, color film sales had overtaken black-and-white, even though the price of color was almost double, and a flashbulb had to be used for most indoor pictures. The success of color had created two problems, one of manufacturing, the other marketing. Declining black-and-white film sales left assembly machines idle; and the entry price for Polaroid photography suddenly jumped higher than it had ever been before.

The company pulled an answer to these concerns off the back shelf of the camera design closet: a simple, inexpensive, fixed-focus black-and-white box camera that Polaroid had discussed and rejected on several previous occasions. This camera's chief advocate was Stan Calderwood, who wanted a camera priced below $20. Its chief opponent was Bill McCune, who was concerned that the quality of the pictures the camera produced would not measure up to the standards so painstakingly improved since 1948. Stan attacked on all fronts at once with his customary energy and a blizzard of overhead transparencies that showed the profitability of the little camera projected well above the current Colorpack line. He also touted the incremental benefits of reactivating idle black-and-white machinery modified to produce the new Type 20 film; and he painted the attractive prospect of a new generation of Polaroid buyers, young, unspoiled by exposure to any other camera, ripe for later conversion to more expensive Polaroid color cameras.

Land remained aloof. He watched the controversy between his two most powerful captains with interest and perhaps some amusement. The problems associated with the surface tension of color film, experiments with an additive color technology, and his dissatisfaction with the film transport mechanism of the new pack camera occupied his attention. He did not attempt to prevent, or to settle, the scrap between Calderwood and McCune. When Calderwood's arguments proved irresistible to the bureaucracy, Land applied his imprimatur to the project in the form of an invention.

Although the new camera had no focus system, its aperture had to be adjusted to the light of the scene. Land contributed an ingenious exposure control device. When the photographer gripped the small red stalk that projected above the shutter bezel, a tiny electric bulb inside the camera illuminated a checkerboard display in the viewfinder just above the image of the scene to be photographed. By rotating the phallic control stalk, the photographer could open or close the aperture to admit enough light to balance the brightness of the bulb, which was keyed to the light sensitivity of the film, about 1,200 ASA. When the two brightnesses were balanced, the illuminated checkerboard spelled the word *yes,* indicating that the picture could be taken. Simple, precise, never tried before or since, this exposure control system made the camera very easy to use. It was, however, the camera's sole distinction. The other aspects of its design harked back to the earliest Polaroid cameras. Boxy and ugly, it used roll film that produced small, undistinguished black-and-white pictures. Its attractions were the small size of the camera, its list price of $19.95, and the fact that the pictures, such as they were, developed in ten to fifteen seconds.

Doyle Dane Bernbach listened impatiently to the exhaustive briefing prepared for them, then with characteristic but creative perversity fastened on what seemed to Polaroid the least important feature of the camera, a little wrist strap that hung from one white plastic corner. Bob and Phyllis, given as ugly a duckling as had emerged from a client's production line since the Volkswagen Beetle, decided the camera would only look good hanging from the wrist of a beautiful girl. Bob called Joan Wolf from the studio in his Pound Ridge home, where he and Phyllis worked most mornings. "Find the most beautiful girl in New York who hasn't been used in a commercial," he growled past his cigarette. "She's got to be a teenager," he added. "This camera is supposed to appeal to kids even though it looks like it was carved out of a bar of Ivory Soap."

"What are you going to call it?" asked Joan.

"Phyllis wants to call it The Swinger. We'll show it swinging from the girl's wrist."

"The client will never buy that name."

"We're betting they will. Phyllis says no one in Cambridge knows what a swinger is."

"But the kids will."

"That's the beauty part."

"Well, I know just the girl. She's gorgeous, she's never been in front of a camera, and she has the sexiest walk in America."

"Who is she?"

"She's a stylist for a fashion photographer. I met her a year ago when she was renting antiques for a shoot. Her name is Ali MacGraw."

"How old is she?"

"She looks seventeen."

"How old is she, Joan?"

"She's twenty-seven. Trust me."

Abaco was one of the least developed islands in the Bahamas. The DC-2 from West Palm landed on a bumpy strip where the island's taxi fleet — three in all — was waiting by a tin-roofed shed to take the crew to Treasure Cay. Our driver told us in the space of an otherwise unremarkable journey through Norfolk Island pines and tarpaper shacks that he was the great-great-great-grandson of a Tory; that his ancestor had fled the American Revolution and started a cotton plantation on Abaco; that the island's thin soil had supported two fine crops of cotton and then no more; and that he had never been farther off-island than Eleuthera. We heard essentially the same story from the desk clerk at the little hotel where we registered and from every other Abacoan we encountered.

The beach at Treasure Cay lived up to all Joan Wolf's promises. Client, agency, actors, and production crew gazed with delight at the lovely peach-colored crescent, virgin of footprint or Polaroid negative, at the gentle swells of the Caribbean lapping at its perimeter, at the reefs frothing lazily fifty yards out in the green water. Clad in shorts, T-shirts, straw hats, and sandals, the New Yorkers gathered to plan the rape of the beach. Mike Nebbia, the ostensible director, understood that, since it was a Bob Gage commercial, Bob would direct and Mike would handle the camera. The company cameraman would oversee the lighting, in this case a matter of reflecting God's light in the right places. The lighting director wore swimming shorts in anticipation of a relaxed shoot. Neil Schreckinger was present since I was there. Whither the client went, thither went Neil. He dressed in his usual February ensemble — a topcoat, a Ray Milland snap-brim fedora, a baggy gray Brooks Brothers suit, a white oxford cloth button-down shirt, a rep tie, and the only current copy of the *New York Times* on Abaco. The thermometer rested comfortably at eighty-two, the breeze ruffled the girls' hair, and the unfiltered sun spilled over us. "Get the Jeep out there and set up," said Mike. "I want a camera stand with a three-sixty shooting radius. And sweep up all the tracks you make. Ali, come over here. Let me see you." She opened the long man's shirt she was wearing over her bathing costume, and a profound silence gripped the crew. She wore the smallest bikini available at Saks in 1965. "Great," said Mike after a moment. "Give her a camera. I want to see her walk."

Joan looked at me. I looked at Ali MacGraw. "Give her the camera, Peter," said Joan. I gave her the camera. "Ali, take off the shirt and walk about twenty steps down the beach." Joan spoke, as usual, with crisp authority. "Swing the camera from your wrist as you walk, the way we did it at the studio. Then turn around and walk back this way, toward Mike." Ali smiled and with maidenly modesty let the shirt fall to the sand at her bare feet. Then, clad in the transparent armor of Venus, she walked. Her feline stride, graceful and vigorous, seemed to carry her over the peachy sand in linked waves of fluid motion. She did not hurry nor did she tarry. She did indeed look seventeen, but there was in her walk a suggestion of ageless carnality. In forty steps she was back.

"Good Christ," said Bob. "No one's going to notice the camera."

The commercial was built around a jingle, the music composed by Mitch Leigh, who between commercial assignments wrote *Man of La Mancha* in 1968. Phyllis supplied The Swinger lyric. It had a nice bouncy feel to it, perfectly in sync with Ali MacGraw's stride. Mike Nebbia set her to walking miles across the sand of Abaco, around, rather, in a circle, the center of which was his camera, panning smoothly as Ali walked on in time to the music looped on the tape machine. The other boys and girls in the cast swam, ran, played volleyball, and took pictures of each other doing these things, but Ali walked on, her beautiful panther steps never losing their spring, The Swinger swinging from her wrist. Neil, top-coated and felt-hatted, his *Times* over his face, dozed in a beach chair. I cleaned sand out of Polaroid cameras, coated pictures, and supplied Swinger film from a picnic cooler. The crew swept the sand between takes, keeping Treasure Cay fresh for the movie camera. Ali walked.

"Where did you find her?" I asked Joan.

"Ali? She's one of the best photographer's stylists in New York. I've been trying to get her into something for a long time. This is the first time she's been on the other side of the camera."

"How does she like acting so far?"

"She says it's hard on her feet. She's getting blisters. If Bob and Mike don't let her stop pretty soon, this will be her last part." As it turned out, she made four more Swinger commercials for us before going to Hollywood to star in *Goodbye Columbus* with Richard Benjamin. The beach commercial, finished in time for the camera's introduction in June 1965, created a furor. Since The Swinger used only black-and-white film, the television spots were shot in black-and-white as well. In an era when all commercials were in color, they were a surprise. Ali MacGraw was a sensation.

Watching the rough cut in the shabby screening room of the New York post-production house, I worried, not about the reaction of the young television audience we wanted to attract — I knew they were ready for Ali — but about the reaction of Land and Calderwood. They were not prudes, I told myself, but I was crowding the current boundaries of television sex. There was nothing overtly suggestive about The Swinger commercials, just the video eye watching Ali walk. But if someone decided she should have a bigger bathing suit we'd have nothing ready to meet our television dates, or for print, either, since we were using stills of Ali's walk in the magazine ads, newspapers, and store displays.

As it turned out, Land made no comment about The Swinger name or the campaign. Stan turned prudish and made us reshoot the stills for the print material at the last minute, not with a different bikini but from a different, presumably less swinging, camera angle. Ali walked through the television sets of the nation all summer and fall, heading for Hollywood, swinging our camera. The Swinger was a marketing success, selling almost a million cameras in 1965 and three million the year following. Stan was right: it made money and kept the black-and-white film machines running. Bill McCune was right also: although The Swinger was a sales success, its pictures disappointed. Kids bought the camera but quickly tired of it. Its useful life was the shortest of any

Polaroid camera yet. Although it sold well for several years, we were eventually left with several million units for which there was no market. I wound up bartering them for cheap radio and television advertising time. Land probably made a mistake in acceding to The Swinger. Though it sold more units than any Land camera to date, it may have converted many of its customers to conventional photography. Bob Gage was right: the viewers paid more attention to Ali MacGraw than to the camera. I was right, too: I knew that television sold cameras and in Bob and Phyllis I had the best creative team in advertising. I could only hope that the next camera would be worthy of their talents. It was an uncomfortable feeling to know that the advertising was better than the product.

20

The Ninth Floor

Cambridge, 1966–1969

The Colorpack design had always rankled. Two problems distressed Land: one not unforeseen but worse than expected, one a clear instance, in his eyes, of his associates' failure to heed his warnings. Polaroid color prints, left in a dry environment, began to curl, sometimes hours after they were taken, sometimes weeks. The layers of emulsion that received the three sets of colored dye-developers in order to form the positive image shrank slightly when the last of the liquid in them evaporated. Since the plastic paper base on which they were coated was stable, shrinkage of the color layers caused a tension on the surface of the print that produced an inward curl. In its worst manifestation the picture became a tightly wrapped cylinder the length and diameter of a large cigarette, and unrolling the print would sometimes crack the emulsion.

Land invented several cures for this complaint, which was causing Polaroid's telephones to ring almost as hard as they had during the black-and-white fading crisis of 1951. The first was a direct, unsophisticated fix, a pack of eight cardboard squares, each with an adhesive back masked with a waxed sheet. All the photographer need do, Land explained earnestly to me, was peel the cover sheet off the card, position the color print fresh from the camera on the sticky surface of the card, then gently press the still fragile color image flat, using the wax sheet. The card prevented the picture from curling, but the process required dexterity and precision. As many prints would be lost to sticky cards and clumsy fingers as to curl, but my past experience suggested remonstrance would not dent the inventor's enthusiasm. He brushed my comment aside when I told him the cards were as bad as the coater if not worse. Why did each fix have to stick to your fingers?

Land wanted them called *mounts* and proclaimed them a great step forward in the conservation of color prints. Polacolor images thus mounted would last even longer than other color prints. Mounts were to be regarded as a significant photographic achievement. A deck of eight sticky cards was duly included in each box of color film. Land knew, of course, that this solution was only temporary. Despite his poker-faced advocacy of mounts, he set to work in the Back Lab on a more elegant way to balance the surface tension of the color print.

The other thorn in Land's side was the two-stage pull. In the first Land camera design, the photographer pulled the end of the film roll to move the positive and exposed negative sheets, part of two continuous strips, together between the pair of rollers into a development chamber in the back of the camera. After sixty seconds the photographer opened the door to the chamber and removed the picture. In the effort to make the pack camera smaller and lighter, the film rolls were replaced by a pack of eight pairs of positive and negative sheets stacked in a steel box. When the photographer loaded a film pack into the camera he pulled a black cover sheet out of the pack to unmask the first negative behind the camera lens. After he snapped the picture he pulled a small white paper tab from the side of the camera to bring the positive sheet out of hiding into juxtaposition with the exposed negative. Another, larger tab emerged, which was then pulled to bring positive and negative through the rollers and out of the camera, sandwiched together while the image developed.

After ten seconds for a black-and-white picture, or sixty for color, the picture was stripped away from the negative. At that point the photographer had three pieces of paper to handle along with the camera: the print, the negative, and the white tab. If he or she possessed the courage to mount the picture in the field, two more were added, the wax cover and the sticky card. In addition, the cardboard film box, a foil wrapper around the film pack, an instruction sheet, and the steel box that contained the film demanded disposal. In fifteen minutes a diligent photographer could finish a pack of Polacolor film with eight color pictures securely mounted on cards for his grandchildren to admire. Around him on the grass would be strewn a box, a foil bag, a sheet of instructions, a cover sheet, eight negatives, eight tabs, the steel container, and eight wax sheets: a total of twenty-nine disposable items, not including his eight hard-won pictures. Since pack film sales averaged about 15 million units per year in the sixties, some 435 million pieces of Polaroid debris hit the turf every year, each piece bearing Phyllis Robinson's admonition, "Please don't litter the landscape, someone might want to take a picture of it."

The pack camera system worked well, was less bulky than the roll film cameras, and was easier to use, but it lacked elegance in Land's eyes. Though Land had complained about the two-stage pull at the design sessions, no one responded to his lead; no better system came forth. McCune had a 1963 deadline to meet, and the two-stage pull was cast in steel and uncounted tons of paper for the next nine years. Bill, who had become an executive vice president of the company, supervised all of Polaroid's engineering. Camera design took pride of place among the engineering functions because from the design of a new camera all other company decisions flowed. In the jargon of the eighties, Polaroid was a product-driven company. Planning was little influenced by market research, financial concerns, or competition. If products drove the company, Land drove the products. Polaroid competed only with itself. The real competition was between Land and McCune over product planning.

Land's primary scientific fields included optics, chemistry, and physics. He could quickly master, however, any field or technology that engaged his curiosity. He read technical and general literature omnivorously. Since electronics had claimed his interest early, Polaroid was a pioneer in electronic miniaturization, beginning with the wartime Dove missile project and later in the application of electronics to the photographic process. Computers controlled manufacturing at Polaroid long before they were either fashionable or commonplace in industry. The color negative facility at New Bedford, where the production process required emulsion coatings thinner than a wavelength of light, employed one of the first large-scale installations of minicomputers from the Digital Equipment Corporation for computer-aided manufacturing. Land's mind often ranged far ahead of his associates', searching and sorting and trying things on.

To McCune was often left the problem of converting an idea into something tangible and, if possible, economical. He had to work out the tough compromises necessary to meet cost and time constraints. Not surprisingly, McCune's preferred communication medium was the committee meeting, while Land's was a telephone with one person at the other end of the line. If Land produced the brilliant theories, McCune had to make things work in the real world. Both men possessed muscular minds and athletic egos. Each was certain he could play the other's role. When Bill returned from his twice-yearly visits to Switzerland, where he skied, climbed, and visited the Porsche factory across the border in Stuttgart, he sometimes discovered that Land had been spending time with his, McCune's, camera design team. Land neither forgot nor forgave the two-stage pull.

Lever Brothers' soap refinery on Main Street was torn down in 1966 by Cabot, Cabot & Forbes, which developed a complex of four office buildings on the site of the old cracking tower. One of the neighborhood's interesting odors disappeared, and in the still pungent air of Cambridge rose three nine-story concrete boxes and a three-story pork-pie hat. Linden trees and timid squares of grass surrounded the development, christened Technology Square, since MIT sprawled three blocks away. Polaroid, a charter tenant at Tech Square, had the pork-pie building designed to accommodate its management group.

Land appropriated a third of the top floor for his own use, and Terre, his wife, engaged a Newbury Street decorator to design a proper office for him. The result could not have been more unlike the alchemist's lair at Osborn Street. Bright windows gave upon the struggling green of the courtyard. Fluorescent lighting recessed around the spacious main room illuminated deep carpet, leather couches, coffee tables, and a free-form desk supported by strange bronze tree trunks whose twigs snagged the stockings of the unwary. There were bookshelves, of course, but they contained gift volumes, Ansel Adams portfolios, Japanese art books, and ceramic pots made by one of Land's sons-in-law. Those of us invited to inspect this new salon gazed in surprise at the muted, matching colors, the crystal ashtrays, the suede wall covering. Land asserted his delight at the final result, but for several years he visited Tech Square mostly for state occasions: board meetings, greeting foreign visitors, little dinners. His real work continued amid the rich clutter of Osborn Street three blocks away.

Polaroid moved several departments, including some of the engineering groups, into the lower floors of the three nine-story buildings. The rest of the Cambridge contingent continued to inhabit the motley collection of leaseholds, including the ex–candy plant at 730 Main Street, the failed machine shop at 119 Windsor Street, and the former furniture factory at 2 Osborn Street. An old Ford assembly plant on the Charles River, with an automobile test track on the roof, was acquired for light manufacturing in 1967. One day early in 1968, contemplating the twin thorns of curling prints and two-stage film advance, Land quietly initiated a call to Cabot, Cabot & Forbes. He rented the entire ninth floor of 565, the building across the courtyard from his new office. He could swivel his massive glove-leather chair to see it through the spindly treetops. Into this bare space he began to move chemists, optical scientists, draftsmen, lab technicians, and, a little later, camera designers.

Nan Buddy, a Smith graduate, was the latest, but not the last, of the brainy and beautiful "Princesses." Like Doxie Muller before her, she had been given a staggering assignment. Land instructed her to begin thinking about a single-sheet film unit. He called her at 6:30 each morning to discuss a print that could perform all the functions formerly contained first in the roll and then in the pack. This film would have no chamber in which to develop, no sandwich to be peeled. All of the elements of exposure and development — and the cessation of development — must be self-contained. Gone in a stroke would be 435 million pieces a year of what the industry analysts called garbage. Gone also, in this hypothesis, were the intricate paper constructions of the preceding film systems, to be replaced by a complexity of chemical interactions that, if achieved, would be to the current color development process as a Broadway musical is to a junior high school play.

Brushing aside distracting thoughts of problems and difficulties, Land began to explore an exciting new terrain. If the picture unit consisted of a single sheet, there could be two ways to expose it: from the front, the viewing side of the print, or from the rear. Land immediately set Howie Rogers to work investigating both concepts. Since the single film unit theoretically eliminated the headache of both curling and the two-stage pull, Nan Buddy designated the frontal exposure concept "Aspirin" and the rear exposure system "Excedrin," not dreaming that these banal code names would one day be immortalized by a federal judge. While Howie experimented and Nan struggled, Land examined the benefits that would derive from the single-sheet idea. First and foremost, the film pack could shrink. In theory, it would contain just one sheet for each picture plus an initial cover sheet. With the saving in bulk, Land decided he could increase the number of pictures in each pack from eight to ten. Such a film pack involved less work for the customer, allowed him to take more pictures between film purchases, and seemed in all respects more elegant.

In most $500 million corporations such a decision, involving as it did basic interactions between the customer, the dealer, the cost of the product, and its size, in this case measured by number of exposures rather than ounces or grams, would be researched in painstaking detail, if not by the company then by its advertising agency. Customer interviews, focus groups, surveys, dealer interviews, and tests of every ilk imaginable would be invoked to help management come to the ideal balance among content, cost, customer reaction, competitive factors, and — most critical — price. The best solution would be defined as that which generated the greatest income to the company. On this foundation rested the uniquely American package-goods industry. Film qualified as a package good, not quite in the mode of soap, toothpaste, or ketchup, but consumable and broadly distributed.

The idea of such a market research study, however, never crossed Land's mind. He felt perfectly able to decide such questions, testing his conclusions, to be sure, with Nan Buddy or others of the Princesses. For Land, or anyone representing him, to sit behind a mirror window, listening to consumers talk about how many pictures they wanted in a film pack, was as unthinkable as hiring Arthur D. Little to help design the single-sheet film unit. In later years, when I used focus groups to get customer reaction to features of the finished SX-70 system, I kept the knowledge from Land as long as possible. When he discovered that his marketing group was indulging in market research he demanded the names of the actual culprits. I told him he could punish only me, which dampened his zeal and allowed us to continue our nonintuitive exercise.

Unencumbered by other people's ideas, Land raced ahead. If the film pack could be made smaller, the camera could be smaller as well. Land, following his own maxim — Anything worth doing is worth doing to excess — leaped to the extreme. What about a camera only slightly larger than the film box? What about a disposable camera that was itself the film container, which could be discarded with all garbage inside it after delivering ten perfect pictures? These ideas and many others were examined by the growing population of the Ninth Floor, which, although it was a "secret" operation, overnight had become a corporate institution and acquired the status of capital letters. In lieu of a project name, the single-sheet film concept was designated SX-70, the same file code that had designated the first photographic experiments in 1943.

The disposable camera lacked elegance; Eastman Kodak had tried it in the thirties without enduring success. The internal dimensions of any Polaroid camera, and consequently the external dimensions as well, depended not only on the size of the film pack, but on the focal length as well, the distance from the lens to the film plane necessary to expose the full area of the picture. Land's group decided that the picture area would be three and a quarter inches square, slightly smaller than the 3¼-x-4¼-inch Colorpack print. This, plus an additional half inch of length to accommodate a pod for each picture, determined two dimensions of the film pack; its thickness could be guessed, say, three quarters of an inch. Setting aside the focal length question, Land then contemplated a shape that would fit easily into a shirt pocket, about the same size as a pack of cigarettes, but only half as thick. Overnight the pocket defined the external limitations of the camera. The Ninth Floor acquired a closetful of pockets: shirt pockets, apron pockets, pants pockets, coat pockets, both breast and patch, and, the last resort of beleaguered camera designers, commodious raincoat pockets.

The focal length question would not remain in the background, and a number of ingenious ideas were tried to allow the camera to fit into a pocket. Among them was a flat camera whose shutter would admit a thin line of light the width of the picture. The shutter slit was to descend the length of the film sheet, depositing visual information like a scanner as it moved from top to bottom at the press of a button. This solution particularly pleased Land because the focal length was greatly reduced. It proved unworkable, however, and only two alternatives, both unacceptable, remained. The first was a box camera, but with the requisite focal length, no pocket in the closet could contain it. That was out. The second involved an erecting system, a feature of all the previous Polaroid camera designs except The Swinger. Levers or slides allowed these cameras to unfold, moving the lens and shutter away from the focal plane to a distance far enough, from four to six inches, to allow the image from the lens to cover the full area of the print. Conventional cameras had long since dealt with the focal length problem by exposing smaller and smaller areas of film, thus shrinking the size of the image, which shortened the focal length and reduced the size of the camera. A 35 mm camera achieved a short focal length and a compact body by exposing a negative area less than two inches square, from which an acceptable print was produced by enlarging the image in the processing lab. Land had more than nine square inches to cover inside the camera without such luxuries as a lab or an enlarger. The single-sheet concept — the new SX-70 — must fulfill the dream of true one-step photography.

The cumbersome erecting systems of the old Model 95 and the newer pack camera made them far from pocketable. Land's Ninth Floor design team, McCune's design team, began to think about mirrors as a way to shorten the interior dimensions. About this time Bill McCune returned from his chalet in Zermatt tanned, fresh, and full of energy. He called his camera group together, surprised to discover that some of them had been moved upstairs to new offices. The next day McCune received a telephone call. Natalie put Land on the line. He did not say whether he was three blocks away, across the yard, or in the same building. The message was brief. Land alone would direct the SX-70 camera and film development. Bill was not to come up to the Ninth Floor again. Otto Wolf was proscribed as well, presumably because he was close to Bill and not loath to speak his mind. Bill would continue to manage the other engineering activities in the company, which was to say that the captain could look after all the functions of the ship except the direction in which it was sailing.

Bill stared at the dead telephone in fury and surprise: fury that he had been summarily relieved of camera design, a job he had performed brilliantly for almost twenty-five years, and surprise that Land had issued a direct order. McCune couldn't remember when that had happened last. He sat in his office on the third floor of 549, trying to imagine what was going on across the courtyard. He knew the camera designers were playing with mirrors, trying to fold the focal path, even examining the farfetched notion of a through-the-lens viewing system in the classical 35 mm single-lens reflex style. McCune thought it impossible that without him they could succeed with any design that had a hope of being manufactured. He thought of the dozens of men and women, including Dick Wareham, one of his best and brightest, who had been instructed not to speak to him. He knew that some of them would disobey, but why, why in God's name did they have to? Didn't he and Land want the same thing? The answer, as he thought about it in the loneliness of his office, was yes. The answer was control.

21

South Africa

Cambridge and Soweto, 1968–1977

When Martin Luther King, Jr., was assassinated on April 4, 1968, Land stayed up late, watching the news reports on television. He made several telephone calls in the small hours of the morning, and before dawn he began a journey around his company. It had been almost ten years since he had last attempted to speak to everyone in the company face to face. Before the war he could address all of his employees in one room. After the move to Main Street and during the war years, the Polaroid population, growing rapidly, spread to buildings all over the southern, industrial end of Cambridge. Land formed the habit, which became an instant tradition, of visiting every building and talking to all of Polaroid's people in small groups in the course of one day, or gathering them in an auditorium, usually in December before Christmas. By 1960, the explosive growth of the photographic business had created four manufacturing plants in Waltham and so increased the number of employees, three thousand in 1960, seven thousand by 1968, that the Christmas trek became an impossibility.

The day after King's murder, however, Land set out at five o'clock in the morning to talk first to the C shift just finishing seven and a half hours in the W3 pack film plant in Waltham. The men and women of the C shift were surprised and pleased to be called away from their places early. Word spread with uncanny speed: Land had arrived in the building and was going to talk to them. Walking down the rubber-tread aisles, between rows of giant spoolers, slitters, and assembly machines lit by the harsh blue-green fluorescents, the workers wiped their hands of oil or the alkaline residue of the pod machines. As they headed for the cafeteria, the only room large enough to contain the whole shift, they joked and speculated about the reason for this extraordinary visit. Many of the employees had never seen Land in person. He was far more fascinating to them than the president of the United States, his aura on a par with that of Carl Yastrzemski, Bobby Orr, or Bill Russell. As bets were made, the odds favored an announcement of some new invention. What else would Land be there to talk about, a pay raise?

The machines they left were, of course, Polaroid designed and built. In 1959, Land had described his design rationale to an audience at MIT. "One of the fundamental objectives of our machine designers is to make machines that work for people rather than machines that employ people merely in the unplanned and accidental relationship that exists today." At the time he spoke, planning for the pack film program was well under way. Irv Pollitt, a member of the planning team, said, "Our goal was to bring the product to market on time without word leaking out. At the same time, we had a rare opportunity to create a healthy environment for people to work in: to design the building, design the equipment, even design the job. When machinery was being planned, we decided that some functions which could be automated shouldn't be. Our research showed those functions would be fun or interesting, making the job of operating the machine less tedious." In the speech at MIT, Land articulated the two broad aims of the company: "to make worthwhile products genuinely useful to the public, and to make a worthwhile work life for every member of the company."

The first aim was rarely discussed by Polaroid's employees. They saw it as Land's responsibility, and he seemed to be doing an excellent job of it. The Second Aim was, however, capitalized and graven in tablets of stone by the Employees Committee, the negotiating group who, in this nonunion company, represented the concerns of the hourly employees to management. Implicit in the Second Aim was Land's faith in education. "The individual in industry will be better qualified to increase his technical competence, and at the same time make his job fully satisfying, if he continues his education as an integral part of his working career." Almost 20 percent of the C shift were enrolled in courses, either inside the company after work or at Boston or Cambridge colleges. The Back Lab, which turned some liberal arts graduates into scientists, served as a model for Polaroid's educational efforts, institutionalized by an ambitious education department.

Land's democratic and somewhat iconoclastic ideas about industry were present from the beginning of the Land-Wheelwright Laboratories. "Everyone was viewed as a person," said Dick Kriebel, "not simply as a job function. Everyone's expertise — whether it was in wrapping packages or in devising new chemical formulas — was equally respected. It was assumed we all shared certain needs and motivations and that we were all working for the same thing, in that case getting the light polarizing film into production. If you don't have a historical perspective on labor-management relations, it's hard to appreciate how unique it was for its time. Hourly workers had traditionally been paid according to how many hours they worked. If you were sick, if you took a vacation, if you had to attend to personal business, you didn't get paid. There was a sharp distinction between hourly and salaried status. But the sense of equality within Land-Wheelwright, and then Polaroid, led to a rejection of the conventional notions about benefits and privileges being for one 'class' but not for another. Although the concept of unification wasn't formally codified until the late fifties, its principles — uniform treatment of all employees from the hourly to the executive ranks in pay practices, bonuses, promotional procedures, career growth opportunities, medical and insurance benefits, were operative from the beginning. Even in the late thirties parking spaces were precious, and at Polaroid they were allocated not according to rank but by seniority."

Land's ideals were taken for granted by the young factory workers of the C shift. If they thought about them at all they felt a vague sense of pride that they worked for a company that had "ideas" as well as products. Seeing Land in person was another matter; that was exciting. As they crowded into the cafeteria, men and women; middle-aged and young; more than a sprinkling of scientists; mechanics, drivers, operators, secretaries, foremen, sweepers, and engineers: all craned to catch a glimpse of the person who was being helped up on a table at the end of the room. Outside the wall of windows that faced Route 128, the dawn discovered a chill spring day. An occasional truck driver wondered, as he sailed past, at the crowd of people gathered so early in the bright light of the room suspended like a stage three stories above the dark highway, the principal actor rising to address the multitude. As Land stood up, the noise in the room died with a curious ripple of surprise. He was not like his pictures. He was short. He wore a topcoat against the chilly room. He did not smile. He was not going to talk about pay. He looked down at them, and silence pulled tightly across the room. "Martin Luther King is dead," he told them. They were surprised to hear this, not because they had not heard the news — it had been the biggest story in Boston for the past thirty hours. The surprise was this meeting, Land telling this predominantly white audience of workers something they knew already. *Land* telling them. What was it all about? The black members of the shift were the most surprised.

Land talked without a microphone to the silent crowd. He told them that the events of the past day marked a crisis point in American society. He told them that Polaroid was a leader and a model of American industry. He asked for their help in bringing more black workers into Polaroid and, as the astonishment of his audience deepened, he asked them if the company's goal should not be to train and promote black workers to achieve parity with the other Polaroid workers, equivalent to their percentage of the Boston population, about 10 percent — Land paused — *at all levels* of the company. He said that, since Polaroid was growing so rapidly, he believed this would not impose a hardship on anyone, and that Polaroid was the ideal company to take the lead since there was more than enough opportunity for everyone. When he stopped talking the silence stretched tighter than before. Then applause scattered across the room as Land got slowly down from the table. The meeting was over. The C shift walked out without saying much, heading for their cars in the parking lot under bare maple trees. They hadn't said yes to Land's question. But they hadn't said no.

Once before, Land had asked for a similar response from his company. In 1957, at one of the last meetings in which he could speak to the entire Polaroid group, accommodated that afternoon in the tattered seats of a movie theater in Waltham, he raised the subject of inequality. In the language of the fifties he spoke of "those who are less fortunate." Negroes, he called them. He said that a "special effort" was required to redress the lack of education and opportunity that existed for them in Boston and elsewhere, thus anticipating affirmative action by some twelve years. Then he made a remarkable statement: "I will go as far as you will let me." His puzzled audience, which contained few blacks, did not know how to respond. In 1968, a few senior employees remembered Land's words in the Waltham movie house.

Boston had never been a melting pot. It was, rather, one of the most self-consciously ethnic cities in America. If my growing up in Omaha among children of Polish, Lithuanian, Norwegian, and German immigrants had been an intensely American experience, living in Boston continually reminded me of what it was to be Irish, Italian, Greek, or Chinese. Since Colonial times races and nationalities had lived in Boston in enclaves whose boundaries were carefully defined by their neighbors and themselves. In 1968, Irish lived in South Boston, Italians in the North End, blacks in Roxbury, Chinese in Chinatown. The turmoil of the sixties had begun to blur these boundaries. Cambridge in particular had become one of Greater Boston's most racially diverse communities, at least in its industrial, non-Harvard, areas. Blacks, Hispanics, Cape Verdeans, and Orientals moved into the housing projects between Central and Kendall squares, around which were clustered Polaroid's motley collection of offices. They moved out of the projects when they found better, or at least more private, accommodations among the old wooden two- and three-family houses of the town.

By 1968, Polaroid was Cambridge's largest employer and growing much faster than the next two, Harvard and MIT. Polaroid's blacks comprised about 6 percent of the company's total population, higher than most other large Boston-area corporations; but as was commonly the case in 1968, blacks occupied the entry-level categories, largely in semiskilled, low-paying jobs. Land's talk to the company was not reported in the *Globe* or the *Herald,* but the *Bay State Banner,* the black community newspaper published in Roxbury, printed articles and an editorial about it. The *Banner* was skeptical, particularly of the goal of 10 percent black participation in Polaroid at all levels. Did that include the board of directors? What about black women? They were a double minority in industry. While Polaroid had a population of about 35 percent female workers, they were also at the low end of the pay scale, concentrated in clerical and factory assembly jobs. Many people inside and outside the company did not expect Land's words to have much of an effect, for he did not initiate any programs or attend the meetings at which black hiring and training were discussed. He had charted his own emotional course. This time he felt that his alter ego, the company, would respond.

And it did respond with the energy, controversy, and originality it had shown for many of Land's ideas. Land worked in his lab — there was so much to do on SX-70 — but social change began to bubble around him like a retort whose Bunsen burner had been opened to the full.

Polaroid had evolved into a camel of a company: part scientific laboratories; part engineering shops and drafting rooms; part populous factories where workers filled three shifts five and often six days a week; part marketing and distribution; part an amalgam of office functions, including patent lawyers, financial people, personnel and secretarial services. Polaroid required many special skills, few of which were readily accessible to Boston's black community. Saddled with de facto segregated schools in one of America's weakest municipal school systems, Boston blacks had almost no opportunities to learn industrial skills. Polaroid reacted to Land's disturbing and unsettling challenge by listening first to some of the senior black employees, who in turn urged more listening to the black community at large.

One of the first results of this listening was a program called Inner City, housed in unpretentious quarters in Roxbury, far from any Polaroid site in Cambridge or Waltham. Inner City was characterized by its modest size, its limited goals, its lack of growth, and its staying power, attributes unusual for social institutions in the sixties. It taught a course in working for a corporation. This included such basics as attendance, dress, hygiene, use of tools and equipment — and being paid on a regular basis. Inner City prepared people to learn jobs. If those who enrolled completed the basic course, other courses with more specific skills were offered. Inner City students were paid a modest wage as long as they were attending classes and every graduate went to work at Polaroid or one of the other Boston-area companies that began to ask for Inner City alumni. Other black training programs were started in Boston. Some, sponsored with enthusiasm and much initial publicity, collapsed of their own weight, cost, or a change in the level of the sponsor's commitment. Inner City, working in a self-imposed publicity vacuum, trained an average of a hundred men and women a year from its inception in 1969. Its graduates had a high employment retention rate; more than 95 percent not only found, but kept, jobs. Inner City succeeded because it was designed by its clients and backed by Land's challenge: "I will go as far as you let me."

Ken Williams had come late to photography. He lived in several cities before he arrived in Boston from New York; he tried many things before he acquired a camera and learned he had found the right thing. In 1970 the Boston chapter of the Black Panthers was looking for ways to improve its image: the white community thought of Black Panthers as dangerous revolutionaries; the black community viewed them as largely ineffectual. The Boston chapter opted for a new veneer of social responsibility and started a kitchen, an education program, and an arts program. Williams, a lean, saturnine, soft-spoken black man with a small beard connected to a smaller mustache, began to teach photography to black children. Photography was an expensive form of self-expression, and a friend suggested that Williams approach the local photography company for some cameras and a supply of film. Polaroid supported several such classes in Cambridge, and Ken was given Polaroid cameras and some film.

The class lasted only a few months, but in the process Ken met Bill Field, Polaroid's art director. Bill had learned his craft as an apprentice to Paul Giambarba and had grown, as Polaroid grew, to become one of the best graphic designers in Boston. His original ideas about color, influenced by his boyhood in Santa Fe, his bold, simple designs, and his imagination in the use of photographs attracted national attention and awards. Bill kept an eye out for new photographers. A white member of CORE, he was passionately interested in the course Land had set for the company. When he saw Ken Williams's portfolio of striking portraits and ghetto landscapes, Bill offered him a retainer as a free-lance photographer. Ken accepted eagerly. From then on he worked in and out of the art studio on the second floor of 549 Tech Square, directly under Land's office.

Polaroid did not know it had been joined to the political future of South Africa until it read about it in the *Boston Globe.* A story that appeared the morning of October 2, 1970, reported that, in a press conference held the afternoon before, representatives of Polaroid's black workers had called on all black employees to leave their jobs until Polaroid got out of South Africa. The first reaction to the story by the three Polaroid groups most concerned — black workers, white workers, and white management — was puzzlement. What press conference? What is this about South Africa? The first of a thousand meetings was hastily convened. Tom Wyman, who had been running Polaroid's international business since 1967, was asked if Polaroid was "in" South Africa. There was no Polaroid company in South Africa as there was in England or in Japan. At the time Polaroid owned and operated twenty foreign subsidiary companies. Polaroid was an early model of the multinational corporation, but it had not yet learned that this was socially unattractive. Bringing in as it did a substantial flow of foreign currency, it was heavily on the positive side of the country's precarious balance of trade. All of Polaroid's products were invented and most manufactured in America, although there were factories in Holland and Scotland as well. Neither the Russians nor the Japanese had been able to copy the Polaroid system successfully; the technology proved even more formidable than the patents.

What, then, was the fuss about? Wyman patiently explained. There appeared to be two issues. Polaroid did not have a company in South Africa, but it sold to a distributor, Frank and Hirsch, Ltd., there. This little company handled several other lines, primarily office supplies and equipment such as typewriters. It had been Polaroid's customer for more than ten years. Polaroid's South African sales were small by corporate standards, about $300,000 a year, compared to about $3 million in the United Kingdom in 1970. Worldwide sales that year amounted to $500 million, of which four fifths were in the United States. Sales to the South African distributor were therefore less than one tenth of one percent of the world total.

The other issue, Wyman continued, was that Frank and Hirsch sold film to the government of South Africa, and about a third of the passbook pictures were made on Polaroid film. The passbook, he explained, was the document required by law to be carried by every black and colored adult in the country. An internal passport for blacks, it was checked every time they left their homes for work or returned to the black-segregated townships. It was one of the most pervasive, universally hated mechanisms of the official policy of separation of the races known by the Afrikaans term *apartheid*, or "apartness."

"Does that mean that two thirds of the passbook pictures are made on conventional film?" I asked.

"Yes, probably Kodak film. Kodak has a subsidiary there and a sizable film factory. It's the largest photographic company in South Africa."

"Then why us? Why aren't they holding press conferences in Rochester?"

"I don't know. Maybe because they think we'll pay more attention."

Just who "they" were was unclear. Even the Black Committee wasn't sure. As the complexities of a major recruitment program and the even more complicated issues of black training and promotion had begun to unfold, Polaroid's blacks had formed a committee to deal both with management and with the predominantly white Employees Committee, organized early in Polaroid's history. EC members, about fifty in all, were elected at each Polaroid site and by each shift. This group, governed by a central committee and a president elected by the representatives, had evolved into a major force within the company. It fiercely maintained its distance from management and provided advocacy and defense for an individual employee against a supervisor or the company. Disputes were heard in a quasi-legal atmosphere, with the ultimate appeal going either to Land or, in later years as the case load increased, to McCune.

Since blacks were in the minority at all sites, the EC in 1970 had only one black member. If not resistant to Land's challenge to increase the representation of black workers at Polaroid, the EC was adamant that the process not infringe on the rights and prerogatives of white workers. They heard Land's words about the growth of the company and the reservoir of opportunity, but the here and now, the specific job opening, concerned each EC rep. They did not oppose the program, but they watchdogged the company's efforts to implement it. The Black Committee was less formally constituted. While it did not necessarily confront the EC, it consistently urged management to get on with the job. The issue of black recruitment and the entry-level Inner City program worried both groups less than the issues of training and promotion. Since both the EC and the Black Committee represented employees already in place, new workers were of less concern to both than the advancement of their constituents.

Land did not involve himself in these day-to-day struggles. He had asked his company the critical question. It had responded. In the meantime he was doing what the company expected of him, pursuing the first aim, to make new products useful to the public. SX-70 factories were rising like secret cities all over eastern Massachusetts. SX-70 claimed all of his time and attention except that which he kept in reserve for a project, living a secret life of its own in a laboratory on Main Street, devoted to a new process for forming color images, the "additive" project. He had had no time for politics, racial, corporate, or otherwise — until South Africa.

The "they" turned out to be Ken Williams and Caroline Hunter, a young woman who worked in Land's own laboratory. She was brilliant, black, militant, and committed. The day the *Globe* article appeared, she was besieged with requests for interviews from all of the Boston media. Overnight she became the spokesperson for an issue that had leaped onto the front page. Within a month she left the company, claiming she had been fired. Polaroid said she resigned. It was apparent that she wanted to devote her full energies to the campaign she and Ken Williams had begun. No one realized at the time the extent of those energies, the depth of her commitment. Williams, who had run across a reference to the South African passbook in a newspaper article and casually showed it to his friend, Caroline Hunter, seemed surprised at the furor, but he soon discovered that he, too, had little time for photography. Although not as articulate as Hunter, he became a recognizable face on Boston television news. Hunter, however, her thoughts organized, her delivery swift, her demeanor alternately rational and passionate, could rivet an audience. She had a simple, compelling story to tell: Polaroid was selling film to the South African government, which used it to oppress blacks; Polaroid must be forced to leave South Africa.

The young reporters at the *Globe* clamored to cover the story. Eventually twenty-seven different bylines appeared in the *Globe* under headlines about Polaroid and South Africa. The story ran on the front page, the Metro page, the op-ed page, and the Business page. It was simultaneously international, national, and local news. Sports and Food seemed to be the only desks that weren't given access to it. Every story began with an interview with the leaders of the crusade.

The blacks at Polaroid were trapped by the issue of South Africa. They could not ignore it, nor could they assess the questions of right and wrong, guilt or innocence, with which the media so glibly dealt. The white employees were deeply troubled as well. They had lived with the assumption, some of them for all their working lives, that Polaroid was a company with a conscience, that Polaroid was a leader in its efforts to train black workers, that it was, in fact, Land. How could this — whatever it was — have happened? What exactly was Polaroid doing in South Africa? While the management of the company — all white — struggled to assimilate the issues, Caroline Hunter was far ahead of them, lecturing to student audiences at Harvard, talking to black members of Congress, writing letters to the United Nations. Ken Williams stayed close to home and concentrated on the Boston media. He marched with students and television crews around the courtyard at Tech Square, chanting for Polaroid to get out of South Africa.

As I listened to a hundred young voices shouting under the linden trees, I envied them their confidence. They looked so sure and sounded so right. But I had little confidence that we would be able to discover what was the right thing to do about South Africa. It wasn't Mississippi. It was ten thousand miles from Cambridge. I knew, however, that we needed a solution soon. SX-70 had been placed on hold.

Land was forced out of his laboratory, shaken, furious at the interruption of his labors at so critical a time. Despite the fact that he was nearing the culmination of twenty years of intellectual and physical labor, he understood that this issue was not trivial. He abhorred apartheid, as did everyone around him. Better than almost anyone in the company, he understood the power of a simple message delivered forcefully to an unsophisticated audience. He knew also that an attack on his company was an attack on him. He began to receive telephone calls — his number had always been listed in the directory — threatening him and his family with violence. The spate of corporate bombings in New England and New York was at its height. At the suggestion of Jim Shea, Polaroid's tough, able security specialist, an arrangement was quickly made with the Cambridge Police Department to supply off-duty officers to drive Land to work and back and to guard his home. Polaroid paid the cost. The Cambridge police were anxious to cooperate; the arrangement was to become permanent.

When in doubt Polaroid formed another committee, in this instance a broad-based one that included representatives of the EC, the Black Committee, and middle and upper management. Tom Wyman and I were included; Bill McCune was both the organizer and the informal chairman. Twenty to twenty-five men and women, about a third of them black, met almost daily for the next six months, trying to understand the issues, pragmatic and moral, surrounding the company's situation and to discover the best way out of the dilemma. Caroline Hunter maintained the committee's sense of urgency by holding Polaroid's feet to the fire. She commanded the attention of the national media: *Time, Newsweek, Business Week,* all the television networks. There might be two views in the press of China, Cuba, or even Russia, but in America there was only one view of South Africa. That the story could be so easily made local was a revelation. It was heady wine to fight apartheid in Cambridge, Massachusetts. Polaroid was the first American corporation to be singled out. The fact that it had little stake, financial or otherwise, in doing business in South Africa was irrelevant. Ken Williams and Caroline Hunter had raised the issue. Polaroid had to answer. It was a great story.

The committee took more or less permanent possession of Polaroid's dark little mahogany board room next to Land's office on the third floor of 549 Tech Square. The meetings began at eight o'clock in the morning and often continued through lunch and dinner, eaten at the large oval table covered with the unfamiliar detritus of greasy paper napkins and Pepsi cans. The committee was soon impaled on the horns: Polaroid could not get "out" of South Africa because it was not "in." The obvious course of action might be to stop selling cameras and film to Frank and Hirsch. That, however, would not accomplish anything, since the distributor would simply continue to buy from another source: a supplier in the Middle East, another country in Africa, a dealer in the U.K. Polaroid had no way of controlling the flow of its products after they were sold. Thus Polaroid cameras would continue to be purchased and used in South Africa, and film would presumably continue to be supplied to the government. In addition, Frank and Hirsch, one of whose principals had fled Nazi Germany to South Africa, seemed genuinely concerned about the furor. They had telephoned, cabled, and written us, pointing out that their policies concerning their black employees were considered liberal. They offered to do whatever they could to help solve the problem. "I think we should ignore the whole thing," said one Polaroid department manager, his face pink with anger. "We're not in South Africa. We don't have a company there, not one single employee. There's nothing we can do that will affect the situation in that country one goddamn bit. Excuse me, but I think this is nonsense."

"We *are* in South Africa," I said. "Ken and Caroline said so on NBC news last night and they'll say it again tonight. They put us in South Africa. Now we have to do something about it."

The committee agreed early on that the practical solution depended on addressing, if at all possible, the moral problem. After several days of debate about what was best for South African blacks, a figure stood up in the back of the board room. "I'm leaving," he said. Chuck Jones had been one of the founders of the Black Committee. Skeptical and tough, he was not impressed with Polaroid's progress toward greater black opportunity, nor in this committee's chances of arriving at a significant decision. He did not speak often and the table was suddenly quiet.

"What's the matter, Chuck?" Bill McCune asked.

"For a hundred years Whitey has been telling black people what's good for them." Chuck pulled on his jacket, picked up his car keys, and headed for the door. "Now we're sitting around eating lunch and deciding what's right for blacks in South Africa. I don't want any part of it."

"What do you suggest?" Wyman said to Chuck's departing back.

"Why don't we ask them?" he said. "Why don't we go over there and ask them?" The door closed.

Chuck Jones's question provided the committee with its first answer. Land and the management executive committee agreed to send four of the ad hoc committee members, two blacks, including Chuck Jones, and two whites, including Tom Wyman, to South Africa. They would stay ten days to two weeks, travel as much as possible, talk to as many people as they could. Then they would return with a recommendation. Land attended the last meeting of the full committee before the group left to fly to London and Johannesburg. He listened to the review of their itinerary, which was purposely vague in the middle. They would try to visit at least one of the black townships normally forbidden to foreign visitors. They would travel with as little fanfare as possible. No word of their trip would be given to the American press until they returned. They would take their chances with the South African press, which, we had been surprised to learn, was remarkably free, vocal, and often critical of the government. Land made no promises to the committee or its traveling representatives other than to say that, if the recommendation was agreed on by a majority and it was an honorable one, the company would follow it.

The four Polaroid workers, if a senior vice president could be included in that category, were able to travel with few restrictions in South Africa. They stayed for two weeks and talked to a remarkably diverse group of people: Helen Suzman, one of the few opposition members of South Africa's general assembly; Gatsha Buthelezi, chief of the Zulus; members of the outlawed Black African National Congress; Robert Oppenheim, the liberal industrialist. They met — in private — all the black employees of Frank and Hirsch and many other blacks. They spent two evenings in Soweto, the largest of the black townships outside Johannesburg. Smuggled in and out in two ramshackle cars, the whites crouched low so their faces would not be seen on the dark streets, they glimpsed the blocks of grim bungalows as the cars hurried past. In the kerosene light of a Soweto living room whose curtains were tightly drawn against the night, they listened to a message they heard over and over from the blacks with whom they had spoken. "You are a small company in South Africa, but your name is known. Don't turn your backs on us. Do what you can to help us. Help our children get more schooling than we had. Help us to get the same pay as whites get for the same job. If you want to help us, don't go away. Even a small effort will mean much to us."

"What kind of help do you need?"

"Training to get a better job. Education for our children."

"Will the government let us do anything like that?"

"I don't know. You could try."

When the group returned, their recommendation was unanimous: if Polaroid was to be guided by what black workers in South Africa wanted, we should not walk away from the situation; to do that would leave it solely in the hands of the government and the revolutionaries. They proposed that we establish a set of guidelines for Frank and Hirsch which included recruiting blacks; giving equal pay for equal work among black and white workers; setting up an educational trust, to be funded jointly by Polaroid and Frank and Hirsch, for scholarships for black children; and establishing a training program at the distributor to upgrade its black workers' skills. Frank and Hirsch must stop all sales of film and equipment to the government, a largely symbolic gesture, since the government could import film from other sources if it wanted to. If Frank and Hirsch refused, or the government of South Africa blocked any of these proposals, we should reconsider our position. These recommendations were accepted by the full committee, by the management executive committee, by Land, and by the Polaroid board of directors. The board members had anxiously watched the South African storm breaking over Polaroid's head. Those who were on the boards of other companies could only wonder where it would strike next. The Sullivan Principles, promulgated by a black member of the General Motors board, which followed Polaroid's committee recommendations almost to the letter, were still two years in the future.

In a quiet moment after the return of the travelers, I asked Chuck Jones what he thought of South Africa. "I liked Soweto," he said. "Just like home."

Concerned that the company's story would not be told in the press, Polaroid, in 1971, published two statements as paid national advertisements, setting forth the facts about Polaroid's relationship with Frank and Hirsch; describing the process of discussion and debate that had taken place within the company; recounting the delegation's visit to South Africa; and stating the recommendations that had come out of their visit. Somewhat to our surprise, Frank and Hirsch accepted the plan in its entirety. The South African government made no comment, nor did the government of the United States.

In this country the plan was greeted with almost universal criticism from the press. Caroline Hunter and Ken Williams excoriated it. Student groups denounced it. The black and white employees of Polaroid felt, however, that in the main the right thing had been done. The issue subsided at Polaroid, which was immersed in the last crises of the SX-70 development effort. What profit came from sales to Frank and Hirsch was largely subsumed in the costs of the educational trust fund and the incalculable cost of the time and effort expended by the company to unravel the South African knot.

Frank and Hirsch stuck to its end of the bargain for six years. It hired more blacks and instituted a training program. With only one hundred employees in all, of whom thirty-five were black, the company was so small that its actions were important only as a demonstration of what could be done. It encountered no government restraint or interference. Polaroid audited the program carefully once a year. Chief Buthelezi visited the United States and had lunch at Tech Square. The promises seemed to have been kept.

Then in 1977, Bob Lenzner, a reporter for the *Globe* and the London *Economist* who had covered the Polaroid South African story for both papers, called me to say that a Johannesburg source had told him that Frank and Hirsch was again shipping Polaroid film directly to a South African government office. I asked him not to break the story until we could confirm or deny it and promised to tell him the results of our own investigation, no matter what it revealed. His source was correct. We broke off the relationship with Frank and Hirsch. Polaroid and South Africa were done with each other. We were out.

22

Rehearsal

Norwood, 1971

Land always arrived late to a rehearsal. It was a habit that exhibited a certain disregard for his associates, since it usually added hours at the far end of the evening, but it did allow them to solve the mechanical problems of presentation — lighting, projection, sound — that had to be surmounted before the real work of the night could begin. The huge meeting room was black except for a spotlight on the stage that illuminated a spare, black leather and chromium chair and the small white pedestal table requisitioned from my office. An entrance door far in the rear of the hall opened and light streamed in. An omnipresent voice, testing sound on the elaborate network of speakers hanging from the ceiling girders, barked, "Shut the door," as Land and three Princesses slipped inside. An image of the stocky silhouette registered for an instant, then disappeared as the door closed like a shutter. "Sorry, Dr. Land," boomed the voice as the party groped their way to a tiny office at the rear corner. The house lights came slowly up to reveal some fifty people sitting quietly in rows of rented wooden folding chairs, dressed as if for a football game. It was frigid for a Sunday evening in late April. Conversation in the vast room, a factory chamber indeed as long and as wide as a football field, the floor smooth concrete, the ceiling, supported by widely spaced steel columns, about twenty-five feet high, hushed when the voice stopped its dreary counting to three. There were no windows. The stage, constructed in the preceding week, projected about fifteen feet into the room, proportioned like a conventional stage in a high school auditorium. Three thousand chairs faced it in expectant rows.

•

Polaroid's annual meeting was a rite of spring that had few precedents in the business world of the seventies. Most corporations viewed the annual meeting as a necessary evil, prescribed by law, requiring the participation of senior officers taken from more important tasks and offered to an audience that usually included dolts, malcontents, and professional gadflies. This was the era of Wilma Soss, the Gilbert brothers, and Evelyn Y. Davis, the professional stockholders who made a career of disrupting annual meetings and asking difficult, often personally embarrassing questions of the chairman. These confrontations were universally dreaded. Security at most meetings was severe, and they were usually designed to be as short as could decently be managed. Locations were often chosen in inaccessible towns like Dover, Delaware, a state where many companies, including Polaroid, had registered to take advantage of the favorable incorporation laws. Attendees might be shown some charts projected on 35 mm slides, be given a handout or two, hear an operations report and a financial report, be rushed through the dreaded question-and-answer period, vote for the slate of directors and the auditor, and find themselves adjourned.

Land invented a totally different kind of annual meeting. Like many of his best inventions, it served several purposes, was complex, elegant, tastefully packaged, required enormous preparation, and dealt with several audiences on different levels simultaneously. Within the company Land used the annual meeting to push to completion, or near completion, the development project at hand. Research and engineering efforts at Polaroid had a life cycle of their own. No matter with what sense of urgency they had begun, problems soon set the pace of the project, and solutions, not dates, became the milestones.

The SX-70 project was in its second year of intense activity, although research on the film structure had begun in the mid sixties. Land had set extraordinarily difficult goals for the project. The camera was to be small, but just how small was still the subject of emotional debate. It was indeed to be a folding single-lens reflex, an animal that not only did not yet exist in photography, but had never been imagined. The integral film structure would allow development of the color image to take place, then cease at the appropriate moment, entirely within the film unit itself. The chemical processes would take place in the light, not in a dark chamber. The camera was to include revolutionary optics and a complete set of electronic controls, some of which had not yet been invented. Three Polaroid factories were being built simultaneously: a negative plant in

New Bedford, a film assembly plant in Waltham, and the new camera assembly plant in Norwood, scene of the meeting. Each required process machinery that was to be conceived, built, and installed by Polaroid engineers. Many of the most important manufacturing issues had not been solved, since the specifications of the camera and film were still changing.

The SX-70 program was so complex and so extended the boundaries of half a dozen technologies that those who worked on it had difficulty in stretching their faith and their optimism beyond the piece of the whole on which their own energies were concentrated. Land was virtually the only person in the company who knew in detail all the difficulties that had to be surmounted. The rest of us could only guess. "Do not undertake a program unless the goal is manifestly important and its achievement is nearly impossible," Land had said thirty years earlier. This sort of statement could be maddening to pragmatic men and women. The tired people sitting in the hall that evening were wondering what Land was going to show on the stage three days hence. Polaroid's annual meeting had captured the full attention of its internal audience.

Planning for the meeting, held each year at the end of April, began in January. When it became known within the SX-70 project teams that the unformed, recalcitrant, pitiful embryo that they were nurturing might be birthed onstage before an audience of shareholders and the national press, panic, anger, and despair spread like an epidemic. It wasn't fair. It was much too early. The goals were "nearly impossible." That phrase had echoed around the company since SX-70's inception. In January, April loomed as but a few weeks away. Project managers' carefully drawn flow charts and timetables were tossed aside in the face of the terrifying confrontation. No corporate gadfly could induce one-half the fear that a public demonstration evoked. The concerns were the same: exposure, embarrassment, lack of adequate preparation, questions to which there were no answers. Did Land really mean it? Would he really do it? Meanwhile, six months' work was accomplished in six weeks.

Rehearsals for the meeting began a month before the date. Polaroid's meetings in the sixties and seventies were usually held in the newest fully enclosed manufacturing building to be completed, a new warehouse, a camera or film plant, or, in 1968 when expansion had temporarily slowed, a circus tent pitched in a parking lot. The venue had to be a large one, for attendance at the meetings had steadily grown. By 1971, the company's public relations staff was predicting an audience of between twenty-five hundred and three thousand. Few public halls in Boston could accommodate that number, and the need for elaborate technical preparations and many nights of rehearsal ruled out any auditorium with a busy performance schedule. The size of the audience was unprecedented. Contrary to current corporate practice, Polaroid encouraged people to attend, not only shareholders, but their friends and families as well. Far from limiting access, the company provided maps, road signs, parking areas, and shuttle buses to make attendance as easy as possible.

But two factors above all served to swell the size of the audience: the expectation of seeing a new product and Land's presence on the stage. If the SX-70 development team formed the first audience, the second was the thousands who would occupy the folding wooden chairs, a congregation of the converted. They would come prepared to be dazzled by Land's magic. Most of them owned a Polaroid camera. Many were small shareholders who had seen Polaroid stock split and split again: four for one in 1964 and two for one in 1968. The stock price swung erratically, but the trend since 1951 had been steeply up. The stockholders felt they had been invited by Dr. Edwin H. Land himself, the source of all that was exciting and profitable about owning Polaroid stock. Many of his shareholders — he made no bones of the fact that he thought of them as his — attended every year without fail. Many were also employees. If a financial analyst should ask a critical question, or a gadfly attack, the audience reacted so indignantly that the Chairman needed to step in to defend him. "No, no, let him speak," Land would say. "A perfectly reasonable question. Please let him finish." The psychology thus reversed, the critic found himself on the defensive, his intended prey his defender. Many of the questions from the audience were of the sort fans ask of motion picture or sports idols: "How long did it take you to develop color film?" "What are you going to invent next?" The answers were often whimsical: "A new name for instant photography."

Playing to this responsive audience was more than emotionally gratifying. Land had enough feel to understand the nuances of audience reaction to a presentation. His shareholders taught him how the world would react to a new product. The meetings were themselves experiments, products often exposed to an audience in piecemeal fashion. In 1970, Land had displayed some examples of the first integral color pictures, labeled experimental, and given his first public description of the complex layered structure of SX-70 color film. This year it was being rumored in Boston that he would demonstrate the new camera. His engineers felt passionately that it was at least a year too early. But he was clearly tempted to experiment with the shareholder audience. He had another strong motive as well.

Since 1957, Eastman Kodak had been providing Polaroid with all the color negative for Polacolor, the peel-apart pack film that was the foundation of Polaroid's business. Although negative sales to Polaroid produced about $50 million of revenue a year to Kodak, Polaroid's rapidly increasing sales and its high visibility caused increasing concern in Rochester. In April of 1969, two events occurred, one known to Land and his officers, one only guessed at. Kodak abruptly terminated the 1957 agreement, which required Polaroid to disclose to Kodak some of its color technology, including the vital dye-developer concept, in exchange for Kodak's cooperative development effort to improve color negative. Periodic research meetings had long been held between scientists of the two companies to discuss improvements and new ideas, but in April of 1968 Polaroid had dropped a bombshell at one of these meetings, describing in general terms a radically new color film. Six months later Land showed Kodak's vice president of research some photographs made on the new material. Kodak was stunned. A year later it canceled the 1957 agreement, which called for cooperative development.

The second event of 1969 followed rapidly. Kodak launched its own instant photography project on a crash basis. The largest photographic concern in the world, some five times larger than Polaroid in almost any dimension, Eastman had finally been stung into action. It was no longer deemed acceptable by Louis K. Eilers, Gerald Zoronow, and Walter Fallon, Kodak's three senior executives, that Polaroid would continue to capture not only the industry spotlight, but an increasing share of the amateur photographic market as well. Admittedly it was a comparatively small share. About 15 percent of all cameras sold in the United States were Polaroid's; about 80 percent were Kodak's; 5 percent encompassed all the rest of the world's photographic manufacturers selling in America.

The Kodak instant project was code-named PL-976, the three numbers indicating that the target for introduction to the marketplace was to be

1976. It was soon renamed PL-974, as more manpower and more money were poured into the effort. The project then split into two groups. Project 129 concentrated on producing a peel-apart color film similar to Polacolor that could be used in Polaroid cameras. P-129 was to be aborted three years later, after an expenditure by Kodak of $94 million, when Polaroid introduced its SX-70 system. Project 130 began efforts to produce an integral structure similar to the one described in the joint research meeting in 1968. This was to be a film for Kodak cameras only. Before long P-130 would involve almost fourteen hundred of Kodak's best scientists and technicians. On the eve of the 1971 annual meeting, none of this was known to Land. Kodak secrecy was legendary, but the termination of the color negative agreement sent a clear signal that war had been declared in the field of instant photography. With Polaroid's SX-70 project struggling with the nearly impossible at every turn, the tired officers and scientists sitting in attendance at the rehearsal could only hope that Land was going to make the right decision. If he showed SX-70's secrets too soon, Kodak would surely benefit. What if a live demonstration before three thousand people failed in some critical respect? The third audience for this meeting was Eastman Kodak. Its people would not be visible, but they would be watching the show nevertheless, audio recorders running, studying every nuance, looking for clues, hoping for a blunder.

The door of the small office at the rear of the room opened and Land emerged, walking up the dark aisle toward the stage. The sound system, the elaborate stage lighting, most of the theatrical mechanics had been rehearsed. The formalities of the meeting had been reduced to routine. Those parts of the program that did not include Land were pat. Still, nothing important had been decided. It was close to midnight. The stage manager, John McCann, Land's laboratory assistant, was standing at the corner of the stage, dispirited and exhausted, watching his mentor's progress toward the front. Land stopped at one row, then another, to chat. When he paused to talk to one of the design engineers on the camera team, he reached into his right coat pocket. Every eye followed the motion of his hand. He pulled out — something — then replaced it quickly.

In the uncertain light it was hard to see clearly what it was. It was shiny, about the size of a cigar case. Land occasionally smoked cigars.

Was it the camera? Many of this quite senior group had not seen it yet. The issue of its size had caused great pain. That which was nearly impossible became unbearably difficult as the size of the package was reduced. Battles were fought over a millimeter of dimension. Land had described the SX-70 as a "pocket camera" at a previous shareholders' meeting, a name that Kodak quickly preempted and attached to one of its new camera models, just as it had used the name Instamatic for its conventional film cameras in an apparent attempt to capitalize on the growing interest in instant photography. How big was a pocket camera? Word on the camera team, and the film team as well, since they must live or die by the same dimensions, was that the most important person on the SX-70 project was Land's tailor.

John McCann worried as much as any of the rest that Land might show the camera to the audience at the meeting. His concerns, however, were more for stagecraft than corporate strategy. Land could and would do what he wanted. John had to make it work for the audience. There were so many imponderables. Was Land going to take a picture? If so, of what? And how would he show a picture to three thousand people, some of whom would be sitting two hundred fifty feet away? McCann thought rapidly about a video camera and an array of monitors. He'd need at least twenty monitors, hung from the ceiling above the crowd. They'd have a problem with all the speakers already mounted there. A problem, too, with enough light to get a good image of the picture on video. He'd have to load one end of the stage with light. Land finished his conversation, walked up the aisle, and mounted the black-carpeted steps to the stage. McCann checked to be sure his own lapel microphone was switched off.

"Good evening, John." Land looked around, his features heavy under the harsh spotlight, his geniality gone, his mouth grim.

"Hello, Din."

"Is the stage bright enough? I should think another half stop." Land casually expressed ambient light levels in f-stops, the measure of exposure in a camera lens. His accuracy without recourse to a light meter was uncanny.

"We have a larger spot. We can add more. We can bring it all up higher. Do you want to rehearse? Everyone is ready." McCann did not belabor the obvious — that they had been ready for hours.

"I don't think I need to rehearse tonight. Perhaps tomorrow morning."

Land paced the length of the stage and back, getting the feel of it under the balls of his feet.

"Din, what do you have in your pocket?" McCann asked reluctantly, urgently.

The Chairman of the Board, Chief Executive Officer, President, Director of Research, and Project Manager of SX-70 looked out at the sea of wooden chairs and smiled his little-boy smile. "A block of wood," he said.

23

Octagons

Cambridge and Needham, 1972

Land had decreed that the last veil was to fall at Polaroid's 1972 annual meeting. SX-70 would finally be shown naked and entire to an amazed world. Since 1969, he had teased the shareholders, who loved it, and the press and the financial analysts, who hated it, with glimpses, hints, and peeks. He had talked about the new system and described some of its basic features. He had showed sample integral prints in 1970 and played with the wooden camera in his pocket at the 1971 meeting. Each time he had used the imperative of disclosure to the shareholders to advance the development work ahead of a schedule too deliberate for his impatience. This was contrary to conventional business wisdom. A cardinal sin of marketing was to expose the new prematurely, thus making the current product obsolete, in this case the nine-year-old pack camera line.

Land had Polaroid flirting with disaster in the marketplace. We had done everything ingenious people could think of to keep the venerable pack cameras fresh and interesting, including the addition the year before of a self-timer with a buzzer that allowed the photographer to aim the camera on a tripod or a table, press the shutter, and, while the camera buzzed ominously for three seconds, run around and position himself in the picture. In addition to the buzz, a sixty-second development timer beeped when the picture was ripe to be peeled from the negative. A third device went boop when there was too little natural light to make a good picture. Phyllis Robinson and Bob Gage built a charming campaign around buzzes, beeps, and boops that kept the pack line alive while Land told the world that a revolution in photography was just around the corner.

In the late sixties, Stan Calderwood had begun to worry about our ability to continue to sell cameras. He calculated that a Polaroid camera had been purchased by half of America's 40 million households. His research showed that 10 percent of households could be assumed to have no interest in photography at all, that another 10 percent were committed to 35 mm cameras or home movies, and that another 10 percent fell below the poverty line. That left a pool of only 8 million U.S. households from which to fish. I felt Stan had underestimated the American family's appetite for hardware. I asked him how many radios he had in his own household.

"I don't know."

"Of course you don't. Neither do I. But try to count."

"Well, one in the living room, one in the kitchen; another one, a clock radio, in the guest room. That's it. No, a little portable in my workshop in the basement. Wait, one in the garage. That's it."

"How about your stereo?"

"Yes, it has a tuner."

"How many cars?"

"Right. Two cars, one radio in each."

"That's nine radios for two people, and I'll bet you've forgotten a couple."

"Well, radios are not cameras."

"How many cameras do you have?"

"That's not fair. I've been collecting cameras all my life."

"How many?"

"I don't know."

"Ten?"

"Maybe. But I'm not typical."

"How many television sets?"

"Two. No, three."

"So, you and Norma Jean have nine radios, two cars, more than ten cameras, and three television sets."

"Peter, we are not typical."

"Everyone I know has at least nine radios."

When Stan left the company in 1971, convinced that Land would never make him or anyone else president, we had been selling cameras at a worldwide rate of 4 million a year. When I took over the marketing reins from him, we sold 3,600,000 cameras in the face of Land's SX-70 striptease. The next year, 1972, with a full-blown disclosure of the SX-70 system, but only a few thousand that were salable, we still sold 4,600,000 of the old cameras worldwide. We sold between 4 and 9 million Polaroid cameras a year every year for the next ten without reaching market saturation.

From this evolved two theories. First, Land was correct to ignore conventional wisdom: he was teaching the American public, and by extension a world market, that the Polaroid camera was not a lifetime acquisition, but an evolving idea, an ongoing adventure, an exploration of technology. If that sounded like an improbable marketing plan, it had proved itself since 1950. Second, yard sales were invented to get rid of old Polaroid cameras. We knew with considerable certainty that amateur-owned cameras, Polaroid, Kodak, or Japanese, had an average useful life of three years, with the majority of film use in the first year. Polaroid's film usage curve was even more heavily skewed to the initial year of ownership than that of conventional cameras. Thus, if we continued to change camera designs every three to four years, the pattern in the sixties and seventies, we could hope to rekindle the interest of an owner whose camera had departed in a yard sale or was gathering dust on a closet shelf.

The 1972 shareholders' meeting was planned for the main warehouse building in the distribution center in Needham. Since all the new SX-70 buildings were occupied and being heavily utilized, tons of fragile cameras, film, and industrial products had to be moved from the floor of the warehouse, one of Polaroid's largest buildings, to rented space nearby. The warehouse went through the requisite installation of a professional sound system, theatrical lighting, a control booth, internal communications, thousands of rented folding chairs, and the last-minute planting of grass, flowers, bushes, and full-grown trees, stuck like stalks of celery by large machines around this undistinguished pudding of a building. The warehouse was one of Polaroid's oldest buildings outside of Cambridge. Its roof leaked in every rain and had once collapsed under a load of wet snow, killing one person. It had resisted the best efforts of the building engineers who had repaired and rebuilt it three times, then gave up and collected the rainwater in interior gutters and drains.

A month of preparation made an amazing difference; freshly painted and sodded, it looked quite presentable outside. Inside, the customary chaos reigned. The major problem of this meeting, beyond producing a sufficient number of workable SX-70 cameras and enough film, was security. The meeting would take place late in April, as specified in the company bylaws. SX-70 would be demonstrated to all and sundry. No date, however, had been set for the sales introduction of the system. Discussions, meetings, and word fights abounded. Manufacturing was starting up on all the elements, both at Polaroid plants and in vendors' factories all over the country. Glitches occurred daily. The flat battery that supplied power to the camera from each film pack was a source of mysterious and frustrating problems that kept a team of Polaroid engineers in residence in Appleton, Wisconsin, home of Ray-O-Vac, the supplier. The Polaroid camera plant and the SX-70 film assembly plant were down as often as they were up. Only the new color negative plant in New Bedford, the facility on whose success the destiny of the entire system depended, had achieved uninterrupted operation under its imperturbable manager, Mac Booth. The film people in particular were concerned about what would happen at the meeting. Land was up to his old tricks. They did not feel ready; too many questions needed answers. If an SX-70 print fell into the hands of a financial analyst, a reporter, or — worst case imaginable — Kodak, valuable secrets would be revealed. The system might not go on sale for another year. Why must the company again risk everything so early? Paranoia rose to flood level.

I had two concerns of my own. We had to continue to sell pack cameras until SX-70 was ready for market, and I was unsure for how many months after the April meeting the life raft would have to be patched. On the other hand, I could not ignore the anxiety of the film and camera groups. Nothing would be worse than to trumpet the Second Coming, then be forced to retire to the back room for hasty repairs or redesign. Land alternated between serene and ferocious, but as usual, he took the positive view. He felt he had solved a dozen of the toughest problems of his or anyone's career. He had whipped or cajoled nature into submission on seemingly insoluble technical questions: the optics of the camera used the cast-plastic technology developed during World War II for Patton's tank sight to fold light through the internal lenses and mirrors in ingenious ways; the surface of the print, opaque to light in the initial phases of development, became transparent as the colors appeared, adding yet another chemical process to the already extravagant molecular choreography taking place within each piece of film; not only did the colors of the final picture emerge brilliantly, but the pairing of metal molecules with the dyes gave the pictures an astonishing permanence. The great goals had been achieved. Enough of these insignificant manufacturing delays, give me an audience!

Land decreed that there would be no turning back from a full presentation of the system, or rather, with characteristic reticence, he issued no decree at all. He simply alerted team leaders that their services would be required for the meeting. Overnight the entire company, in which communications were normally haphazard, since Polaroid occupied twenty-nine buildings in seven eastern Massachusetts towns, became aware that SX-70 was about to come out of the closet. The management executive committee, whose meetings Land attended sporadically if at all, accepted the fait accompli with grumbling and dire reminders by each of us of the risks involved. The major question was still unanswered. What followed? When would, how would, we decide when it was time to turn SX-70 over to the dealers and customers? When would we begin to recoup some of our $750 million investment?

Land shared the film group's concern for security of the SX-70 pictures. An invention was needed. He wrestled with the problem of demonstrating a camera whose pictures had an image area three and a quarter inches square and whose resolution and color were the final criteria by which the whole system would be judged without putting the pictures in the hands of his audience. Television, which had been used before in similar circumstances, was ruled out; a step removed from the real image, it would degrade resolution and color. The door to his study closed, and for several days he was closeted with Nan Buddy and several of the other Princesses.

When they emerged they proclaimed not one invention, but two. The first was an octagonal stage. Six octagons would be situated behind the audience area in the big Needham room. Each octagon would be a picture-taking center. Ideas were solicited for the visual themes, although it soon became evident that Land and the Princesses had planned them already. The second invention was a picture rail, slotted to hold the pictures securely by their lower margin, with a pin inserted through each empty pod so that they could not be removed. The rail ran around the octagon at eye level behind a barrier of flowers, far enough back to

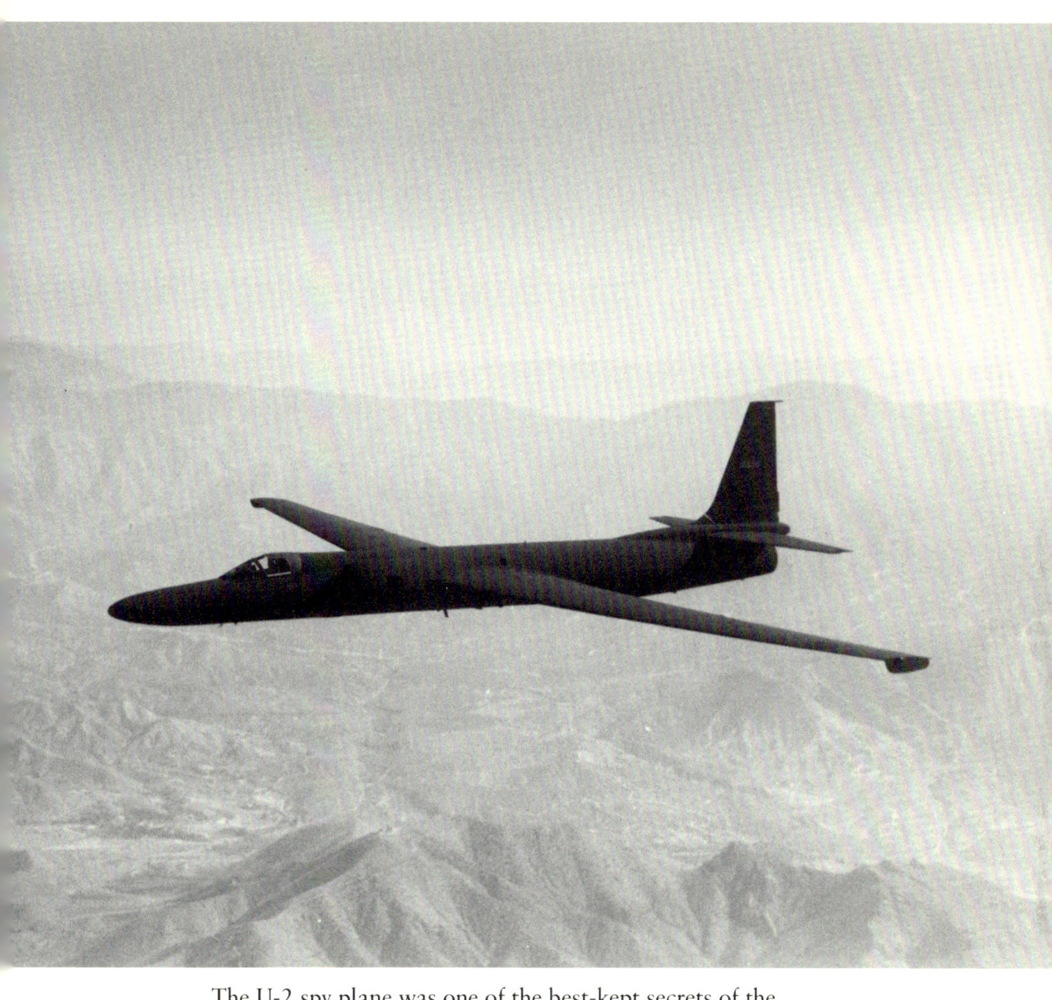

The U-2 spy plane was one of the best-kept secrets of the Cold War. (Courtesy *Lockheed-California Company*)

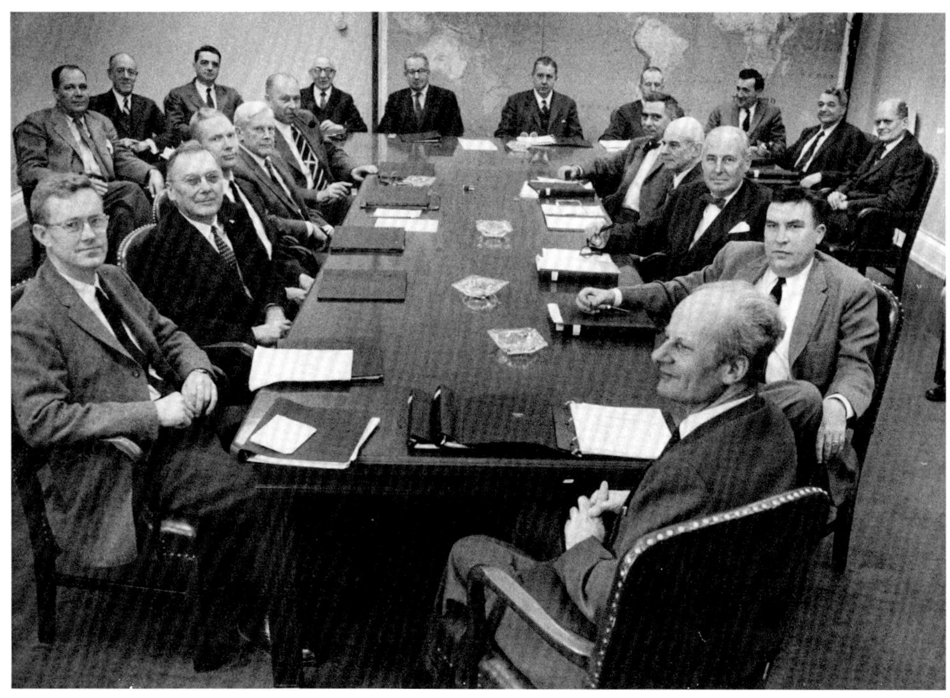

The U-2 was the creation of President Eisenhower's science advisory committee. Land (third from left at the rear) and James R. Killian (sixth from left) played leading roles. (Paul Schutzer, *Life* magazine. © Time Inc.)

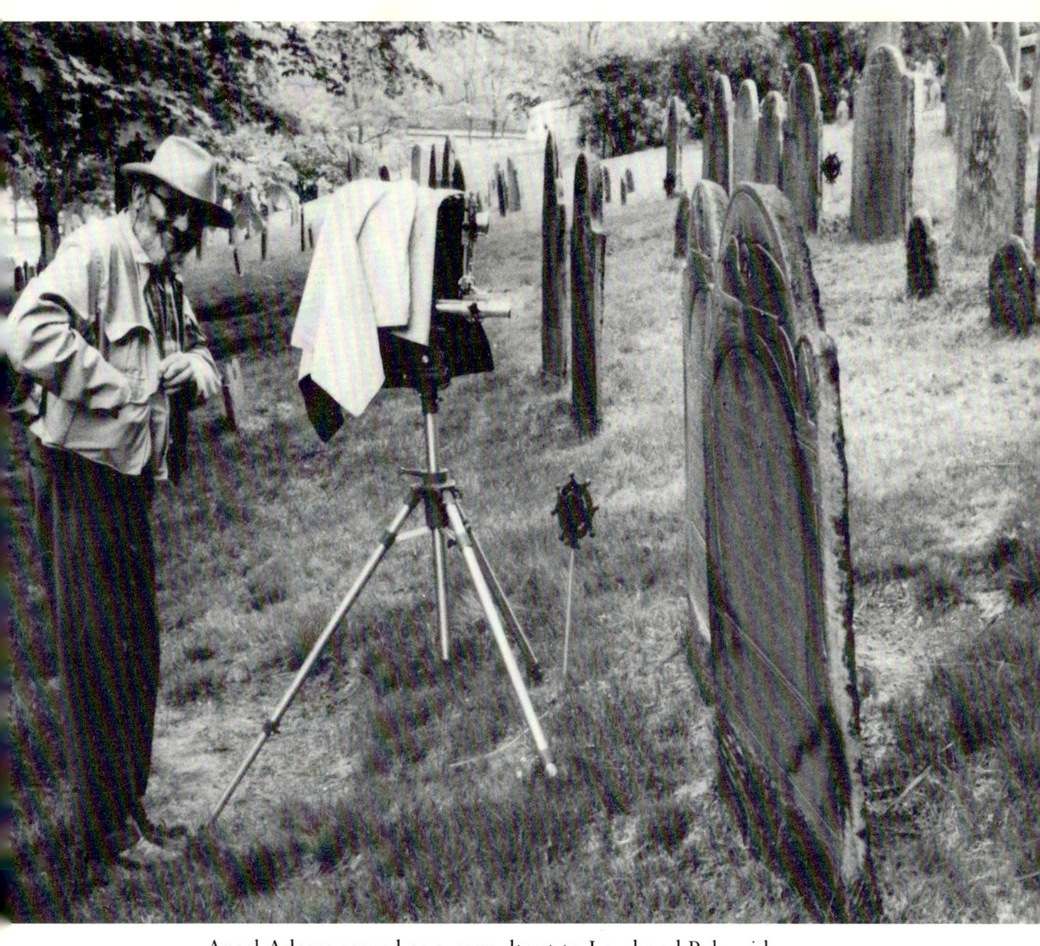

Ansel Adams served as a consultant to Land and Polaroid from 1948 until his death in 1984. He personally tested virtually every new camera and film type and trained many of the company's photographers.

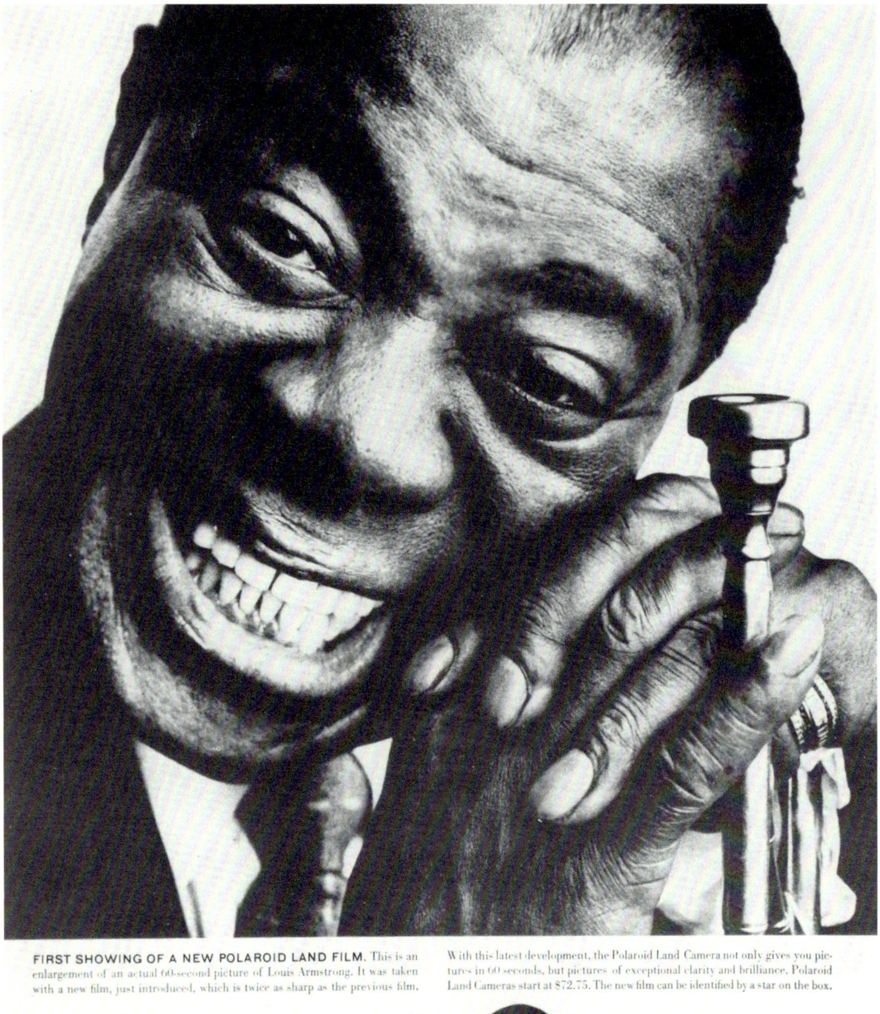

FIRST SHOWING OF A NEW POLAROID LAND FILM. This is an enlargement of an actual 60-second picture of Louis Armstrong. It was taken with a new film, just introduced, which is twice as sharp as the previous film. With this latest development, the Polaroid Land Camera not only gives you pictures in 60 seconds, but pictures of exceptional clarity and brilliance. Polaroid Land Cameras start at $72.75. The new film can be identified by a star on the box.

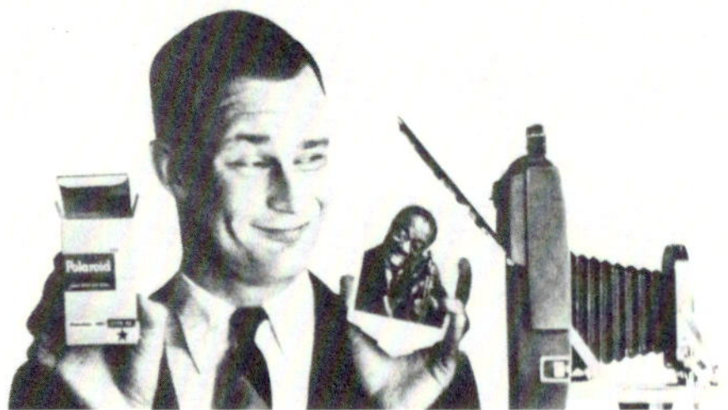

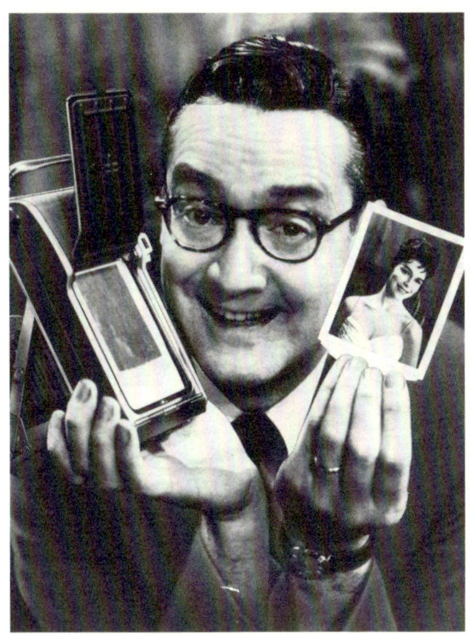

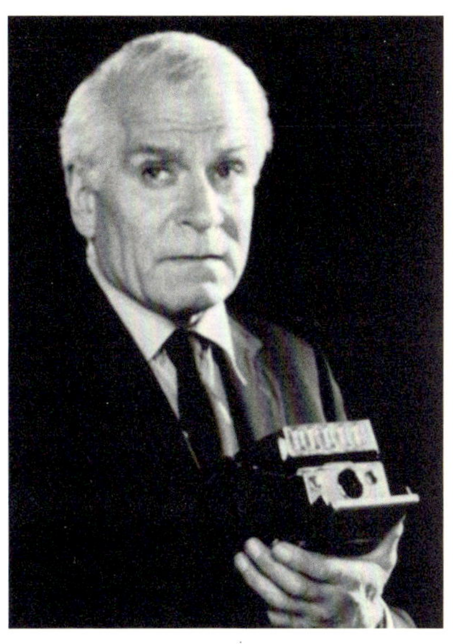

Many personalities have represented Polaroid on television and in print, among them (clockwise from top): Steve Allen; Sir Laurence Olivier, who introduced the SX-70; James Garner and Mariette Hartley; Garry Moore; and Louis Armstrong, in the image made by Bert Stern for an advertisement in *Life*.

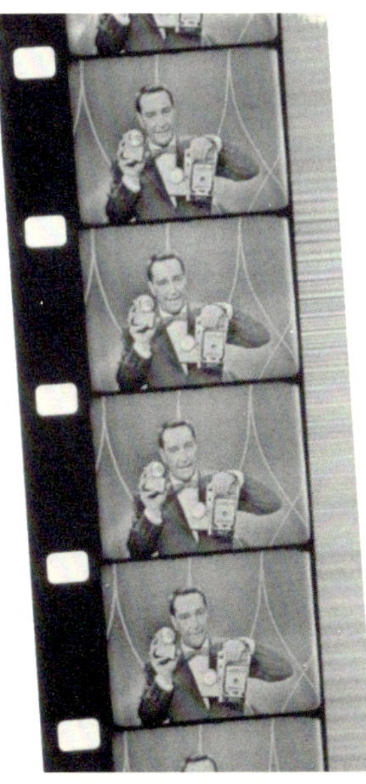

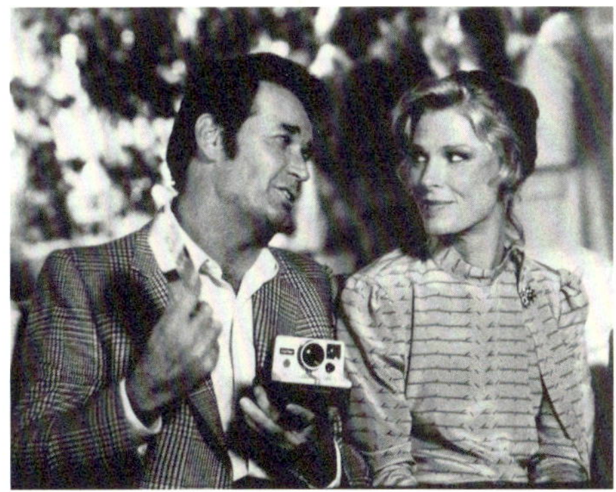

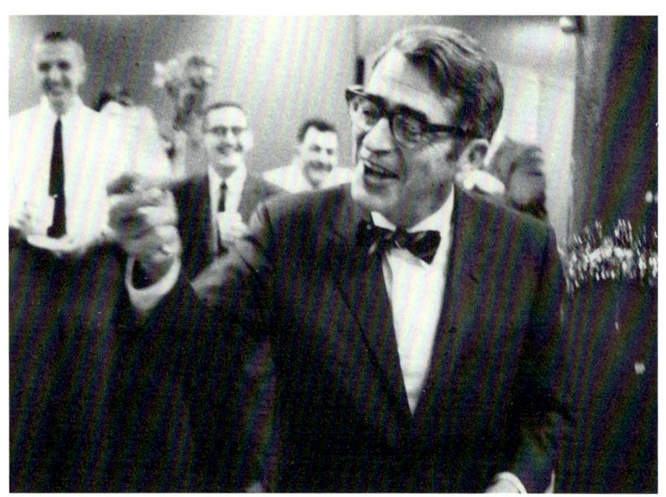

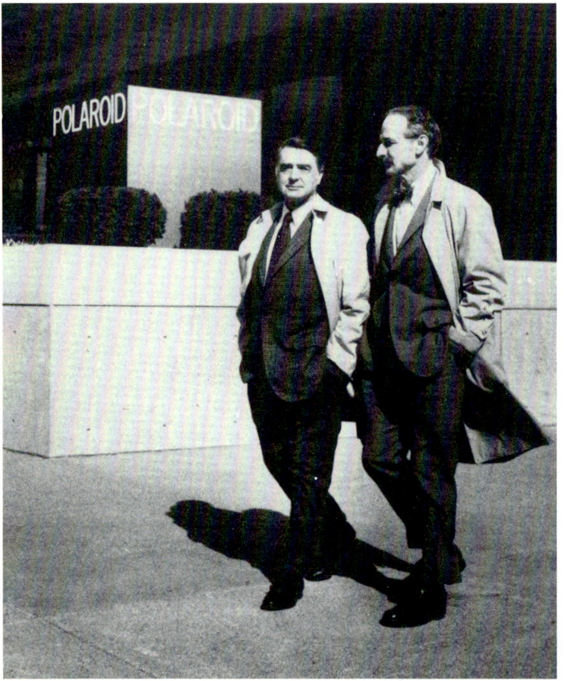

Richard Kriebel articulated Land's vision of Polaroid not only for the general public, but for Polaroid employees as well. *Left:* Land and McCune in front of Technology Square on the eve of the introduction of the SX-70. (*Michael Peirce*/Polaroid)

OPPOSITE PAGE

Howard Rogers, right, and Elkan Blout, second from left, confront some of the thousands of compounds they examined during the research on instant color film. (Fritz Goro, *Life* magazine. © Time Inc.)

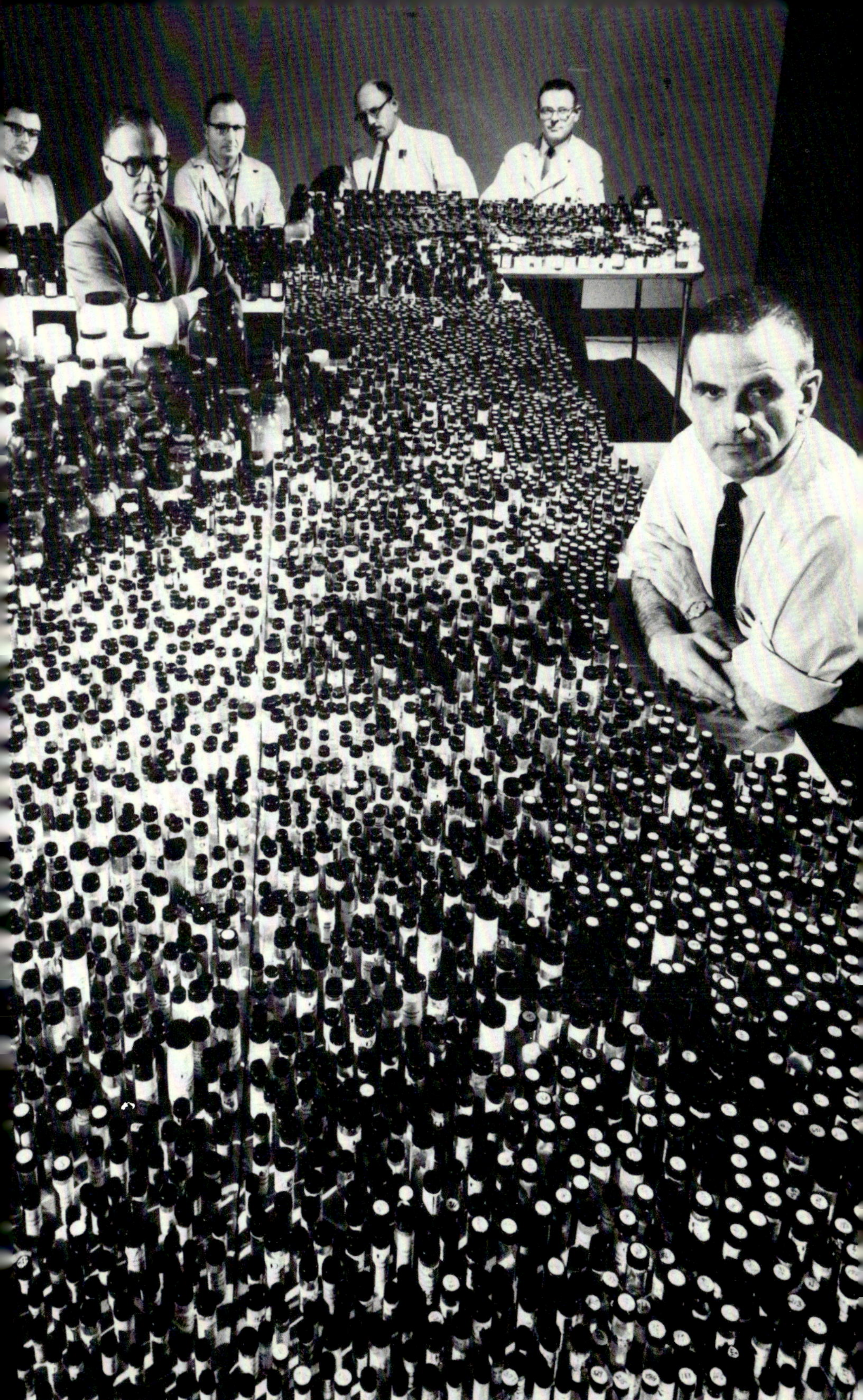

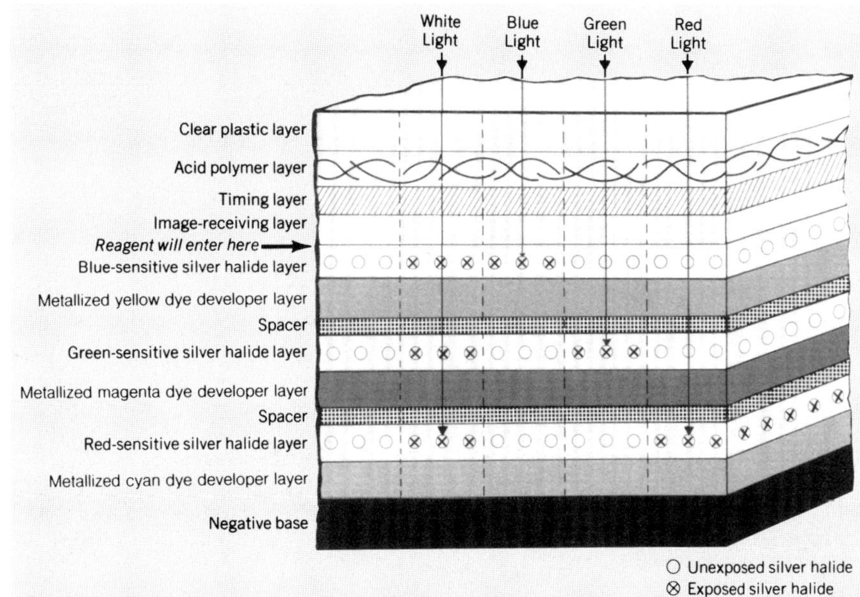

SX-70 color film consists of eleven precisely coated layers behind a clear plastic window.

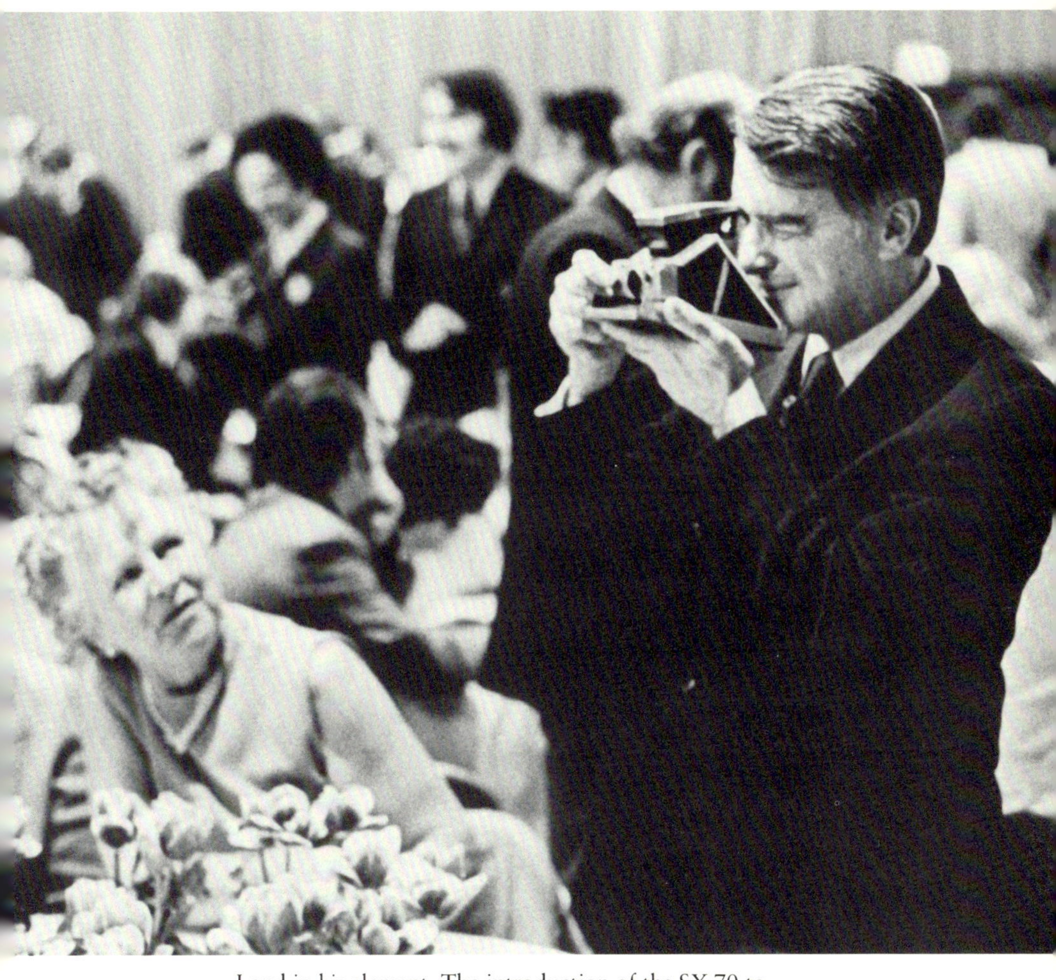

Land in his element. The introduction of the SX-70 to Polaroid shareholders in 1972 was Land's most spectacular corporate extravaganza.

OVERLEAF

Land was never happy with this superb 1977 group portrait of all the people who had been with Polaroid since the inception of instant photography. (© *Arnold Newman*)

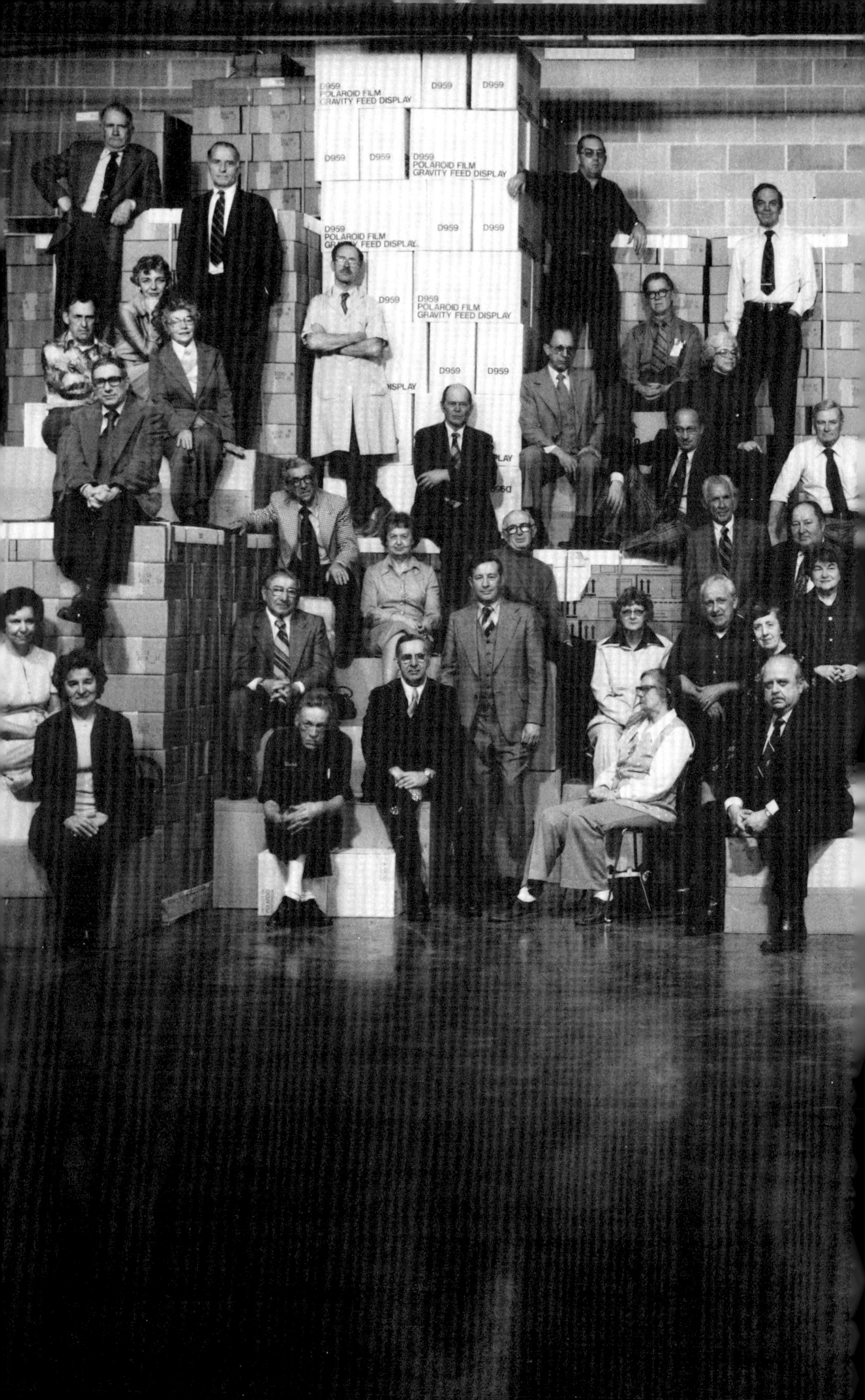
D959
POLAROID FILM
GRAVITY FEED DISPLAY
D959
D959
D959
D959
D959
POLAROID FILM
GRAVITY FEED DISPLAY
D959
POLAROID FILM
GRAVITY FEED DISPLAY
D959
D959
D959
POLAROID FILM
GRAVITY FEED DISPLAY
D959
D959

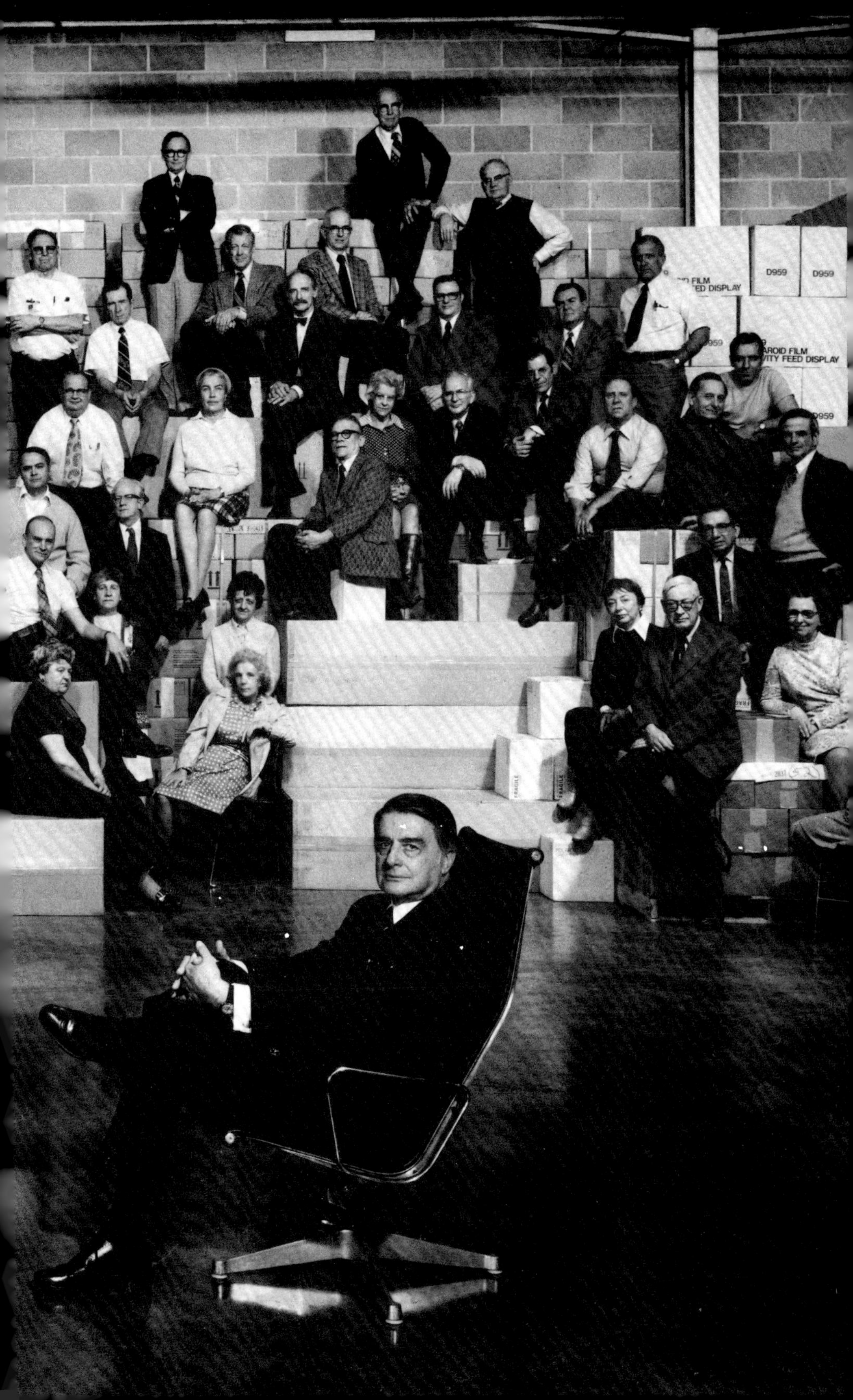
D959
D959
FRAGILE

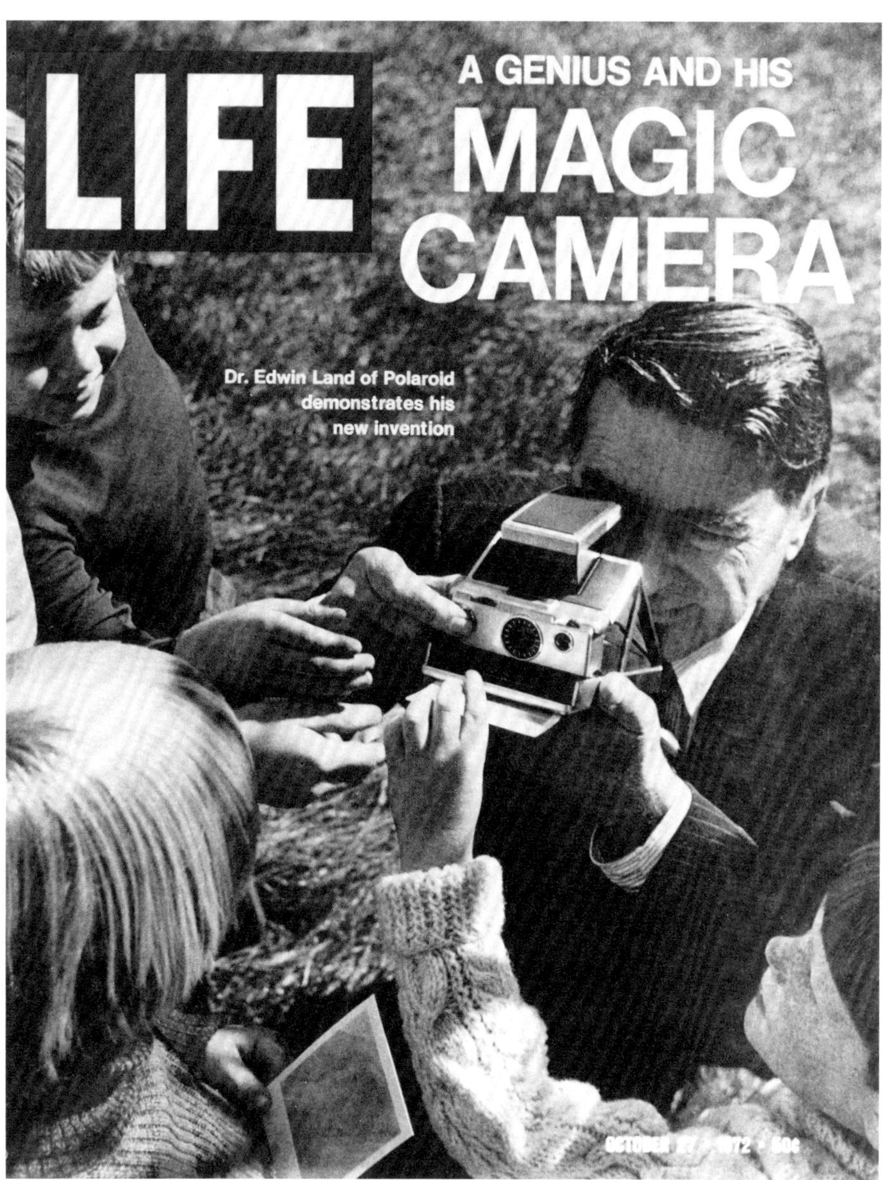

Land hid behind his camera for the cover of *Life*, October 27, 1972. (Co Rentmeester, *Life* magazine. © 1972 Time Inc.)

prevent them from being touched from the floor, near enough for the pictures to be seen and studied. In his office, Land described these inventions with the same genial lack of modesty that one might use to announce a cure for cancer. The room was crowded with people, including company officers and carpenters, who had been invited to examine a section of octagon and a short length of picture rail, put together in the preceding twenty hours by the model shop. I surmised that the major expenditure for this meeting would be for lighting. We would need hundreds of spotlights, perhaps a thousand. In the final event the greatest cost was for flowers.

On the day of the 1972 meeting, Land, surrounded by people in various stages of panic, anxiety, uncertainty, and despair, radiated joy and confidence. During the formal portion of the agenda his wit enlivened the mandatory reports, which were dispatched with more haste than was seemly. Gone was his microphone fright of years earlier, dissolved in empathy with his audience, the moment, the product. The formalities ended, Land mounted the stairs of an empty octagon, brightly lit in the center of the otherwise dark hall. He seated himself in a simple chair, picked up his pipe from the little Eames table purloined as in the past from my office, charged his pipe, lit it, and said, in a quiet voice that was superbly audible to the farthest corners of the room, "Photography will never be the same after today." The audience, a few less than four thousand, heard and believed. I believed. I had staged the show and still I believed. Even now, from the vantage of fifteen years, I am sure that with the SX-70, Land changed more of the commonly accepted mechanics of photography than any man since Fox Talbot.

The innovations of the SX-70 system were truly revolutionary. Why did they not create the surprise, the lasting wonder, of some other modern inventions, in fact of the first instant camera in 1948? The American public, with its appetite for new technology, swallowed SX-70 with a hiccup of appreciation and wondered what might come next. Land himself had taught them that there would always be another idea, another invention, another feature, if only a beep or a boop. This system, which most of us at its debut devoutly believed to be an ultimate, met with instant and enthusiastic acceptance, but was perceived as another step in a continuum. Pop technology marched on. What would come next? Video games, little computers, mood rings, home video? Bring it on. And keep it coming. Nevertheless, many of us in that warehouse room felt a small jolt at the back of the spine, a lump in the throat; saw it as a moment we would remember beyond most other moments. I knew that *I* had been changed by SX-70, and photography was far from the most important thing in my life.

Land chatted happily with his audience while I worried about the segment to come. We had written a script for him to use to describe the features of the system while slides illustrating them were projected on a huge four-sided box of screens suspended above his octagonal stage. Since the four projectors changed slides simultaneously, Land had to proceed smoothly, allowing Arnie Zunick in the control booth to advance the slides on cue. Our rehearsals taught us that to stop or go backward invited disaster. Once they got out of sync, the projectors were unfixable. True to form, Land had used every trick in his repertoire to avoid rehearsing with the script and the projectors. Each detail of the photographic subjects on the octagons commanded his attention: the arrangement of peaches in the fruit stand, the colors of the children's clothes, the decoration of the painter's studio. He was the *kitschmeister*. At one point during the night before the meeting, he asked that the baby ducks be taught to dive one at a time from a rock into their pond for the photographers. One of his retainers eagerly accepted the assignment, but time was too short. Land hated to read onstage, primarily, I thought, because it was one of the few chores that required him to don his glasses. At the meeting itself he made sure his spectacles had been left back in his office. After starting the narration, stopping, searching his pockets for the missing glasses, and thoroughly confusing Arnie, Land invented his way out of his dilemma.

He stepped down from the stage and found a seat in the darkness between two delighted female shareholders. He cast the script aside and with his wireless microphone told Arnie to proceed with the slides, slowly. As they flashed on the screens, he provided a folksy ad-lib commentary. "Oh, yes. Here's the Flashbar. That's the new flash device we invented. You see there are five bulbs on each — Wait, yes, there it is being inserted in the camera. Notice — Not so fast, please, Arnie. Now here we're taking a flash picture . . ." On he rambled, an absent-minded professor describing his vacation as the slides clicked by. The audiovisual professionals gnashed their teeth. The audience loved it. We stared at the huge pictorials of shutters and lenses suspended above the uninhabited stage, as the smoke from Land's pipe curled in the air above the empty chair. His desire to be there without really being, to lead without commanding, to achieve omnipresence and invisibility at the same moment, was for once fully satisfied.

Two hours of photographic vaudeville followed. The touch was perfect — a little amateurish for my taste, just right for the shareholders. Thirty-nine hundred strong, they roamed from one octagon to another, watching clowns juggle for the photographers, toddlers pose, ducks swim but not dive. As hundreds of pictures were snapped, they were handed by the photographers to assistants who quickly checked them for flaws such as incomplete developer spreads. An imperfect picture disappeared down a chute, never noticed in the excitement. A malfunctioning camera was instantly swapped for a fresh one and the wounded SX-70 spirited to an aid station hidden in the back of the room. All in all, cameras and film performed very well.

The pictures pinned in the slotted rail behind banks of flowers were clearly visible to the spectators, who were offered magnifying lenses if they wished to study them closely. As they walked from one octagon to another, the audience could admire but not touch. Security guards in shareholder suits were stationed at each stage. As each picture was pinned in the slot, its milky white face slowly began to exhibit a faint image, then cleared to reveal colors that became brighter and brighter. In two minutes development was complete. Anyone who attempted to reach over the rail was gently dissuaded. Even so, a few pictures vanished. The financial analysts and the press, unable to get close, tantalized by the sight of this incredibly complex new system apparently working perfectly, but unable to ask all the tough questions they had brought with them, fumed. They were not charmed by the ducks, the kids, the flowers. They knew Land had eluded them again. They wrote their stories and reports. They praised SX-70. But they bided their time in impatience.

About fifty financial analysts covered Polaroid on a regular basis. For some like Brenda Landry, who had once worked in my marketing services group, Polaroid was almost a full-time preoccupation. She made four times her previous Polaroid salary at White, Weld, and investors large and small paid a great deal of attention to what she wrote about the company. Analysts fell into two categories. Some worked for institutional investors like Morgan Guaranty Trust, the "buy side," whose reports were available only to clients. Others worked for brokerage houses like

E. F. Hutton, the "sell side," whose recommendations were circulated more broadly. Analysts were really specialized reporters whose success depended on the perception by their audience that they had somehow garnered information about a company that was not available to the individual investor.

Believing it was against the laws of God, man, and the New York Stock Exchange to give company information to one person and not all persons, Polaroid had attempted for years to keep the analysts at arm's length. This policy, which reflected Julie Silver's conservatism as much as Land's antipathy, was anachronistic among major companies. Most corporations found a way to give information even-handedly to the financial community, but Polaroid stonewalled: the annual meeting, the annual report, press releases, nothing more. The analysts resented this policy, and Land was the focus of the resentment. Analysts and financial reporters were both allies and competitors. A reporter like Dan Dorfman would call an analyst, perhaps two, before writing about a company in his "Heard on the Street" column for the *Wall Street Journal*. He was more likely to call an analyst than the company itself, assuming that he would get better copy. The smart analysts always responded. A quote or two every week in the national financial press kept their reputations bright, whatever their current batting average on predicting stock price movements. Reporters, for their part, fought to be included in analyst meetings with company officials. Analysts were present at most press conferences. I read a wide variety of analysts' reports on Polaroid and was impressed by the amount of whole cloth cut for their clients. However, since Polaroid's door was closed, we had no one to blame for the lack of accurate information but ourselves. Still, for many wrong reasons, the analysts were often right in their conclusions.

The great stock market of the sixties was cresting like a tsunami, with a few issues riding the foam on the brow of the wave. Polaroid, Xerox, and Avon were part of the nifty fifty, at the very top of the upper tier of the two-tier market. Shortly after the 1972 annual meeting, Polaroid stock hit a modern high of 149½. This represented a price-earnings ratio of more than one hundred, each share of stock selling at one hundred times its anticipated earnings per share. Earnings in 1972, depressed by heavy expenditures for the development of SX-70, were $1.30 per share. The glare of the spotlight was intense on stocks with P/E ratios far less extreme than Polaroid's.

Our stock was often heavily traded. Polaroid management, however, was usually unavailable for comment. And the Chairman took no pains to conceal his contempt for the professional market-watchers for their single-minded concentration on the movements of the stock price. He felt, with some justification, that they were less concerned with growth, creation of value, research for the future — the things that motivated him — than dollars to be made in the purchase or sale of the company stock. Their short-term focus, from one quarter to the next, particularly galled him. He had been working on SX-70 since the early sixties.

Land's personal holdings, those of Terre and of the Rowland Foundation, the nonprofit foundation Land had established in 1965, 4,914,192 shares in all, were then worth about $735 million. As had been his custom from the beginning of the company, Land sold few shares, although some of the foundation's shares were sold occasionally to finance its charitable and scientific activities. Land was not motivated by wealth; he did not think much about it. His other drives were far more intense. His only indulgence, if it could be called that, was philanthropy. Land was enormously generous to Harvard over the years, always insisting on anonymity. The American Academy of Arts and Sciences, MIT, and many other institutions in Boston also benefited from Land's generosity. But almost always with a stipulation of secrecy.

The 149½ price not only etched Polaroid's high-water mark, it came close to measuring the top of the bull market. At the same moment that SX-70 was first displayed to the public, the great tide crested and began to recede. By the third quarter of 1972, the stock had fallen as low as 107¼, a loss of 42 points from the high in less than four months.

In the meantime, the final SX-70 birth pangs racked the company. Crises flared, meetings were organized, task forces formed to find solutions. SX-70 had slipped from the inventor's hands the moment the meeting was over, into the arms of the bureaucracy. The crises were all too real, however. The battery continued to generate more concern than electric current. The quality control people had started shelf-life testing as early as possible. They felt, correctly as it turned out, that accelerated tests would not accurately predict the decay of the battery's power over time. Nestled as it was like a foil-wrapped graham cracker inside the film pack, the battery would determine the longevity of the film. The only way to be sure how the battery would behave in six months was to wait six months to see.

In addition, a significant number of people in the company were having difficulty in focusing the camera. Land was particularly proud of the elegant full-field focus mechanism of the SX-70. As the photographer turned the focus wheel, he looked at the scene through the camera lens, in the classic single-lens reflex mode, seeing exactly what the camera saw. As the lens came into focus the entire scene became less fuzzy, then suddenly sharp. For anyone with normal eyesight this was perfectly useful. Land, of course, had eyes like an eagle. Someone with short sight, thick glasses, or bifocals could not easily tell when the scene had crossed the invisible line into sharpness. A group of optical designers and customer service people braved Land's wrath by suggesting that a split circle be added to the viewfinder optics. This aid to focusing was used in many 35 mm cameras. As critical focus was reached, two halves of a small circle in the center of the viewfinder came into register, easier for some people to see than the sharpness of the entire scene. Land raged and would have none of it. Of course people could use the viewfinder he had designed! They must be taught. It was marketing's responsibility to teach them. He passed this message to me several times a week.

In the meantime Polaroid's dealers were growing restive. Though SX-70 was receiving a great deal of publicity, no on-sale date had been announced. The important Christmas selling season was just around the corner. Land feared the Polaroid bureaucracy would not solve the last round of problems without an irrevocable deadline. He had already played the annual meeting card. As in years past, the organization had responded with a frantic effort in which six months' work was compressed into weeks. Now he turned to me. "What are we going to do?" he asked disingenuously.

"Do about what, Dr. Land? Din."

"How are we going to get SX-70 — what is the word you use — launched?"

"Are we ready to go?"

"What do you think?"

"Well, the system performed beautifully at the meeting, but all I hear about are the problems. I'm not sure what to think. Will we ever be ready? So many things about it are essentially untested."

"Exactly. We have to test in the marketplace. That's the only test that means anything."

"We've been thinking about another Miami introduction. I suppose we could set up a massive customer service operation in the field to deal with the problems. But we would have to be prepared for anything and everything. I wonder —"

"That's a very courageous decision. Why don't you write a memo saying that you're planning to, ah, launch SX-70 in Miami? How soon can you be ready?"

"Well, Dr. Land, we need as much time as we can get. There are a tremendous number of things to do. Training for the sales force, a dealer meeting, the customer service thing —"

"November." It was not quite a question.

"Maybe by November." This was June. Could we really be ready to sell the product in four months?

"Yes, excellent. November. Early November. Specify the date in the memo. Address it to me. I'll see that it is circulated. I congratulate you. A courageous decision."

As I left, I wondered about my courage. I was almost certain there was another name for it.

24

Market Research

Charlestown, 1972

Co Rentmeester was a handsome young Dutchman, blond, tall, and very professional. He had made his reputation with a series of photographic essays for *Sports Illustrated,* shooting color with a 35 mm Nikon. In a sports situation he used three loaded cameras, each with a different lens so he need not pause to change lenses in the midst of action, just drop one camera and grab another. He had done very imaginative work with American college football, perhaps because he came from Holland and saw the game with fresh eyes. I was surprised to hear that a sports photographer had been assigned by *Life* magazine to shoot Land. We had been working with *Life* for six weeks on an SX-70 cover story. Don Dery, Polaroid's public relations director, was reassuring. "He's a good choice. Land will like him. He's a pro and he's a gentleman. His English is a little rough, but he knows how to fade into the background. After five minutes no one will know he's there. And he's very good."

"Where are we going to work?"

"I don't know yet; outdoors, I think. I want a place that Land can walk around in, not be confined, let the situations develop. And it would give Rentmeester some room. He's at his best outdoors. But we need some ideas."

Although Land would not come out and say so, he did not want his face on the cover of *Life* magazine. In a long discussion with him several days earlier, I repeated all the imperatives. *Life* was America's leading magazine. It still had a weekly circulation of 5.5 million copies, although television had seriously eroded it. *Life* was an exciting mix of photographs and features, but with enough news-focused stories to remind people that still pictures and text could sometimes tell more about the events of the week than hastily edited videotape footage on a small screen. *Life* was the only large-format, slick-paper magazine left in the United States, its page almost twice the area of *Time*'s or *Newsweek*'s. More than size, it represented quality. Its photographers were still the best in the world. A *Life* assignment took precedence over any other photography job. Even though it might not pay as much, and it paid tolerably well, the prestige of the *Life* photo credit was all-important. Exposure to a big audience on a big page well laid out by editors who understood the visual: that was what photographers dreamed about. Celebrities and politicians dreamed about having their face on the cover of *Life* magazine. I knew that was part of the problem. Land did not want to be considered the former and was certainly not the latter. "Why do you need me?" he protested irritably. "The camera should be the celebrity."

"But, Dr. Land, the magazine wants it. The readers relate to people. People always want to read about people. They want to know about SX-70, but they want to see the inventor."

"Why?"

"I'd hesitate to say. It's the way people are. And editors know it. That's why you have to come. Besides, it will be fun. We'll have a good photographer with us and just walk around outside and take pictures. We'll choose a day with good weather. There's some good color in the maple trees, and the grass is still nice and green. You'll enjoy it. I'm sure you could use a break."

"Let's find some children then," he said. I took that as agreement and departed. Land vanished into the Back Lab. He did not need sunshine and green grass to enjoy himself. The real world was always waiting for him behind the lab door.

We were walking in a park in Charlestown. Children spilled from a nearby schoolyard into the park, making important noises in the September sunshine. Land and Co Rentmeester walked together, Rentmeester with a Nikon on a wide cloth strap around his neck and two more in his camera bag. Land had his own camera in his pocket, where it had gestated like an overdue marsupial for the past five years. He was describing the optics of the SX-70 to Rentmeester, who would be doing some studio shots to illustrate the revolutionary light path of a single-lens reflex camera that, unlike the bulky Nikon around the photographer's neck, could fold into a flat, leather-covered, pocket-sized package.

The afternoon was soft and green, the grass still bright. The two men paused by a bed of chrysanthemums. Inge Reethof, the Polaroid lab photographer, knelt to take some close-ups of the flowers. Focusing down to ten inches, she snapped a picture, and the SX-70 devoured the image, then stuck out its tongue, emitting a sound like a small animal eating a bee. Two children came over to look. Inge showed them the blank picture. They expressed disappointment, which a moment later turned to joy. "I see it; it's coming," a little girl said as the image began to appear on the print. Land smiled. Slowly, the yellow emerged, then, more rapidly, the other colors of the flower appeared. More children came by to watch this magical spectacle, not realizing that they were selecting themselves to appear on the cover of *Life*.

"Hello, Carly," said Land to an eight-year-old. "Is your mother here?"

"Yes." She indicated a woman sitting on a bench near the street. The woman waved and Land returned the greeting.

"Would you like a picture?"

"Yes, please."

"You can look at it and show it to your mother, but then you have to bring it back and give it to Inge." SX-70 pictures were guarded like rubies, since the introduction was still a month away and security was unforgiving, even to the inventor. Land bent down and lifted the camera to his eye. He focused on the girl and snapped the picture. As the print issued from the chin of the SX-70, he proffered the camera to Carly. Solemnly she plucked the picture from the slot and studied it. The other children pushed in to see. I kept my eye on Rentmeester, who was twenty feet away, shooting with a long lens that afforded him an intimate view of the scene. Land kept snapping pictures, the children grabbing for them as they came out of the camera. They were all enjoying themselves immensely, no one more than Land.

"Is this a cover or is this a cover?" said Dery. He could not refrain from rubbing his hands in glee.

"Don, did you choose this park? How does Land know these kids?" I asked.

"Land picked it," said Dery. "He said it's where he does his market research." We watched the squealing children running with pictures to show mothers and friends until the SX-70 film ran out. On October 27, the new issue of *Life* went on sale. The cover caption read, "A genius and his magic camera. Dr. Edwin Land demonstrates his new invention." The cover was crowded with children laughing and reaching for a picture coming out of the SX-70. Not much of Land's face was visible, just the shock of dark hair, the heavy brows. The principal elements of the composition were the camera and the children.

25

Management

Cambridge and Paris, 1972

Land's management style, like most of his relationships with people, was unconventional, indirect and elliptical. He seemed able to manipulate parts of his company without managing them. When I proposed Laurence Olivier as the spokesman to introduce the SX-70 on television, Land frowned and was silent. I told him it would be a coup, that Lord Olivier had surprised us by agreeing to our proposal, that he had said he would not consider making a television commercial for any other company but Polaroid. "It is a tremendous compliment," I said, then, as Land's frown deepened, immediately wished I hadn't.

"Let's discuss it later," we said simultaneously and parted.

I closed the deal with Olivier's agent and flew with the group from Doyle Dane Bernbach to Paris, where four television spots were to be filmed on the stage of the Théâtre Nationale. Time was extremely short. In five days the segments were shot and flown to London, where they were edited, music added, and the commercials made ready for air in one additional week. When I returned to Cambridge, Land asked me what was being done about television. He was acutely aware that the introduction date for SX-70 was rushing up on us, but technical problems occupied him twenty hours a day. "What about that English fellow?" he asked plaintively. "What was his name? I think we should discuss that further."

Olivier, for his part, had been superb, pacing the boards in Paris with the camera cradled in his big hands. His voice was an instrument of unbelievable range and subtlety, but he had difficulty, as many others were to have after him, saying "SX-70."

“*S*X-70. S*X*-70. SX-*70*.” He was dissatisfied. The pacing continued; the noble brow furrowed with thought. Then he paused, smiled at the empty seats and said, “Of course. I have it now. *Essex*-70.” That was, of course, perfect.

Olivier approached the making of television commercials with the same intensity he brought to every part. He did thirty takes of one line, not because the director asked for them, but to play variations with that magnificent musical instrument, each reading different. Bob Gage, directing for Doyle Dane Bernbach, was enchanted. The two settled into a comfortable relationship, professionalism overriding the unfamiliarity of the situation. “Please call me Larry,” said Olivier to the crew, to all of us, when we stumbled over “Sir Laurence” or “Lord Olivier.” He confided at lunch, a box containing the sandwich and banana that is served on movie sets all over the world, that the $350,000 he was being paid would go into a trust fund for the education of his two young daughters. The only restriction he imposed on the contract was that the commercials not be shown in England.

Land did not see the finished commercials before they were simultaneously broadcast on all three networks the evening of November 28. He did not comment to me on Lord Olivier's performance if, indeed, he saw it at all. It soon became apparent that Olivier's presence in an American television commercial had created an overnight sensation. Having heard as much from his friends, particularly those at Harvard, Land would smile and nod as they complimented him on his coup. “SX-70 deserves nothing less,” he said.

26

The Stock

Cambridge, New York, Miami Beach, and Boston, 1972–1974

The financial analysts who followed Polaroid in 1972 devoted a good deal of energy and ink to describing the way they felt SX-70 should be introduced to the public. Their reports, addressed ostensibly to investors who held the stock or potential investors who might buy it, read like memoranda to the company management. Land's approach to the project, reinvention of all the elements of the photographic system, backward integration into camera and negative manufacturing, commitment of three quarters of a billion dollars in research, manufacturing development, factories, and equipment, made them extremely nervous. They would have organized the product development cycle differently. Land, however, did not see this effort as cyclical. He had pushed the plunger down and awaited an explosion that would blast the old to atoms and leave the new — clean, glowing, pulsating — at ground zero.

Since Polaroid had not heeded them about product development, the analysts busied themselves with the product introduction. The price of the camera particularly concerned them. Polaroid had made no announcement; the question was still hotly debated within the company. The cost of manufacturing the camera rose almost by the week. Assembly in the new Norwood plant, fed by the subcontractors all over the country who supplied electronics, lenses, castings, and the notorious leather panels, made young men older faster as the last days of 1972 slipped by. Ultimately we agreed on a list price of $180, about $60 above the price the marketing group had used in its original planning, but not as high as the manufacturing and financial people wanted, given the escalating cost of the camera. Don Dery proposed a last-minute series of press calls to be completed before the introduction meeting in Miami Beach at which the camera would be given to dealers, press, and, we decided at the last minute, the analysts. No more out-of-reach pictures, no more security guards; the camera had enjoyed its carefully planned debutante ball; now it was to be pushed out of the house into the rude hands of the public. Since some of the newspapers would not send reporters to Miami, and most magazines had lead times of a week or more, Don prepared a road show that included demonstration of the camera, a briefing on the technical specifications of the system, a description of the festivities to be held in Miami, and the marketing plan. This plan, of course, revealed the pricing details.

Don made his rounds a week before the Thursday, October 26, 1972, introduction date. The advance briefing implicitly assumed that the release date, the day of the Miami show, would be respected. If one publication jumped the date, all the others would be angry and we would be suspected of favoritism. Don got, he thought, routine release date agreements from all the publications on his list. As he was briefing the *Wall Street Journal* in its 30 Broad Street offices to a surprisingly large gathering that included editors, some of the management, and a group of interested reporters, Don noticed someone slip out the back of the conference room. He shot another SX-70 picture and passed it around so that the group could watch the in-the-light development. A sinking sensation developed simultaneously in the pit of his stomach. The briefing over, reporters and editors threw questions at him, but Don, noticing more activity at the door, began to hedge his answers. As the session ended, he stressed again the critical nature of the release date.

When the room emptied, Don packed up his cameras and raced to the lobby. The Dow Jones printer had already spelled out the story, the entire story, including the $180 camera price. It had been put out on the wire as he briefed the group upstairs. The *Wall Street Journal* does not hold a story for anyone, he was told. "You know that. It's always been our policy." Don tried to control his famous temper until he got me on the telephone. By that time I had read the story in Cambridge, tearing the sheets out of our own printer in surprise. It would be picked up, of course, by every paper in America next morning.

"Don, don't shout, you're hurting my head. It's not a calamity. So the price breaks early. That's the only item that wasn't already known. There's nothing we can do about it anyway."

"Sons of bitches" was followed by much more.

"No matter. No real harm done. I'll see you in Miami on Monday."

As it turned out Don was delayed a day. I had to phone him from the Fontainebleau with the news that a lawsuit specifically naming Land, Wensberg, and Dery personally, since those names had been mentioned in the *Journal* story, had been filed by a shareholder against Polaroid. It charged that the camera price, a factor in making a decision to buy or sell the stock, had been leaked to the *Journal.* Since the "leak" resulted in the immediate dissemination of the information by the broadest possible medium — the DJ wire is used by every major publication in the country as well as most brokers and financial institutions — the suit did not stand on very firm ground. Being personally named in a $3.5 million lawsuit was, however, a new experience for Don. It caught my attention as well. With the stock market sagging, Polaroid stock, one of the highest of the high fliers, was extremely vulnerable. It had come down some forty points since the April meeting. We now heard a chorus from the analysts that the camera price was too high and that they would have to revise their sales predictions accordingly; but as most of their estimates exceeded our struggling production capacity, we were not disappointed.

The Miami Beach meeting was almost as extravagant as the Polaroid stockholders' meeting in Needham, but of course it lacked the impact of surprise as well as Land's personal showmanship. He sent half a dozen of his staff and made sure that I called him several times during the course of the evening. From a pay phone in the hall outside the gaudy auditorium I told him we were fanning the flames he lit in April. This audience, the photographic dealers of metropolitan Miami, less genteel than the one in Needham but no less enthusiastic, would be the only dealers in the world to sell the camera until production allowed us to broaden our distribution. The Miami dealers were being handed a golden franchise. They crowded into the Fontainebleau, their eyes alight with calculation. Searchlights leaned around the sky, limos sniffed each other in the noisy street, flags snapped in the courtyard, crowds elbowed for position at the entrance to the ballroom. The dealers watched a spectacular sound and slide show, saw Laurence Olivier demonstrate the camera in the television commercials, listened impatiently to recorded

Mozart, watched a film by Charles Eames. They were given a camera, film, and Flashbars and trained in how to use them. The $180 price was brushed aside; many dealers would sell the camera for twice that price as long as the supply remained limited. Nor were they concerned about how many they could sell. How many could they get? Visions of sugarplums danced in their heads although it was only October. Visions also of large cabin cruisers moored in local marinas: a few months later *Photo Dealer* pictured just such a thirty-eight-footer, *SX-70* in gold leaf on its broad transom.

While the dealers were being trained, the flower of the financial world gathered in an adjacent room. Each of them also received a camera kit boxed in a carrying case with the legend of the meeting emblazoned on its side. They paid scant attention to the hard-working camera demonstrators, more to the Polaroid officers who were present and whose names would be dropped in future reports whether they opened their mouths or not, and most to the buffet and the bar. Any question about the public reception of the system was answered by the sight of the dealers in the next room, circling like hammerhead sharks in a feeding frenzy around the order desk.

Two images of that analysts' gathering stayed with me always. A young man, his turnout suggestive of Princeton and the Harvard Business School, sauntered to the hors d'oeuvres table and opened his Mark Cross case. Empty, it was soon filled. As he snapped the brass locks smartly shut, I could only hope that the lobster puffs would not stain the lining. As the evening drew to a close and most people were leaving, camera case in one hand and attaché case in the other, I saw a securities analyst set his camera on the floor to shake hands with an attractive woman. A third colleague walked past, noticed the camera, paused, reviewed his options, and with a graceful motion reached down and scooped it up, departing with briefcase and two camera cases while the other continued to make his good-byes.

The SX-70 sold as fast as we could ship it, but the trickle of camera production with which we entered Miami grew with agonizing slowness. Dealers did most assuredly demand and get $300 to $350 a camera in the first few months, since Polaroid was prevented by law from more than suggesting a list price. Miami drugstores and ma-and-pa camera shops filled telephone orders from New York, Los Angeles, and London, or rather filled lists of orders, collecting deposits in advance against eventual delivery. Polaroid set up a network of storefront customer service offices in shopping malls and empty grocery stores.

The service staff, shipped down to Miami for an indefinite tour of duty, gave out free film if a customer had picture problems and traded a new camera to anyone who brought one in for repair. We kept a telephone line open to Cambridge, and a steady stream of engineers and manufacturing and quality control people trooped through the service centers. Every Polaroid employee of whatever rank, from camera repairman to vice president, who made the trip to Miami spent at least one hour behind the counter talking to camera users. I was determined that Land get the test in the marketplace he had asked for and that the results be reported quickly and accurately.

The mood of the Miami crew bounced from tense to euphoric to anxious again, depending on whom we talked to last on the customer side of the counter. Most exciting were the people, not a few of them, who came in just to show off their pictures. They found us a responsive audience. All in all, the system performed much as Lord Olivier promised every night on Miami television. Focusing the camera, however, was and continued to be a stumbling block, the reports of which did not receive a warm reception at Osborn Street. Land would not be dissuaded from his contention that it was an educational, not a design problem.

John Wolbarst had been an editor of *Modern Photography,* had written in earlier years a column on instant photography, and had authored *Pictures in a Minute,* the book Stan Calderwood and I had made a modest best seller. When Wolbarst agreed to head the customer service group at Polaroid, he asked me what his job was to be. I told him he had been installed to protect the customer from the corporation. That was all he ever needed to hear. A distinguished photographer in his own right, he was stubborn, realistic, and quite unimpressed with bureaucratic shenanigans. More than any other person he supported the safety net we spread in Florida to keep the SX-70 introduction together while the last of the tough problems were analyzed and solved. He knew from the moment his eye touched the viewfinder that a focusing aid of some sort was needed. As he patiently explained, demonstrated, and argued with the camera design group, still firmly under Land's control, the opposition hardened. Customer complaints seemed unable to influence the situation. John asked that I arrange a personal interview for him with Land. Each time I requested a meeting something prevented it, often at the last minute and once when John and I were sitting in Land's outer office, waiting. Finally, on a day when I was out of town, Natalie called to say that Land would see Mr. Wolbarst.

Pulling his tan corduroy jacket over the red suspenders he wore to hold trousers on his skinny frame, John prepared for battle. Armed with reports and transcripts of customer interviews, he walked briskly from Tech Square to Osborn Street. He was admitted forthwith. Land stood. They did not shake hands. Although John was a senior company manager and a respected figure in the photographic world, Land saw him in one light only, not as the defender of SX-70, the glue that bound the Florida introduction together, the focal point of the test in the marketplace. Wolbarst was the enemy. He stood in opposition, vocally in opposition, to an aspect of the camera design that Land had identified as one of its essential and immutable features. Full-frame focusing was simple; it was elegant; it was unique. But John doggedly presented the case against it while they stood there in the book-lined study. Land nodded curtly. He had heard the evidence. He had done what I asked of him. The interview was over. John made his escape. Reason did not triumph over elegance for another six months. Land never spoke to Wolbarst again, not even on the occasion of his retirement at sixty-five, one of the most respected customer service figures in the country.

After the Miami introduction, Polaroid's stock price bounced from a high of 134½ to a low of 104. In the first quarter of 1973, in the face of a descending market it hit 140⅜ again, but then dropped back to 103¼. The SX-70 domain slowly grew by cities in Florida, then by counties, finally by states. The production of cameras was increasing more rapidly than that of film, but our ability to supply an adequate quantity of film to each camera purchaser limited our expansion into new territory. In these early months customer interviews suggested that SX-70 film consumption would run well ahead of historic levels. Land had proclaimed that the camera would average "a picture a day without decay." No one asked him if he was serious. The life of the battery continued to concern everyone in the film group, but since SX-70 film did not remain long in a dealer's store, its shelf life was more hypothetical than real.

As the system's novelty lessened, film usage began to descend to regions on the curve more in keeping with our pack film experience. Since the universe of SX-70 users was still relatively small and constantly changing, our sampling techniques were not very accurate, but as 1973 wore on it became apparent that film production was beginning to overtake the camera supply. Polaroid's forecasters did not have a firm fix on film usage; they were arguing among themselves, desperate for more data. Ed Bedrosian, the only Polaroid financial manager authorized to talk to the analysts, no longer constrained to keep them on hold, answered dozens of calls each day. He began to suggest the need for a full-blown analysts' meeting before the end of the year to respond to their concerns about SX-70, made more acute by an uncertain stock market. That request antagonized both Land and Silver, who had no desire to liberalize communications. Ed was allowed, however, to speak to the analysts on the phone as long as he repeated the same message, approved by management, to everyone.

The stock price reached a high of 143½ in the second quarter of 1973 and floated along, defying the gravity of the bear market that was hauling down less volatile issues. SX-70 expenses mounted. Batteries and film packs were scrapped in disheartening numbers. The cost of maintaining instant customer service in an area now almost half the size of the country grew enormously. SX-70 camera production lagged again and, as expected, in the face of the glamorous new system Polaroid's revenues and high profit margins on the old pack system fell off. Still, sales in 1973 represented the least of Polaroid's problems: they increased by more than $100 million, or 22 percent above 1972. However, ahead stretched the rest of the rollout, the upper reaches of the production curves, the unknown later life of the battery. Despite reams of advice arriving daily from securities analysts as to what course to follow in these and other areas, Polaroid was not awash in confidence or high spirits.

The Museum of Science, one of Boston's younger institutions if compared to the Boston Symphony Orchestra or the Museum of Fine Arts, had, under the tirelessly enthusiastic guidance of Bradford Washburn, a renowned explorer and cartographer, grown from a small facility where children fondled owls and snakes to a rambling red brick castle on the Charles River Dam. The cap of its eight-story tower obtruded on the Boston skyline just below the State House dome. A three-hundred-seat auditorium occupied the basement, its rear windows looking down the Charles River Basin just a few feet above water level, a fact that would seem prophetic in retrospect. We chose this location for Polaroid's first formal meeting with financial analysts in several years because it was cheap, Polaroid being a modest benefactor to the museum, because it was handy to Logan Airport, and because, since it was a temple of science, the location might remind those in attendance that Polaroid served the gods of science as well as Mammon. Mammon, however, was breathing hotly down Polaroid's neck.

The stock price stood at 124 when the company surprised the analysts with the invitation to the Museum of Science. The first reaction came from the financial press: they called Don Dery to let him know that they would attend, invited or not. After some waffling, we decided that repelling them by force would be inappropriate, and the doors would be open to the press as well. No seat in the auditorium went unoccupied. Even standing room was at a premium, in spite of the absence of bar, buffet, or souvenirs. Land, of course, was not present. Tom Wyman, general manager of the company and widely believed by this group to be Land's heir apparent, was the principal speaker. He described to an audience busily scratching in their notebooks the balance between SX-70 sales and manufacturing, demand still far ahead of supply. He went into some detail about the heavy expenses attendant on the "ramp-up" as he termed it. As usual, he was low-key, straightforward, not a particularly graceful speaker, but ultimately convincing. The meeting proceeded without incident to the question-and-answer period. I was asked about the marketing schedule. Tom was quizzed about manufacturing. Ed Bedrosian was asked by Jim Awad, an analyst for E. F. Hutton, what he thought the earnings outlook would be for 1974. Ed had been instructed to avoid predictions, but no one had instructed him to avoid the truth. He hesitated for a moment, then, choosing his words carefully, said, "I'd be surprised if we make three dollars a share." The room was still.

"Would you mind repeating that?" asked Awad, whose earnings projection was well in excess of that figure. Ed repeated himself, and the room all but emptied as three hundred fifty people rushed for the three pay phones in the corridor. The stock lost close to sixty points in the next several weeks. That represented $295 million of Land's holdings, about $2 billion of the total value of the stock. But Ed's statement was not inaccurate. Earnings in 1974, reduced by continuing expenses for SX-70 and development expenditures for a new system that would be called Polavision, not only did not reach three dollars a share, they fell below one dollar — eighty-six cents to be exact, the lowest since 1953. The architects of that meeting, I among them, were not congratulated by Julie Silver, whose personal loss in the "adjustment," as an irreverent person dubbed it, was considerable. Land stopped calling me on the telephone early in the morning — or at any time of day — not, I felt, because of the stock — personal wealth was probably Land's least concern — but because John Wolbarst was being proved correct about SX-70's viewfinder.

The year 1974 opened full of the mingled promise of rising sales and rising expenses, major manufacturing problems yet to be solved, and customers still full of enthusiasm for SX-70. An extremely high index of customer satisfaction sustained us in the face of all else. The public was telling us that Land was right, that his gamble would pay off, that his genius was recognized and appreciated. On the other hand, the analysts were in full cry at Polaroid's heels. We had fallen from grace with a heavy thud, dropping into the bottom tier, no longer flying high, not nifty at all. Could Polaroid be considered a growth company? they asked, forever trapped in their own jargon. Our sales were certainly growing, at the rate of more than 20 percent a year, but where were the big earnings? When would we begin to pay off that huge research and development investment?

In fact, we had paid for the development of SX-70 as the expenses were incurred, the company had not a nickel of debt, and we owned one of the significant technical monopolies in the world. These details, however, were trampled like bugs into the pavement by the elephantine strides of the analyst community at the charge.

In the early part of 1974, SX-70 film sales began to fall behind our estimates. In a year and a half we had not succeeded in creating an accurate film usage "model," a formula using data collected from dealers each month that could tell us how much film was being used by an SX-70 camera of a given age. Our production planning sorely needed a dependable model, as did our financial planning. "A picture a day without decay" had not come to pass. No one expressed surprise except the Chairman. Because our model for pack film usage, tuned over many past years, consistently proved accurate, our forecast group remained confident they could achieve the same for SX-70, but as they carved out the model each slice reduced our expectations of SX-70 film usage. Ed Bedrosian began telling the analysts, most of whom were calling him twice a week, that the SX-70 film stream was "disappointing," carefully using the same words with each caller. As it became apparent that our second-quarter 1974 earnings would be the lowest in twenty years, the ragged veterans of the near-fatal encounter at the Museum of Science urged Land and Silver to let them try again.

The potential for an explosion had to be defused. The consequences of an extremely poor quarterly report would be worse if we did not offer some explanation. As this was being discussed, Brenda Landry, the White, Weld analyst, a vivacious brunette who, it was erroneously believed, had a pipeline into Polaroid, issued a sell recommendation for the stock, citing Ed Bedrosian's "disappointing" film stream statement. She reported only the information the other analysts had heard and not acted on, but her report, quoted in the *Wall Street Journal* the next day, caused Polaroid to drop fourteen points, the biggest single-day loss in the stock's history on the Exchange. Land's fortune shrank by another $68 million, in this instance between breakfast and teatime. We had come to realize that the second quarter would barely show a profit, probably less than ten cents a share. Land and Silver reluctantly agreed to another meeting with the analysts. We promised to stress customer satisfaction.

For good luck we chose the Museum of Science again. A dozen extra telephones were installed in the hallway for the day. An elaborate agenda did not seem to make much sense, so we planned short, informal presentations by each of three spokesmen, followed by what Ed insisted on calling the Q and A. The self-appointed victims would present themselves onstage like clowns waiting to be dunked in the water. It was clear the analysts would bring their own baseballs. I was to talk briefly about marketing; Bill McCune would describe camera design changes, including the new split-circle focusing aid just being phased into production; Tom Wyman would report on manufacturing; Ed Bedrosian would act as moderator. Of the lot, I had the best story. We were selling every camera we could get out the factory door. Our marketing problems were mostly on the supply side. Tom had the most thankless assignment. There were still no clear answers to questions about battery shelf life or the frequent production delays in almost every facility. Bill could at least talk of design problems corrected, while Land gnashed his teeth across the river. As the auditorium was filling with Romans in three-piece suits, each of us patrolled a separate, clearly defined territory backstage. Once, as Ed passed me in our pacing, I asked him, "What do they want to know?"

"Whether we're crooks or just stupid," he replied. I couldn't decide whether I was thirsty or needed to find the men's room again.

The meeting itself was a shambles. Customer satisfaction was dismissed out of hand. To Ed fell the explanation of why the second quarter had produced earnings of seven cents a share. Tom and I disagreed publicly on the critical question of how much pack film was being sold. Bill McCune was all but inarticulate. As hundreds of attaché cases clicked shut, and Brooks Brothers and Lord & Taylor departed for Logan, I turned to Ed, searching for a shred of comfort.

"I don't think they think we're crooks," I said.

In the weeks that followed, the stock went from 28 to 14⅛. Land lost another $68 million. In the twenty-six months between May 1972 and July 1974, in the face of a spectacular product introduction, instant sales of every SX-70 camera we could manufacture, enthusiastic acceptance by the public, raves from the photographic press, and a $200 million increase in Polaroid's revenues, the price of our stock had tumbled from 149½ to 14⅛. Land lost $660 million, the shareholders in toto $4.4 billion. Polaroid was not the only body on the trading floor, but it had fallen farther faster than most. The analysts had taken revenge on what seemed to them our arrogant refusal to take them into our confidence until it was too late. They were right, for what seemed to us all the wrong reasons. For every seller there was a buyer. Brokers collected their commissions all the way down. The analysts polished their reputations. Short sellers of Polaroid stock prospered, while value was sucked out of the stock like water out of a bathtub until the bottom appeared, $5.00 a share below the $19.39 book value of the company. Small comfort that the market was universally stricken. SX-70 was being discredited. The public had accepted it, but Wall Street would not. Now we had to prove the system, Land's system, to the world. We owed it to him.

27

The President

Cambridge, 1975

Succession was not an issue that troubled Land. He had always run the company; all the titles of power and command were his. He drove with a light rein as long as the buggy was headed in the direction he wanted to go. I had the freedom to do the job I wanted to do as long as it pleased Land. I wanted to represent the company with style and quality and good taste in its marketing. Land wanted the same and seemed content to let my taste and my choices stand. Although I spent upward of $50 million of Polaroid's money each year, his concerns usually focused on details. Once in a while he would ask for a change in a photograph for an ad, and he liked to design the annual report with the Princesses. However, almost every aspect of Polaroid's corporate effort was determined by product choices and product timing. Land made those choices, not without a great deal of thought, because he knew the success of the company depended on them, but without self-doubt. He had done so for forty years with only a few missteps, such as the 1950 picture-fading fiasco.

Fortune magazine found in Land a fascination that only increased as the years went on. In a 1970 article about Polaroid, the *Fortune* writer asked the Chairman about his successor. "Land launched into a description of such a paragon of talent, intelligence, and virtue that even he paused, laughed, and said, 'We're making him down in the laboratory.' " That remark was not lost on Land's associates. Stan Calderwood was one of the first to realize that Land had no flesh-and-blood successor in mind. Stan was at least as energetic, ambitious, and restless as the other senior officers.

Although he had joined Bill McCune as an executive vice president of the company, he came to understand that he would not progress much further. One implication of Land's *Fortune* statement, which would be quoted around the company for years to come, was that Polaroid was destined to be run by a great scientist. Land defined that as a class of one.

Stan, realizing that he was not, nor ever would be, included in the class, resigned in 1971 to seek his fortune elsewhere, finding it eventually in the financial environs of State Street in Boston. When he left, his two senior managers, Tom Wyman and I, were given new responsibilities. Tom, who had supervised the international business, became general manager of the company and inherited the personnel headaches that attend a half-billion-dollar company on a trajectory to double itself in the next six years. I was put in charge of marketing. We were the two most senior nontechnical officers in the company. Using a headhunter, Stan had recruited Wyman from Nestlé in Switzerland, beginning for Tom a long and mutually successful relationship with the executive placement industry. When Tom became general manager in 1971, the analysts, skeptical of Land's "making him in the laboratory" remark, decided that Wyman was the ideal candidate in spite of, or because of, his business background. Tom, who maintained an impressive network, did nothing to discourage this speculation, but his popularity with the analysts was not an unmixed blessing, especially in Land's eyes.

Nineteen seventy-four had turned out to be one of the most trying years in the company's history. To those who remembered the past, it was 1950 all over again. U.S. sales declined for the first time since the advent of instant photography, although total Polaroid sales, bolstered by gains overseas, were up. The crises of SX-70 kept the management running from one brushfire to another. At any moment we expected to glance up to see the forest burning above our heads, set aflame by the latest battery or film flare-up.

Early in 1975, Wyman had lunch with Land and suggested that it might be the appropriate time to strengthen Polaroid's management by making him, Wyman, president. Land was not amused. The company had all the presidents it needed. He had no intention of making any changes, but he dissembled. Within the hour he had called Julie Silver away from the golf course in Puerto Rico, where he was vacationing. Julie arrived in Cambridge the next day, sunburned but stoic, ready as always to give Land the best advice he could provide. In the meantime,

Bill McCune had caught wind of the events Tom had set in motion. Bill told Land and Silver he would not work under Tom. He suggested that he, McCune, should be made president. A tense round-robin of conversations took place among the contestants that day. Less than a month earlier, the company had laid off almost a thousand workers, most of them in manufacturing areas that were operating below capacity. It was a dash of icy water, the first Polaroid layoff since the defense contracts had been canceled at the end of World War II, and it left many, both within and without the company, shaken and uncertain.

Julie, ever the realist, told Land that the company could not afford to lay off a thousand workers, report earnings of eighty-six cents a share, and accept the resignation of Bill McCune, its most senior technical officer after Land, in the span of three months. In his quiet, flat voice he advised Land to accede to Bill's "suggestion." McCune was indisputably the most able technical administrator after Land. Howie Rogers, while a brilliant scientist with creative insights often equal to Land's own, was not an executive, nor did he have ambitions to become one. There were no other scientific contenders.

The succession crisis was the first time since the company had entered the photographic business that Land felt himself at a complete loss. This was not a problem that could be solved by Herculean efforts in the laboratory. His statement to *Fortune* returned to haunt him. If anyone had been developed in the lab, Bill had. Try as he might, Land could find no alternative. He knew that Julie was right; the company was on thin ice. While Land had radiated confidence in every public statement for a year, he knew better than anyone the stubborn technical problems still surrounding the SX-70 battery and the film. But he also knew Bill's opposition to Land's pet "additive" color film project and Bill's desire to develop other, less expensive, hence less elegant, versions of the SX-70. Land was torn. But wouldn't he still retain control? Chairman; Chief Executive Officer; Director of Research. Wasn't that sufficient?

That evening Land told McCune that he would announce the following day that Bill would be Polaroid's new president. He asked that Bill try to persuade Wyman to stay. McCune drove to Tom's house and broke the news to him. Wyman, who had an offer in hand to become president of Green Giant, a food company in Minnesota, smiled skeptically. "Land will never let you run the company," he said to Bill. A few years later, William Paley made Tom the latest in a long line of CBS presidents.

The day after Julie's hasty flight from the Caribbean, to the astonishment of all but four members of the company, Polaroid's board of directors named William McCune president, the second in Polaroid's history. The board also appointed him a director and a member of the executive committee of the board. Land designated him chief operating officer and welcomed him at a meeting of the company's officers with a careful little speech. McCune annexed all of Wyman's responsibilities to his own portfolios of engineering and manufacturing. Nothing changed overnight except the title. But since Land had always held the title before, everything had changed.

28

The Ritz

Boston, 1975

I sat biting my knuckles. The suite on the sixth floor was cheerful with birch logs burning in the fireplace and the draperies pulled close against the nasty weather beating against the windows. I opened the curtain a crack to peer out over the Public Garden. The traffic on Arlington Street moved slowly under streetlamps blurred by sleet, the sounds of the evening rush hour muffled. I wondered for the twentieth time what I hoped to accomplish. What the bloody hell I thought I was doing. With characteristic naiveté I had rushed ahead. Acted, not thought it out carefully. Acted and assumed that something good might come out of it. Watching taxis move past the hotel entrance, I wondered why I always thought of the upside. There was, of course, a downside as well. Naiveté was the habit of never examining the downside. I had been called naive at least twice recently, once by my wife, once by Ted Voss, my advertising vice president. The coincidence had prompted me to look up the word in the old *Webster's* I kept at home. The definition was not helpful: ingenuous, artless. I looked the next day in the *American Heritage* College Edition Jean Caloggero, my secretary, kept by her typewriter. That was more specific: lacking worldliness and sophistication; simple and credulous; "lacking critical ability or analytical insight." A little farther down, it got to the bone: "*naive* generally implies lack of perception, or intuitive judgment, that is the basis of sound behavior in a practical world."

It was not sound behavior in a practical world to invite two powerful men whose passionately held beliefs put them in conflict with each other to take dinner with a junior who desired to achieve some kind of reconciliation, or at the very least a reduction of tension, or at best a hope of a more united approach to the direction of the company. Those vague ideas seemed the most I could come up with to visualize the upside. What was the downside? Land might not come at the last minute. McCune might not come, although that would be uncharacteristic. They might be offended. They might be amused. They might be just plain furious. They must certainly be surprised by my temerity; I was appalled by it myself.

The maître d' opened the door to the small dining room. "Would you care for a drink while you are waiting for the other two gentlemen?"

"No, thank you, Nino. Yes. A Jack Daniel's on the rocks."

"Yes, sir. And here is the menu for this evening. I trust everything is in order." I glanced over it quickly. It was a gold-edged card with the courses listed in handsome calligraphy. I smiled for the first time since driving over from Cambridge. At least we're going to dine. That was one way to trap the Chairman and the president together in the same room for three hours, maybe the only way. Feed them well. For God's sake, they had ample reason to be cheerful. The year was, to all intents and purposes, over. It was apparent that it would be a bonanza. Sales would exceed $800 million and, although the bean counters wouldn't pronounce until late January or February, earnings should be double the showing of the previous year, about $28 million, close to $2.00 per share. SX-70 had become the acclaimed success that Land had assured everyone it would be. The bugs in the camera had for the most part been exterminated. The film was performing brilliantly. Even the battery problems had receded to a manageable, if still very expensive, level. A large brown drink was handed me by the waiter. It was one thing for Land to proclaim SX-70 as the Second Coming of Christ. It was quite another to actually make it happen. Somehow the company, not just some people, but virtually the entire collection of machine operators, scientists, secretaries, technicians, salesmen, and broom pushers, all 13,387 had pulled off a series of major and minor miracles. It was akin to the triumph of an earlier era when every employee had pitched in finally to tame the J-machine and Uncle Dudley. McCune and his protégé, Mac Booth, had willed a brand-new film negative factory designed from the ground up to perform from the moment the first switch was pulled. It had produced faultlessly the one element of the system that was indispensable, an incredibly precise, multilayered negative tuned like a harpsichord to minute but significant differences in color definition, film speed, and exposure latitude. The negative plant in New Bedford was one of the major miracles of the SX-70 project.

The design engineers had accepted, sometimes with considerable reluctance, one after another of Land's impossible goals for the camera and somehow pulled it all together at the expense of their hair, their stomach lining, and their families. SX-70 was an improbable instrument, the likes of which had never before existed except in Land's imagination. It could make beautiful instant pictures and it fit into a medium-large pocket. I put my drink down carefully on a napkin, went to the closet, and took an SX-70 from the pocket of my trench coat. I set the camera on the coffee table before the fireplace. Best to have something to break the ice when they arrived, if they arrived. So many groups had struggled with the almost impossible: the film team who created and recreated molecules and laid down coatings of emulsion thinner than a wavelength of light; the optics group who produced the plastic lenses and Fresnel mirrors for the folding through-the-lens viewing system; the electronics group who had designed the shutter controls and the operational electronics for the camera; the materials people who found a plastic that could be chromium plated like metal and then developed a way to make leather adhere to it.

That was so typical of Land, I thought, to insist that the camera be covered in leather. Not a leather-look-alike plastic, but real cowhide. Expensive, hard to handle, difficult to bond to the surface of the camera body; but it smelled good and it felt good. Land had an instinct for packaging. He listened to all the arguments about the cost being three dollars a camera more with leather, then he overrode them. He was right, I thought. I looked at the camera on the table in front of me. Land was a great marketer, but he would never admit it. Marketing was not one of the attributes he wished to be recognized for. Science, engineering, social philosophy, the quality of his expository prose, yes; titles, honors, degrees — but not Doctor of Marketing.

The door opened and the Doctor of Marketing entered. He was not smiling. His driver, Leon, a Cambridge policeman, nodded a greeting and departed. Land walked to the coffee table without removing his overcoat. His black hair was beaded with moisture. He picked up the camera and turned it in his hands. With a snap of his wrist he opened it and examined the lens. "Is this yours?"

"Hello, Din. Yes. It's the one you monogrammed for me." Earlier in the year Land had acquired a leather stamping device from a luggage shop and installed it in his office. He used it to imprint gilt initials on the leather panels of cameras, taking great delight in operating it for his intimates until he realized that people all over the company were taking their cameras to Jordan Marsh and Filene's to have initials stamped on them. The machine disappeared from his office.

"This is not current. It doesn't have the improved lens."

"I know, but it makes excellent pictures. It's mine, and I'm used to it. Let me take your coat." The waiter materialized and then departed to bring a scotch and water. Land sat down and stared at the fire. His eye fell on the menu. He smiled for the first time and picked it up.

"A handsome *carte*," he said. He read it with a reasonably good accent: "Menu. Le Consommé Paysan. Le Carré d'Agneau Rôti Diablotin. La Bouquet de Légumes. La Laitue de Prairie au Cresson. Le Fromage Continental. Le Sorbet au Citron. La Demitasse. Le Vin — Château Cheval Blanc, St.-Emilion, 1961. Polaroid Corporation Dinner. The Ritz-Carlton, Tuesday, December 9, 1975." He looked into the fire again. "You are feeding us well," he said. "How many members of Polaroid Corporation will be in attendance?"

"Three, as I told you. You, Bill, and I."

"You are always good at presentation."

"I have nothing to present except dinner."

"Well, that looks as though it will be well presented. Where is your other guest?"

"He seems to be a little late. I'm sure he'll be along shortly. Here's your drink."

"And what do you want to accomplish with this well-presented dinner?" He looked around the gold and white room, then back at the fire. He held the drink untasted.

"I just want to get you and Bill together in the same room for an evening. You hardly see each other lately except at board meetings. Perhaps we can talk about some of the things you two talk about separately. You each tell me things to tell the other. I'd much rather you'd speak to each other directly." Land scowled and was silent. Direct communication was not the mode he seemed to favor lately. There was a tentative knock on the door. It was opened to admit Bill McCune, wet, harried, ill at ease.

"Come in, Bill."

"Sorry I'm late. The traffic from Waltham was awful."

"Did you drive the Porsche?"

"Yes. I don't really like to leave it out in this weather. Do you think it's all right in the hotel lot?"

"I'm sure it's fine. I left my own car there." McCune gave me a little smile that suggested that, since my car was not a Porsche, had not been ordered directly from the factory, had not been extensively modified by the owner, and was not given the kind of care that few automobiles in private hands ever receive, the comment was irrelevant. He ordered a scotch and stood by the mantel. A painful silence fell until the drink appeared.

"I just thought — " I began.

"Did you hear Purcell's lecture the other night?" Land asked McCune.

"No, I didn't. Were you there?"

"Yes. It was quite well attended. Elkan Blout was there. We had a discussion afterwards about some young people he wants me to interview. One is doing some interesting work in electromagnetics."

"I'd like to meet him."

"She's at Harvard." Electromagnetics held the floor for a while. I got up to glance into the small dining room. The captain was lighting the candles. The doors were opened, and we went in to dinner.

After the consommé had been served the captain brought the wine. Torn between his duty to the person who had chosen the wine and would sign the bill and a powerful natural inclination toward celebrity, he presented the bottle first to Land, who looked at it, then waved it in my direction. The wine was identified, tasted, accepted, and poured. I lifted my glass. "I just thought — "

"I would like to propose a toast," said Land. He laid the camera on the table under the candles. "To the SX-70, a camera whose elegance reflects the elegance of mind of those who created it. It could not be changed in any detail without marring the perfection that has made it so successful." We drank thoughtfully, McCune silently reviewing all the changes he wanted to make in the camera design, Land gazing at the leather and chrome oblong in front of him with the expression of a lioness regarding her cub, while I wondered if either of them understood that advertising was what sold cameras, whether they were covered with cowhide or fish scales.

"The SX-70 is elegant," I said after a pause. "I'm glad you insisted on the leather, Dr. Land. It makes it look like something valuable. It was a great marketing stroke." I immediately wished to recall my words. Both men frowned deeply.

"It was *not* a marketing ploy," said Land. "It *is* something valuable. It couldn't possibly be enclosed in plastic. The camera deserves leather."

McCune, once again firmly in control of the camera design group, which had a plastic version of the camera well along in development, said to the table at large, "Do you have any idea how high the quality control rejects are running for the leather panels? It's the biggest single quality problem at Norwood."

"Gentlemen, the entrée." The captain presented the lamb, then began to serve. The meal went quickly. The conversation touched on Land's latest trip to Washington, on McCune's chalet in Zermatt, on the abominable Boston weather. At one point McCune inquired politely about my plans for Christmas.

"We plan to spend it at home, as we always do. Andrea and the boys — "

"Excuse me, gentlemen. Would you care to have your coffee in the other room?"

"No, you may serve it here," said Land.

"Some port? A cognac?" Drinks and coffee were distributed at the table. Cigars were offered and declined, though Land cast a longing glance. Sleet rattled against the windows.

"Dr. Land — Din. Bill. I feel, and a lot of other people feel, that you two must find a way to discuss the product-planning issues that are so important to the company. We're having a superb year. We're going to have another great year next year. But you're going in different directions. Kodak is coming into the instant field. We have to have a product strategy that everyone agrees on. Product decisions are the most important decisions in the company. Everything else stems from that." The two looked at me as if I had said that a dog barks. I searched for words. "Isn't there some way we can improve communications between the two of you?"

"We communicate quite well," said Land.

"I've got to be going," said McCune. "Thank you for the excellent dinner. It was nice." He paused, also apparently seeking words. "It was *very* nice. I will think of it with pleasure," he said stiffly, but with a little smile in my direction.

"Indeed," said Land, rising. He picked up the menu. "It was a pleasant evening. Talk to Elkan, Bill, about those young people." He took out his pen and wrote something on the bottom of the menu. He handed it to McCune with the pen. "My driver is waiting in the lobby. A very pleasant evening." He put on his coat. "Communication is not a problem" — he smiled warmly — "especially among such accomplished communicators." The two of them left together. I leaned on the back of a chair and sipped my brandy. Nino appeared with the bill.

"Was everything satisfactory, sir?"

"The dinner was excellent." I signed the check.

"Did the other gentlemen find the arrangements to their satisfaction?"

"Yes. They seem to have found the arrangements . . . satisfactory." I picked up the menu. Land had written carefully at the bottom, in a hand that imitated the calligraphy, "The Old Friend — Din." McCune had written "Bill" in one corner. I sat for a while trying to think, with the perception and intuitive judgment that is the basis of sound behavior in a practical world, about the evening. I considered both the upside and the downside.

The two men had worked closely together for thirty-five years. I had been with them for — what? — seventeen. It had been a reasonably pleasant dinner. Even though I was junior to them in every way, including the most critical from their point of view, my lack of technical background, they had accepted the effort at conciliation with reasonably good grace. They were both gentlemen. They understood the niceties of polite social intercourse. They enjoyed the dinner. The Cheval Blanc was superb. They carried the evening off as gentlemen, but gentlemen in deep disagreement. Nothing had changed. Nothing had been decided. Nothing had been solved. They did not agree on how the company should be run. McCune felt that Land had made the SX-70 effort unnecessarily difficult and expensive and was resisting the changes that were essential to make the system more dependable and more profitable. Land was certain that the product was as close to perfection as human hands could make it. He wanted — expected — every family in the Western world to buy one. He saw it as a classic product that would sell for years without basic changes.

Land planned now to devote the company's resources to Polavision. Bill was deeply concerned about the movie project. He was doubtful of the additive color technology at its heart and worried about the cost of developing a salable system. There was really no misunderstanding between them. As Land said, they were good communicators. I'm the one who has not been getting the message, I thought. I'm surprised that they are so patient with me. I guess that's the upside. The downside seems to be waiting for us somewhere in the future. I wondered how far away it might be. I shrugged on my coat, pocketed my camera and the menu, and headed for the elevator. I may be naive to think you can read the future, I thought, half aloud, but is it naive to think you can change the present? I didn't know the answer any more than I had three hours earlier.

29

Additive

Cambridge and Needham, 1968–1977

Three primary colors form an image in color photography: blue, green, and red; their complementary colors are yellow, magenta, and cyan. In the so-called subtractive color process as used in the Land-Rogers instant color film, successive layers of emulsion were coated on a negative base, three of which were silver halide emulsions: one sensitive to blue light, one sensitive to green, one sensitive to red. Beneath each of the emulsion layers was a layer of dye-developing molecules, unique to Polaroid, in the complementary colors. In the subtractive process, when blue light entered the camera lens and struck the negative, it exposed the blue-sensitive emulsion layer that blocked the layer of dye-developers immediately below it, in this case yellow, from transferring color to the positive sheet. The magenta and cyan dye-developers, however, were free to pass through to the receiving sheet, where they mixed to form a blue image. When green light reached the green-sensitive layer, the magenta dye-developers beneath it were blocked, but the cyan and yellow dye-developers were allowed to move to the positive, where they formed green. In the same way red light blocked the cyan dye but allowed magenta and yellow to combine on the receiving sheet to form red. Most commercial films made by Kodak, Ansco, Ilford, Fuji, and others, as well as by Polaroid, used the subtractive process for color prints and transparencies.

The additive color process, as the name suggested, formed a color image by red light depositing a red dye, green light depositing a green dye, and blue light depositing a blue dye in the final image. Although seemingly simpler, this process posed a number of problems, among them the density of the completed image. Land had been intrigued by the additive color process since 1948; by the fact that, although the principle was as well understood as the subtractive process, no major film manufacturer had adopted it for broad commercial use. His experiments over a span of twenty years led him to the conclusion that a color transparency film could be devised that contained an ordinary black-and-white emulsion with no color dye-developers whatsoever, but still produced a full color image when white light was projected through it. Land envisioned and eventually produced in 1968 a screen of tiny transparent stripes of red, green, and blue, repeated in triads, one thousand sets per inch on the surface of a film base. These microscopic triple lines allowed red light to pass through the red line, blue through the blue line, green through the green line. The light then struck the silver halide in an emulsion layer and exposed it. When developed, the exposed silver halide turned to black silver. Thus, the final transparency was a combination of a mask and a matrix, the mask a black-and-white image formed by the silver halide, the matrix the screen of colored stripes in sets of three. When light shone through the transparency, the silver halide mask allowed rays through the precise portion of a red line in the matrix to recreate the red of the original scene. A yellow spot in the projected image was created by light passing through a spot on adjacent red and green lines. Shades and hues were produced by light shining through the requisite combination of triplets that blended together when projected on a screen or a viewer. The result, when seen in front of a powerful light source, was beautiful, rich color.

The manufacturing problems inherent in this concept were formidable. One thousand triplets, three thousand lines, per inch had to be embossed into a transparent sheet, to be dyed red, green, and blue with utmost precision across the face of the material and then combined with the silver halide emulsion layer. Land conceptualized this process as well as the film itself and hypothesized a continuous manufacturing cycle that would produce the intricate color base material in a nonstop series of operations. The Land Line, as the manufacturing process was christened when it was still in the planning stage, was to be capable of turning out additive color transparency material by mile after endless mile. From the beginning, the instant transparency was characterized as a monumental product. The need for massive manufacturing capability was never questioned by its designers. If demand was discussed among Land's scientists at all, it was assumed that instant transparencies would generate at least as much consumer demand as instant black-and-white or color print film had done. Actually, the market for transparency film was only a fraction of that for prints, both in the United States and abroad.

Land's additive color technology was a tour de force. In true Landian style, it solved a classical problem in totally unconventional terms. He had pondered the additive problem for twenty years. He devoted more than ten years of intensive work to it, his own and that of one of his personal research groups, headed eventually by another brilliant woman, Lucretia Weed. As usual, he did not seek technical or marketing guidance. The system, as it evolved from a concept, to a laboratory prototype, to an exposure and development system, to a viewing device, was almost entirely his. It was so unusual, so out of the mainstream of current or traditional photographic thinking, that it could hardly have come from anyone else.

Lucretia Weed was not only bright, she possessed unusual resources of patience and determination. She somehow managed to keep the additive research alive for years while her mentor's attention was constantly demanded elsewhere. Because she most often saw Land on the fly from one crisis to another, she learned to compress reports of her progress and important questions into the briefest conversations. If she got one or two answers a month from Land, she considered it a signal victory. She was not immune to frustration, however.

One evening Land, who had promised to meet Lucretia hours earlier, returned to Osborn Street close to midnight, to be greeted at the door by a new security guard on his first night's duty. Land's car had just departed, its driver instructed to return in an hour. The guard asked Land for the identification card, produced on the Polaroid system with a photograph of the owner, that every employee carried. Land smiled and said modestly, "I'm Dr. Land."

"Sorry, I can't let you in without identification. Let me see your driver's license."

As was often the case, Land carried no wallet, keys, or money. Realizing that he was facing an officer of commitment and integrity, he looked wildly around for someone to vouch for him. It was snowing outside and he did not want to wait an hour for his driver in the weather.

To his relief, Lucretia came clattering down the steep stairway, the last person in the building at this hour.

"Lucretia, thank goodness; please tell this gentleman who I am," Land called to her in a plaintive voice.

She favored him with the briefest of glances. "I've never seen this man before in my life," she said as she brushed past them to her car.

The uses of the additive system were obvious to Land. It was not suited for making prints, since it required a bright projection light to mitigate the density of the color; but instant transparencies, he was sure, would be at least as popular as his magic pictures. In the years since World War II, the standard of the transparency field had become Eastman Kodak's Kodachrome, a subtractive material most widely used in the 35 mm slide format, where its beautifully consistent color characteristics were prized by professional as well as amateur photographers. This mature, highly refined film had gained about 90 percent of the American transparency market and a major share abroad in competition with German, Japanese, and other manufacturers. Transparency film was used in large quantities by the motion picture industry, for commercial and industrial slides, by commercial photographers, by amateurs to record vacations, birthdays, and weddings, and in home movies.

All of these market segments had reached a plateau, and the occasional technical advance, such as an increase in film speed, to around 200 ASA, or the addition of sound to home movies did little to stimulate an increase in demand. The home movie market had begun to decline in the seventies as videotape technology, evolving rapidly, loomed like a thundercloud on the amateur horizon. Equipment for movie projection had hardly changed, either in the theater or the home, since the thirties. The standard 16 mm projector for office or school auditorium was still the Bell & Howell Filmsound, a rugged piece of machinery whose sharp sprocket wheels were a trap for the unwary.

J. Harold Booth, Polaroid's first professional in the marketing field, came from Chicago's Bell & Howell in 1948 to Cambridge, where one of his newly hired assistants was a brash ex-newspaperman named Stan Calderwood. Early in his Polaroid career, Stan was struggling to rewind a sales film on a Bell & Howell projector while his audience waited restively in the dark. "I wish I could meet the idiot who invented this," muttered Stan as he poked his flashlight around, trying to thread the film under the drive sprocket.

"Please see me after the meeting," came the sepulchral voice of Mr. Booth from the back of the room. Booth was one of the first Polaroid employees to retire on the profits of the company's stock. He converted some of his shares into a yacht and sailed toward sunny weather in 1961.

One of the earliest camera concepts based on the as-yet-unnamed additive film was a small 35 mm camera designed to expose and develop slides ready for projection. The Polaroid design engineers produced an attractive package, but the sensitivity to light of the additive film was so low that it was not possible to make sharp transparencies with the little hand-held camera. Since the film needed so much light to be exposed through the color stripes, the shutter speeds were necessarily slow, and the image was often blurred by movement of the camera. Work on the film went on, under the supervision of Dr. Richard Young, who came to Polaroid in 1961 from Monsanto to work as Land's assistant director of research. Land and Young began to explore motion picture concepts in addition to the still camera designs. In a motion picture, slow film speed, while a detriment, was less critical than for still pictures. The continually changing sequence of pictures in a movie was integrated by the eye into the illusion of connected motion. A single frame of movie film, projected and examined by itself, often appeared blurred and unsharp, but, seen as a flow of related images, the impression of sharpness was supplied by the viewer's eye and brain.

Another serious problem was inherent in the additive transparency, however. The beaded screen, which was chosen because it reflected the greatest possible amount of light from the film, was narrowly directional, that is, the viewer needed to be seated directly in front of the screen to perceive the full color and detail of the projected image. Seen from an angle at either side of the center of the screen, the image appeared dim and colorless.

Finally, the film was so dense that an extremely powerful light source was needed for effective projection. Movie theaters used large, intense projection lights, not because of a density problem, but to throw the image a long distance, often one hundred feet or more from the projector to the screen. Additive film did not allow even a moderate projection distance. The projector had to be bright and it had to be close, or the image appeared dark and muddy.

In the meantime, to the few in the company outside Lucretia's development team who had glimpsed the new technology, it was apparent that the concept that had made Polaroid so successful, its primary distinction in the competitive world of photography, had been mislaid in this project. Instant photography involved interaction between the photographer and the subject. The picture was immediately available, either to admire or to remake immediately if it was less than satisfactory for any reason. Several methods of on-the-spot development had been contrived for the additive film, but viewing was another matter. Transparencies and motion pictures required a screen, a projector with a source of electricity, a darkened room, an audience in chairs, in short, preparations and equipment. Spontaneity and immediacy had vanished.

In the meantime, SX-70 rushed forward to the marketplace. Although the additive project had grown to sizable proportions — in 1972 more than three hundred people were working on it — the urgency of the SX-70 program overwhelmed it. The company was so heavily committed to SX-70 in every direction — research, engineering, manufacturing, and marketing — that mortal men and women could focus only on the crisis at hand. Before, during, and after SX-70's introduction in Florida, it was apparent to everyone in the company, from the Employees Committee to the board of directors, that the survival of Polaroid depended on the success of the SX-70 system. For once there was unanimous agreement in the corporate culture. Politics and bureaucratic advantage were forgotten. The issue *was* survival. No one was more conscious of this than Land. No one worked longer hours; no one contributed more intellectual and animal energy; no one was more resourceful in surmounting the obstacles that nature stubbornly presented to hinder, thwart, and delay. Yet even in the midst of this effort, the additive project moved doggedly forward with Land's participation and his constant, if fragmented attention. It was as if during the Battle of Britain Churchill had been making plans for the colonization of the Antarctic.

Because of the density of the film and its slow speed, instant transparencies worked better as instant movies. Although the format changed, the film speed was still distressingly limited, varying from 5 ASA to 10 ASA at the fastest. Dick Young had been pulled off the project by Land. Bill McCune found Young a new assignment supervising Polaroid's rapidly growing international business, where in spite of his former concentration on science, or perhaps because of it, he discovered hitherto unsuspected talents for general management.

In 1975, the additive project acquired a name, Polavision, coined by Land and the Princesses, now all fully involved with the project. Since most of the current group were married and several had produced attractive children, the Princess progeny crawled or tottered through the test reels of film being shot with increasing regularity. Screen projection had been abandoned reluctantly. The directionality of the image and the lack of any practical means of immediate viewing drove Polavision into a box. The viewer was a self-contained movie system that projected the image from within onto a screen somewhat smaller than the average portable television set. The film was enclosed in a cassette, a marvel of chemical and mechanical functions packed into a small space. About the size and shape of an audio tape cassette, it could snap into a camera, the functional cousin of the conventional Super 8 home movie cameras then commonly available. After exposure, the cassette was inserted in the viewer, which needed a household power source to operate it. The cassette then quickly and automatically ran through a development cycle that rendered the negative transparent. It then rewound itself and was ready to be viewed, or "played," as Land preferred it to be termed. The Polavision player exhibited two and a half minutes of color motion pictures, could be slowed, stopped, and restarted, was dependable and easy to use. Land visualized a system where the cassettes were stored as books or records in a library, to be taken down and played on impulse. The cassette format, two and a half minutes long, he described as an important new medium, more exciting, revealing, and satisfying than still pictures, but escaping the inevitable tedium of a full fifteen-minute reel of edited or, worse, unedited home movies.

As in most of Land's product pronouncements, there was more than a grain of truth in this one. But as in the past, the final product combined elements dictated by what he could do and what nature would not let him do. The Polavision effort had more than a passing resemblance to the American moon landing decreed by John Kennedy and pursued by Lyndon Johnson while the Polaroid program struggled its way through the laboratory. Both were initiated by fiat; both were enormously expensive on the respective scale of nation and corporation; both were pursued by technologists intent on what could be done and how. *When* became a function of cost and the ability to overcome obstacles. The *why* was never examined. The technology developed in both programs, again viewed in the appropriate scale, possessed intrinsic interest and value, the difficulties of the mission provoking unique and ingenious solutions. But there the analogy ended.

SX-70 shouldered past Polavision. They could not squeeze through the doorway to the public at the same time. By 1978, instant photography was at the height of its popularity. More than nine million cameras were sold that year, and Polaroid finally surpassed the profit level Jim Awad and the other analysts had expected five years earlier by earning $3.50 per share. When in 1977 Polavision finally made its first appearance outside the nursery, more than ten years of active development had taken place, not to mention the twenty years it had prowled the corridors and cathedrals of Land's mind. During the tumult of the SX-70 introduction, its test in the marketplace in Florida, its faltering production, the recovery, and its eventual success, Polavision had been incubating under laboratory lights, rarely seen or used by anyone outside the development group.

Light continued to be one of its major problems. The film speed, now about 40 ASA, required huge amounts of light for exposure. Bright sunlight was adequate for outdoor filming, but indoors the situation was critical. A brilliant electric torch, known to photographers as a Sun Gun, could provide reasonable exposure, but no child and few adults could look a Sun Gun in the face without a grimace. Test cassettes often displayed one expression of pain after another.

A second problem was Polavision's lack of sound. Conventional home movies had sound in 1977, as did the emerging generation of home videotape machines. Polavision did not. Land would not recognize either of these problems — the very word ruled them out of his presence — which were essentially related to the needs of the customer, until late in the development process, when Land's own chemical, optical, and mechanical concerns had been at least partially satisfied. Just before the introduction of Polavision, which after many delays finally took place in April 1977, Land and his team invented an ingenious hand-held light that produced less direct glare than a Sun Gun and almost as much usable light. Nevertheless, it still caused babies to cry and strong men to turn aside. Sound was belatedly addressed, but Polavision with recordable, playable sound never came to fruition during the brief lifetime of the product.

Bell & Howell was approached to build the basic Polavision player.

Donald Frey, one of Robert McNamara's whiz kids at Ford, president of the company, was invited by Land to come to Cambridge. After one of the best of the little dinners — rack of lamb and a Château Margaux, followed by a beautifully orchestrated Polavision demonstration — Frey returned to Chicago full of enthusiasm. He responded promptly with cost estimates, unfortunately well above Polaroid's expectations. Bell & Howell's photographic division was lagging behind some of its recent efforts at diversification, such as business products and training courses. Polavision seemed a good bet for the company if the production volumes were great enough.

However, before the first Polavision player was produced, Frey opted out of the contract, perhaps impatient with the continual stream of design changes that emanated from Cambridge, leaving a residual dispute over the ownership of the manufacturing tools. Polaroid's Dr. Sheldon A. Buckler, in charge of the project, always under Land's direct supervision, embarked on a hasty search for a new contractor and came up with Eumig, a small Austrian manufacturer of movie cameras, record players, and music equipment. Eumig, also facing difficulties with its basic business, jumped at the opportunity and proved a patient, reliable supplier of both Polavision cameras and players. Meanwhile, as design changes, vendor changes, and delays in the new film factory stretched the schedule, costs increased every month. The player and camera, which would be sold together, had been tentatively priced at about $100 at retail when the program had first taken shape in the early seventies. By 1977 the cost had escalated to almost $700. The film cassette had risen in cost also, but no reasonable combination of unit price or production quantity could begin to bite into the investment that had been made in the Polavision film plant in Norwood.

No innovation had been overlooked in the design and construction of the Land Line: clean rooms, computer controls, laser knives, and a unique conveyor system that moved the film web on jets and cushions of air. Like an iridescent snake, the additive film raced around the factory, climbing to the ceiling, shooting among the rafters, plunging to the basement, flying from process to process in one of the most technologically imaginative factories ever built. As usual, all the design and construction of the key production machinery had been done by Otto Wolf and his group. Everything about the Land Line was proprietary, revolutionary, secret, and extremely expensive. The unit price of a cassette of Polavision film became an abstraction when faced with the amortization of the major capital investment in the Land Line from which it sprang.

The total investment in Polavision had not yet reached the level of the SX-70 program, but it was climbing fast. Julie Silver had insisted, with Land's concurrence, that the company continue its policy of paying development costs as they were incurred. Polaroid in 1977 was still without significant debt and enjoying the most profitable years of its history. Earnings, return on the stockholders' equity, and unit sales of cameras and film were all at their peak. Unfortunately, research and development costs, capital expenditures, and the employee population, then in excess of twenty thousand souls, had peaked as well. Julie Silver, in whom prosperity aroused a primal caution, could recognize danger signals. He redoubled the sermons of conservatism he delivered on biweekly trips from New York to Cambridge and at the monthly board meetings. He was outraged when he discovered that the first contract with Eumig ordered fifty thousand sets of players and cameras. "Why not five thousand?" he asked. The unit price was lower for fifty thousand, he was told. "Are we suddenly trying to save money on this program?" he demanded.

The driving force behind Polavision procurement was, of course, its inventor. He recognized a lack of enthusiasm for the project among many of his officers, chief among them Bill McCune. Never comfortable with the additive concept, Bill was fully and continuously occupied in trying to bring SX-70 costs down; still, he supported the Polavision program, if reluctantly. The company was booming. Sales had approached the billion-dollar mark in 1976, and the freshman term of Bill's presidency was off to a flying start. He shared Julie's concerns, however. McCune had doubts about some of the optimistic projections he had been shown for the growth of the world photographic market. Listening to Julie's counsel, Bill doubted that the tree could reach the sky. And the Polavision program frightened him.

Stung by Bill's lack of commitment, Land went to the board of directors in 1977 and demanded that he personally be put in charge of the Polavision program. No less surprised by the ultimatum, so different from Land's usual mode of address to his directors — each of whom he had carefully chosen, courted, flattered, and confided in over the years — than by the demand itself, they readily agreed. Aren't you personally in charge already? they asked the Chairman and Director of Research. What was so obviously de facto, they granted without hesitation. Movies in a box moved toward their belated meeting with the American public. Land, becoming ever more self-isolated in his company, felt himself a prophet without honor, a general whose captains lagged behind. How many times had he proved to them that what they could not see was really there? How many times had he done what they thought was impossible? How many times had he been right?

As expected, Polaroid's shareholders saw Polavision before anyone else, at the April 26, 1977, annual meeting. The show that Land and his faithful inner circle produced for the meeting outdid any previous effort. Held in the fully equipped theater for four thousand that doubled during the year as the warehouse in Needham, this extravaganza showed evidences of strain. What had in the past been bright, fresh, and ingenuous exhibited in this stressful year a harder edge.

As always, the staging was professional. After the routine part of the meeting had been dispensed with, the members of the audience were invited to come behind the stage, where they were given a Polavision camera and encouraged to wander through a carnival of color and motion. Following the design of the SX-70 meeting, there were twenty booths to be photographed. Where the SX-70 octagons had offered color, beauty, and even some quiet humor, the mood here was frenetic. Clowns and mimes and dancers vied with each other on a noisy midway. Each set was lit with powerful overhead spots and floodlights to accommodate the film speed. When the guest photographers had finished their cassettes they were invited to sit in a blessedly quiet alcove where the cassettes were developed and played back to them. The rehearsals and the unsparing effort of the preceding months delivered a flawless performance.

Without question Polavision under those circumstances was impressive, most impressive to those who were most knowledgeable about photography. The anomaly of a unique new system based upon one of the oldest ideas in photography did not pass unnoticed. The intricacy of the cassette, its unusual exposure system, its elegant development chemistry, its mechanical complexity, all enclosed, never to be seen before or after playing, beggared the imagination. The player was as complicated as a sewing machine, emitting a menagerie sequence of purrs, buzzes, and barks as it rewound the cassette, pulled it through the development cycle, rewound it once more, and then played it for the viewer. Only the Polavision camera looked familiar, modeled as it was on a conventional Super 8 design about five years old. The new conventional home movie cameras were undeniably sexier, with bigger lenses, long zooms, and built-in microphones. The electronic competition was still bulky and heavy, with large battery cases that had to be carried with the video camera. But aware of the Japanese talent for miniaturization, the analysts in the crowd were primed to ask Land about the future of videotape and how it would affect Polavision. The crowd of shareholders, employees, reporters, and analysts wandered among the booths, impressed with the system, amused by the show, and a little puzzled. They had seen something new, but the sudden recognition of an inevitable idea was missing. They had been shown a dog in a top hat walking on its hind legs, but they were not sure why.

Land paced the stage, challenging the audience reseated in front of him. Not reticent, not evasive, not modest, he insistently taught them the wonders of Polavision. Behind him had been projected a series of charts whose evidence of his company's success was irrefutable. Polaroid was the second largest photographic enterprise in the world. If the largest, Eastman Kodak, dared challenge his patents with an inferior copy of an instant camera, he was prepared to fight to defend — a pause — "our blood." I had never seen him more animated, more in command. He was immense in retreat, I thought. The critics, the complainers, the faint of heart, can attack him if they dare. As he stalked back and forth, Land carried a pointer to emphasize the record sales and profits displayed on the screen behind him. Now he wielded it like a rapier in parry and riposte as the questions about Polavision came from his old enemies, the analysts scattered through the crowd. The questions concerned costs, estimates, profit and loss. He answered with science, research, technology, and creativity. Two cultures challenged each other across the footlights, not communicating, not even acknowledging the existence of the other point of view. The moms and pops among the shareholders, the Polaroid employees who owned stock and had followed Land all their working lives, the retirees who had invested in 1950 and gone to live in Florida on the proceeds, watched the rising storm of debate and acrimony with concern. What was happening? What was wrong? This was Polaroid, wasn't it? This was Land, after all. He had always been right. If he said Polavision would be successful, well, hell, I'll bet on him!

An analyst, speaking into the microphone extended by an usher, acknowledged with faint praise the technology embodied in Polavision. "But, Dr. Land," he said in frustration, "what about the bottom line?"

Land paused in his pacing, stricken. The blooded point of his sword touched the boards of the stage. "The bottom line?" he cried. "The bottom line is in heaven!" The moms and pops rose as one and cheered him to the echo.

30

Prior Art

Cambridge and Boston, 1976–1986

Bill McCune's secretary, Gail Pick, called just after lunch to summon Polaroid's senior officers to the board room. I was already headed up the back stairs, taking the gray concrete treads two at a time, followed by our New Jersey salesman, who was carrying an Adidas bag. Land, McCune, Howie Rogers, Milt Dietz and Dick Wareham, the two senior camera designers, Cliff Duncan, the SX-70 program manager, and half a dozen others were standing silently inside the room, waiting for us. It was not to be a formal meeting. We extracted three Kodak instant cameras and six boxes of film from the bag and cast them out on the big oak table. Land reached for a camera. Milt Dietz toyed with a surgical-looking screwdriver. I opened a box of PR-10 film and handed the rectangular film pack to Land, who frowned at it, turned it over in his hand, examined it from various angles, then inserted it into the open camera. He took a flash picture of Milt Dietz, who flinched, and we watched with hostile awe as the first Kodak instant picture rose out of the top of the camera into Land's waiting fingers. The EK instant camera had been anticipated for more than three years, but Kodak's justly famous industrial secrecy had allowed no details of the system to leak from Rochester. The analysts had been able to do no more than guess about it. Seven years earlier, almost to the day, in April 1969, when Kodak had terminated the color development agreement with Polaroid, that had been a signal that Kodak's instant program had begun.

Color had always been Land's goal. Back in Cambridge, after the Optical Society demonstration in 1947, he had pushed Howie Rogers into a chair on the other side of the long worktable in the lab and told him to begin thinking about how to extend the basic process, which at the time produced only sepia images, to color. Howie sat, as Land bade him, for several years, thinking about color, assimilating the techniques of the laboratory. Then, according to Land, he stood up and muttered, "I'm ready to start." He and Land labored for eight years on the color puzzle, which was much more than three times as complicated as black-and-white.

In 1957, Rogers had achieved the first working prototype of a one-step color film. He had discarded the traditional color chemistry in which a "coupler" would be joined to a "color developer" in each of the three layers of the exposed negative to form a dye. Rogers, having tested literally thousands of compounds, created a new animal, which he and Land named a dye-developer, a combination of preformed dye and developer in a single magnificent molecule. When the prototype color film was shown to Eastman Kodak that year, the company agreed to assist Polaroid in making it ready for production. Polaroid had no negative production facility of its own and had relied on Kodak for all of its black-and-white sensitized material since 1944.

The manufacture of photographic negative was generally acknowledged to be one of the most difficult processes in the world. Color negative involved the coating of many layers, each precise in its thickness and its molecular structure, all laid down, of course, in the dark. Thus, the color agreement between the two companies was twelve years old in 1969, encompassing six years of production development from the 1957 prototype to the Polacolor introduction in 1963 and six years of rapidly increasing production volume.

A year earlier the second color film prototype had been described to Kodak. In October of that year, Land laid some integral color images on the desk of Dr. Henry C. Yutzy, Kodak's vice president of research. This forerunner of the SX-70 film opened Kodak's eyes to the power of Polaroid's research. Seven months later Eastman negated the agreement and, it was obvious to Polaroid, embarked on an instant program of its own. After it abandoned its first direction, P-129, a peel-apart film that was to be compatible with Polaroid pack cameras, Kodak focused all its energies on Project 130, taking the direction it knew Polaroid was pursuing with SX-70.

By early 1972, unknown to Polaroid, Kodak had developed a camera called the Lanyard, which advanced the film through developing rollers by pulling a cord. Although the camera contained no motor, it was quite bulky, and when Land showed the svelte SX-70 camera to his shareholder audience in April, it devastated the Kodak marketing group. The "P-130 program, as earlier defined, is no longer desirable," wrote the Kodak marketing committee in the corporatese companies use to communicate with themselves. The Lanyard was hoist by its own petard. Working with virtually unlimited resources and fourteen hundred people assigned to the program, Kodak still grounded on one reef after another. In late 1971, it was evaluating two different dye-release processes, but neither had sufficient speed for a workable system. In 1972, color stability continued to generate anxiety at Kodak, which considered its conventional print film the standard of the industry. Eastman could ill afford to put on the market an instant color film that might fade. In addition, it was struggling with problems of the mordant, the chemistry that fixed the dye into an insoluble compound, and the opacification process by which the image was shielded from the light during development.

In October 1972, SX-70 had gone on sale in Miami. Even though enormous quantities of money were being thrown at it, the Kodak program was mired in difficulties. Eastman purchased SX-70 cameras and film by the gross and sent them posthaste from Florida to Rochester, where P-130 teams began exhaustive testing and analysis of the rival system. For four months they dissected SX-70, examining the molecules of the film as carefully as the camera's gears and electronics. In January 1973, the Kodak marketing group caucused and pronounced the P-130 project in its current form only "marginally acceptable." They acknowledged that they had to equal SX-70, which had pushed the ante very high, higher than they had ever anticipated. It was estimated that a "me-too" program would take another two and a half years to produce a design that still might not be competitive with Polaroid's. In September 1973, Kodak's development committee made the extraordinary statement to the program managers that "development should not be constrained by what an individual feels is potential patent infringement."

In fact it was almost three years before Kodak introduced the EK-4 and the EK-6, and the instant color film designated PR-10, at a press conference in New York City in April 1976. These cameras were similar in many ways to the SX-70: an electric motor drove a train of gears, a "pick" pushed the picture through a pair of steel rollers, which ruptured a pod to begin development. Unlike the SX-70, the Eastman picture was exposed from behind, rather than in front. The camera was not a single-lens reflex: it used a viewfinder. It was larger, bulkier, heavier. The picture image was rectangular and slightly bigger, and it emerged from the top of the camera rather than the front. Neither the EK-4 nor the EK-6 could fit into a suit-coat pocket, but they produced excellent color pictures. Kodak gave cameras and film to the press at the New York announcement.

Our New Jersey rep, who had bought two EK-4s and an EK-6 from a magazine editor who wasn't particularly interested in this story, caught the shuttle to Boston, a scout racing back to headquarters from reconnaissance, the enemy's guns unmasked at last. An atmosphere of impending battle charged the Tech Square board room. The engineers were elated to discover that the Kodak system was neither original nor superior, but clearly a me-too effort. The EK cameras had none of the elegance, the technological élan of the SX-70; nor were they particularly pleasing in design or styling. We discussed the retail prices quoted at the press conference. They were considerably below the price of the SX-70 for both camera models, though the film price was pegged exactly at the Polaroid price point. But the shining fact remained that we were sure we had the better product. For all their resources, for all their serried ranks of scientists and engineers, for all their billions, they had produced a copy. It appeared to be, as the salesman had told me on the way to the board room, "a goddamn knock-off." Land looked agitated. I asked him what he thought of the system, the room around us an excited babel punctuated by flashes from the Kodak cameras.

"I expected more from Eastman," he said.

Six days later, on April 27, Polaroid filed suit in the United States District Court, District of Massachusetts, against Eastman Kodak Company for infringement of twelve of its patents relating to the art and technology of both camera and film. Kodak denied infringement and alleged that all the patents were invalid or unenforceable or both.

Section 101 of the United States patent statute provides that "whoever invents . . . any new and useful process . . . may obtain a patent therefor." Section 112 requires that the specification contain "a written description of the invention, and of the manner and process of making and using it, in such full, clear, concise, and exact terms as to enable any person skilled in the art . . . to make and use the same." The statute also requires that the patent set forth the "best mode contemplated by the inventor of carrying out his invention." Each patent must teach new art. Instead of concealing secrets of technology and process, it must show others how to create and manufacture. The art it teaches must not repeat prior art; it must be genuinely novel. The patent examiner studies all related prior art before granting a patent, which guarantees the inventor, if his invention withstands challenge, protection for twenty years.

Application of the patent privilege had been a routine aspect of product development at Polaroid from the beginning. Don Brown applied for Land's first patent, for an extensive synthetic sheet polarizer, in 1929, and it was granted in 1934. As chemical and mechanical inventions emerged from Polaroid laboratories, patents were sought whether the inventions were incorporated in a finished and marketed system or not. Polaroid's patent department developed over the years into a highly skilled group of lawyers, about twenty in 1976, who not only knew American and much foreign patent law, but were also well versed in chemistry and engineering. Polaroid protected its patents vigorously and had engaged in some twenty litigations over the years, most of them relatively minor, most of them successful. No case had approached the magnitude of the Kodak challenge, however, which struck at the heart of Polaroid's business. At its height, instant photography never represented as much as 2 percent of Kodak's more than $10 billion in sales. The converse was true for Polaroid; instant photography was indeed its lifeblood. It accounted for more than 90 percent of the company's sales of about $1 billion.

The lines were quickly drawn. The case was assigned to Judge Rya Zobel of the United States District Court in Boston. Two patents were quickly dropped from the suit, one on a motion for summary judgment by Kodak, a film patent that was held invalid by the court, the second, a camera patent for which the lawyers for both parties agreed to waive their claims of infringement and invalidity respectively. Ten patents were left, four camera and six film patents, two of which were so similar as to constitute a single issue. Thus, nine inventions remained in contention. Eastman Kodak set out to prove invalidity and/or unenforceability, Polaroid, infringement and liability. Judge Zobel would constitute findings of fact and conclusions of law as to the issues among some of the most complicated and abstruse questions of chemistry and engineering ever presented to a court. Both parties claimed attorneys' fees, the loser to pay all costs. Polaroid, charging willful and deliberate infringement, sought increased damages, which could be trebled. The issues of compensation were reserved by the judge for a second, postliability phase of the trial.

In 1959, two years after the color work had first been shown to Kodak and several patent applications made for it, Land addressed the Boston Patent Law Association. Characteristically, he extolled the importance of the individual's contribution — Ptolemy, Copernicus, Galileo, Newton, Faraday, Maxwell, Einstein — rather than science as a group effort. He derided the notion of teamwork as the ideal framework for scientific endeavor. "There is something warm and appealing and cozy," he said, "about this picture of the human race marching forward, locked arm in arm and mind to mind; and there are insecure ages in life and insecure people in life to whom this vision of progress by phalanx brings comfort and strength. But I, for one, think this is nonsense socially and nonsense scientifically. I think human beings in the mass are fun at square dances, exciting to be with in a theater audience, and thrilling to cheer with at the California-Stanford or Harvard-Yale games. At the same time, I think, whether outside science or within science, there is no such thing as *group* originality or *group* creativity or *group* perspicacity."

While some in the audience grappled with the notion of Land having fun at a square dance, he went on. "I do believe wholeheartedly in the individual capacity for greatness, in one way or another, in almost any healthy human being under the *right* circumstances; but being part of a group is, in my opinion, generally the *wrong* circumstance. Profundity and originality are attributes of single, if not singular, minds. Two minds may sometimes be better than one, provided that each of the two minds is working separately while the two are working together; yet three tend to become a crowd."

Further, he stated the foundation of his defense against attack from without. "No one today could run the risk of creating a new section of industry without absolute conviction that the substantive contributions he had made justified the patents received, and without full knowledge that the form of the disclosure, the adequacy of the disclosure, and the thoroughness of examination were such that if the patents on which the company based its new industry were ever contested, the company could go into court with sureness. Such sureness," Land continued, "implies the kind of confidence that can be transmitted in the atmosphere of a courtroom only when it is apparent that the inventors know their field, know its history, know the great fundamental problems, and know, most of all, that to this field they have brought genuine creativity and the full solution of problems which might have remained unsolved for many years if they had not undertaken their own effort. When a company enters a field having made this kind of contribution, it has no fear of being stopped in its manufacturing operation by honest or dishonest contenders who came later into the new domain."

Great trials move to stately fugues of law. Polaroid retained two sets of outside lawyers: the Boston firm of Foley, Hoag & Eliot and the New York firm of Fish & Neave, to which was assigned primary responsibility. Each side of the suit was presented by a dozen lawyers who were clearly more comfortable marching forward arm in arm; they, in turn, were supported by scores more of clerks and paralegals, as well as the respective corporate legal departments and patent lawyers who supplied research and staff work as needed. The first great movement of the fugue was the pretrial discovery period in which almost a hundred depositions were heard and thousands of documents produced from the files of each side. Each party could demand what it wished from the other, as long as it could describe it and show that it had a bearing on the case. Thirty-five file cabinets were filled with Xerox copies. Each party could question under oath anyone from the opposing side. Forty-four from Polaroid were deposed, and an equal number from Kodak. Their testimony was taken in informal hearings, usually held in a law office, but under oath, recorded by a legal secretary, presided over by a court-appointed referee, and represented by counsel. The deposition transcripts were available to both sides and could be entered into evidence in the trial to come. Depositions consumed great rations of corporate time and energy in the preparation as much as in the taking.

To the amazement of the Polaroid officers, discovery continued for almost five years. While the battalions of paralegals filled the cabinets, Howie Rogers found it difficult to maintain any continuity of work. After sleepless weeks of preparation, his deposition took a full month to complete in the New York offices of Fish & Neave. There he was grilled by the aggressive Kodak lawyers about everything, it seemed, that he had ever done in the laboratory since he sat down in Land's chair to begin thinking about color. In his patient, quiet voice, Rogers explained the logic that had brought him each step down the road from conventional photographic color chemistry to the new idea of dye-developers. His work on the opacifier, the chemical curtain that allowed development to take place outside the camera, was examined, as he explained the many routes he and Land had followed to solve the problem of shielding development from the light in an integral print. He detailed his experiments with the exposure of the color print from both the front, Aspirin, and the rear, Excedrin, and the dates the experiments were undertaken. The dates of the patent applications were of course on the record.

When Rogers's ordeal was completed, Land was summoned. His deposition proved equally long and searching. Three of the ten patents were in his name, three in Rogers's name, four in the names of other engineers and scientists at Polaroid. But Land, of course, had been much involved with each. His deposition was dignified, precise, measured, guarded. As the questions were fired at him, the outlines of Kodak's defense began to come clear to the only person who held all the science of the two competing systems in his head. Depositions cut both ways. As he responded to the questions of learned counsel, themselves coached by Kodak's scientists, Land prepared his lesson.

The trial began in October 1981, five and a half years after the action had been filed. Judge Zobel, relatively new to the district court bench, was hard for the antagonists to assess, but her demonstrated intellectual credentials were impressive, and Land felt that he would be far better off teaching to a single first-rate mind than a jury of unknown intellectual capacity. In the months before the trial he retired to his office and the Back Lab, emerging only for board meetings or other unavoidable occasions.

Land had become increasingly bitter about the failure of Polavision, which he saw as a failure of his associates, a failure of marketing, and the fact that product development, except for Polavision, was being directed primarily by McCune, by committee. A third iteration of the SX-70 had been introduced early in the year. The new Sun Camera incorporated improvements in electronics, focused by using inaudible sound waves to measure distance. It used a supplementary flash for almost every picture, and its film was greatly improved in color resolution. Land had not been excluded from product planning, but he often excluded himself, preferring not to participate in progress by phalanx. Group creativity was not for him. He could not contemplate a lesser role when he had played the dominant for so many weary, triumphant years in the past.

Land turned his mind almost entirely to the trial. His preparation for it was more meticulous than for any public appearance he had ever made. He spent months working with the Princesses, teaching himself the ways he would explain to an unfamiliar audience the intricacies of the art he had practiced in his laboratory over the past thirty-seven years. He could not contemplate failure. For Kodak to prevail, the judge would have to rule that the patents were based on prior art, were not original, were not the creations of individuals who had brought genuine creativity to the solution of problems that might otherwise have been unsolved for years or forever. In Land's view, to lose this battle would be to reward the results of committee effort, groupthink, legal cheese-paring, the cynical assumption that no individual can stand in the way of a large, powerful, well-equipped phalanx. Individual greatness *must* prevail against groupthink. If he could not win that battle within his company, he would win it for his company, and for himself, in court. He worked until the small hours, wearing out one after another of his assistants. The company might look after its affairs without him. He was sure, however, that no one could look after its fate *but* him.

The measures of the fugue had rolled on with majestic deliberateness: challenge and counterchallenge; pretrial discovery; an interval of waiting — a year; and then the trial itself. It lasted seventy-five days. Courtroom 3 of the district court in the old building in Post Office Square in Boston was as drab and shabby-magnificent as any movie set. It was rarely filled with spectators. After their initial visits, reporters looking for a story, or industry analysts seeking enlightenment, quickly realized that much of the testimony was beyond civilian comprehension. Dozens of witnesses were called from the eighty-odd who had been deposed. Several thousand pages of testimony were recorded. Each of the ten patents was examined, analyzed, dissected, disputed, disparaged, defended. The lineage of each was scrupulously traced. Prior art was claimed and rebutted. Each patent consisted of as many as a dozen claims, each claim itself debated at length. Other patents were cited by Kodak as having disclosed processes or features claimed as original by the Polaroid patents, including French, German, and Russian as well as American patents. Throughout the seventy-five days, Judge Zobel took notes. She often asked one witness or another for clarification of a point. Charts, diagrams, enlarged mechanical drawings, and chemical formulas were offered in evidence. The press and the financial analysts drifted away. The substance would be largely incomprehensible to their audiences.

Land attended every day, every hour. He was the witness called most often by both sides. His sureness, his confidence in the knowledge of his field, its history, the great fundamental problems, were monumental. His ability to teach the field above that of other witnesses, beyond the reach of any challenger, was apparent even to those who could not follow the detail of the arguments. Frank T. Carr, one of Kodak's battery of lawyers, contended that one patent was closely related to a drawing in an earlier patent. "The patent is about how to do it right," Land responded. "This drawing is about how to do it wrong." Land was seventy-one. The years fell from his shoulders, however, as the teaching progressed. He felt comfortable with his audience, comfortable with the setting. It was not a stage, not a public performance before a large, appreciative crowd. It was a lecture hall, dusty, dignified, somewhat lacking in comfortable chairs and friendly lighting, but illuminated by the desire to learn, the need to discover the truth, the exciting contention of opposing ideas. He had never been more magisterial. He spoke in a quiet voice that discouraged interruption. Kodak's lawyers found it hard not to act respectful.

The next movement of the fugue produced frustration, impatience, and finally resignation on the part of the antagonists. After hearing the final arguments, the judge adjourned. She had an enormous volume of testimony and evidence to consider, almost all of it by experts in their fields, filled with subtleties and nuances of science, one half diametrically contrary to the other half. Three years, 1982 to 1985, passed without word or ruling from Judge Zobel.

In the meantime, Kodak sold 16.5 million instant cameras and the film to go with them. Polaroid's sales of instant cameras increased at first under the dual impetus of heavier Polaroid advertising and the advertising of Kodak, which effectively more than doubled the public impact of instant photography overnight. In 1978, 14.3 million instant cameras were sold by the two companies. Kodak captured 25 percent of the market, as high as 30 percent in the initial stages of the competition. After that, however, worldwide sales began to decline. Polaroid sold 9.4 million in 1978, but by 1982 that had shrunk by more than half to 4 million. What was happening? Kodak, whose revenues were heavily dependent on conventional photography, promoted the EK instants as "party cameras," with the implication that "real" cameras used conventional darkroom-developed film. The gimmick issue raised its head again. Polaroid felt that there was an effort to degrade and trivialize the instant field and that Polaroid was suffering far more from the effects than its rival, the source from which trivialization emanated. Polaroid's management executive committee despaired at the silence from the chambers of the United States District Court, District of Massachusetts. In the midst of this judicial stillness, Land retired from his company in August 1982.

His leaving was quiet. There were no state occasions, only a gathering of the senior officers and scientists for a quiet dinner at the Ritz, where he was presented with a bound set of his papers and speeches. The meal afterward was subdued. Most of those present had not seen him for months, some for more than a year. There was so much to say that little of it was said. The trial had receded into the past. No one knew how it would turn out, or when. Land accepted the collection of his words bound in calf and stamped in gold. He held the volumes to his chest in much the same way he had received a gift at the annual meeting four months earlier. There, on the stage of Symphony Hall, we had listened to a brass quintet and watched Land and McCune sitting side by side, facing the darkness as the notes of Handel soared across the footlights. Land had been taken completely by surprise when he was presented with two bull mastiff puppies to replace his beloved mastiffs, Per and Se, both long since dead. He stood alone, holding them tight, their wrinkled faces pressed to his, tears coursing down his cheeks, unable to speak. There were no tears shed at the Ritz, no puppies to unlock them. We departed feeling unfulfilled and unexpressed.

When Judge Zobel finally issued her Memorandum of Decision on September 13, 1985, it was 122 pages long, a masterful and detailed analysis of every argument in the case. It announced a stunning victory for Polaroid and for Land. She had weighed the merits of ten patents, including the two that were considered together. The Rogers patent for a negative dye-developer, the Excedrin patent, which related to exposure of the print from behind, had emerged as the critical issue in the trial. SX-70 used front exposure with a mirror to reverse the image. The EK cameras exposed the image from the rear without a mirror, so that when the image was viewed from the front it appeared correctly oriented. Rogers, however, had thoroughly explored both methods of exposure in the early days of SX-70 development, and both had been patented by him.

The judge ruled the Excedrin patent valid, despite the many challenges by Kodak, and infringed, a major victory for Polaroid. The Land patent for polymeric acid stabilization — cessation — of the development process was ruled valid and infringed by Kodak. The Land patent for symmetrical supports to prevent curling of the developed print was ruled valid and infringed by Kodak. The two Rogers patents for the opacifier were ruled valid and infringed by Kodak. A patent in the names of two Polaroid engineers, Blinow and Leduc, for a rear-mounted camera motor and an extended gear train was ruled not valid, but infringed by Kodak, not of consequence if the ruling of invalidity stood. A Land patent for a rear-mounted film pick, the arm that pushed the film sheet forward into the rollers, was ruled valid and infringed by Kodak. A patent in the name of Dr. Lloyd Taylor, a Polaroid scientist, for a mordant formula to stabilize the dyes was judged valid but not infringed. A patent in the names of Wareham and Paglia for a light shield to prevent light leaking to unexposed film was ruled valid and infringed by Kodak. The tenth patent, assigned to Paglia, for a detachable housing for the steel rollers was ruled not valid but infringed. Thus, Judge Zobel found for Polaroid in seven of the ten patents. One she found valid, but not infringed by Kodak. Two she judged to be invalid, but infringed. Polaroid, elated, applied for an immediate injunction to prevent Kodak from continuing in the instant photography business.

One month later, Judge Zobel enjoined "Kodak, its officers, agents, servants, employees, and attorneys, and those persons in active concert and participation with them" to stop manufacturing, using, and selling EK-4 and EK-6 cameras and PR-10 film. She gave them until January 9, 1986, to comply. Kodak was staggered. The blow was far more hurtful to its corporate pride than its business, but the public relations spokesman so forgot the situation as litigant before a federal court as to issue a hasty release saying, " 'Our position has not changed. Kodak instant products were developed using our own distinctive technology. We believe that our products do not infringe the patent rights of others.' The company said it has no plans to alter its current manufacturing schedules or marketing plans pending resolution of the appeal. The appeal itself will be filed with the Court of Appeals for the Federal Circuit in Washington, D.C." One month later, Judge Zobel denied the appeal and the injunction took effect. Kodak announced that it would appeal the patent judgment to the Supreme Court, but, accepting the devastation of manufacturing, distribution, dealer confidence, and customer relations, it abandoned the instant business. Many analysts felt that Kodak had never made a penny in it. Some sixteen million EK camera owners were informed, in January 1986, that when dealer stocks of PR-10 film were exhausted no more film would be available. Kodak offered EK owners a $50 credit on other Kodak products, a small conventional camera, or a share of Eastman stock, then selling for $44.50, in exchange for the orphan instants, which had become instant orphans. When speculators began to buy dealer inventories of cameras for $25 apiece to exchange them for shares of Eastman stock, which went up as stocks often do on bad news, the offer was summarily limited to three shares per household.

Polaroid and Kodak began consulting their lawyers again, Kodak having engaged a new law firm, about the next movement of the trial still to be heard to determine the extent of damages. Kodak's final appeal of the Zobel patent ruling was denied several months later. Polaroid had swept the field in the biggest patent case in modern times. The analysts, their vicarious hunger rekindled, proclaimed that Polaroid should demand a billion dollars, perhaps two billion, perhaps four.

A key issue concerning the infringement of Land's polymeric acid patent hinged on the definition of the location of the acid layer in Kodak's PR-10 film. The question was whether or not the acid layer was located "in the photosensitive element." Both parties agreed that the PR-10 acid layer was positioned between the plastic support and the photosensitive layer, but Kodak contended that in the manufacture of the film, the acid layer was coated on one support and the photosensitive layers on another support, the two elements then assembled together into one film unit. Thus, the Kodak lawyers argued, the acid layer was not truly positioned "in the photosensitive element." The judge sensibly said that, regardless of the manufacturing procedure, it *was* where the acid layer was positioned. The Kodak lawyers then cited conflicting definitions of "photosensitive element" in other Polaroid patents. Again the judge demurred in her Memorandum of Decision. The patent in question provides its own clear definition, she pointed out. Furthermore, "a patentee is entitled to choose his own terms and to insist on them so long as he is consistent and does not contravene any single established or accepted meaning," she wrote, citing *Mooney* v. *Brunswick Corp.* and *Harrington Manufacturing Co.* v. *White*. Then in a footnote, she cited a third authority.

> "When I use a word," Humpty Dumpty said . . . "it means just what I choose it to mean — neither more nor less."
>
> "The question is," said Alice, "whether you *can* make words mean so many different things."
>
> "The question is," said Humpty Dumpty, "which is to be master — that's all."
>
> (L. Carroll, *Alice's Adventures in Wonderland & Through the Looking Glass.*)

When he read this citation, plucked from one wonderland to shed light on another no less mysterious one, the master of the lecture hall, the master of his field, the master of the great fundamental problems, but the master of his company no longer, must have managed a wry smile. At least I hoped that he had.

Epilogue

Brattle Street

Cambridge, 1983

Land was asleep. He was talking to me, and he fell asleep at the end of his sentence. His eyes closed, for a moment I thought, but they stayed closed. He sat in the big leather chair in his study in the old house on Brattle Street with the comfortable noises of late New England spring drifting in through an open window. I could hear a lawn mower several houses away. The traffic noises from the street were muted, brush strokes across the warm afternoon. I peered at him anxiously. As usual, he was vexing me, not responding as I expected him to, in this case not responding at all. We had been talking. And then he started sleeping. It was quite annoying. His face was calm and as handsome in repose as it was when animated. His dark hair was thick with a slight wave and the classic seven-point actor's hairline. I wondered, as I often had, if he darkened it; mine had been gray since I was thirty-five. His brows were black, heavy, stern; the nose strong with deep calipers that measured a wide mouth with sensitive lips above a square jaw.

Land, however, had made himself invisible. By closing his eyes he effectively disappeared. It was typical of him to have invented a form of invisibility that he alone could control. The first impression one received when meeting him was that of the eyes. It took a while for the other features to register. The eyes were the man; as long as they were closed he was not present. I recalled Howie Rogers's description of his first interview with Land in 1936. Howie had been pumping gas at the Jenney station in Brighton after he had finished his first year at Harvard, then run out of money. His brother, Nickerson, working as a technician at

Land-Wheelwright, urged Howie to come in and apply for a job. "We need help. It's not like any other company around. You might enjoy it."

"What do you think it would pay?"

"About ten dollars a week, I should guess."

"I'm making twenty-five at the gas station."

"Come in anyway and see what you think of Land."

Howie arrived in clean shirt and trousers a few days later at noontime. Land invited him to Levine's Drugstore across Dartmouth Street for a sandwich and an ice cream soda. They talked about commonplace subjects. Howie did not know enough about the laboratory to ask many questions. "He looked into me," Howie said. "He seemed to be satisfied at what he found. That was my interview."

"What do you mean, he looked into you?" I asked.

"Oh, he just did. Looked into me for a while and that was it. I had to pay for my lunch because Land didn't have enough money to pay for both of us. My father was furious with me when he learned I was going to work there. He thought I was crazy. My plan had been to work for a year or maybe two at the gas station and then go to MIT. Of course, I never went back to school. I learned more from Land in two months than I ever did at Harvard. If I had stayed at Harvard I probably would have majored in math. It's funny that I haven't used math much since then."

Dick Kriebel joined the company the year before Howie. He described Land in 1935 as almost theatrically handsome, with unusual eyes. "Discerning eyes. Disturbing eyes. He never maintained eye contact very long," said Kriebel, "but that was what you remembered about him, his eyes. To this day I can't tell you what color they are."

They are brown, but they were closed. The warm breeze through the window spoke of fresh-cut grass and lilacs. I looked around the room. I had been there several times before. Land and Terre had lived in this large Georgian Colonial house for more than thirty years. It stood three stories high above a lawn and tidy gardens, comfortably close to its brick, wood, and stucco neighbors, which housed Harvard professors, museum directors, symphony musicians, and other Cambridge Brahmins. The two Land daughters, Jennifer and Valerie, had grown up at 163 Brattle Street and on a farm in Peterborough, New Hampshire, where they raised horses. The rooms of the house were tastefully cluttered, except for the rather formal living room with its brocaded furniture, Chinese screen, and sculpture, where Mrs. Land had evidently drawn the line.

The study was full of books and pictures, as indeed were most of the rooms of the house, including the kitchen. A magnificent Ansel Adams *Moonrise* dominated the fireplace. Stacks of framed pictures leaned against the wall. The remains of our sandwich lunch and two empty glasses that had contained iced tea stood on a small table between us. I wondered if I should take the tray back to the kitchen. The cook had gone out for the afternoon after serving us. She had told the Doctor her plans before departing. I picked up the tray and carried it out through a cool, paneled hall, past the stairway and a large room with an antique bar that must have come from some old New England hostelry. Land had laid out stacks of carefully sorted papers the length of the bar, reflected in the grand mirror behind it. I left the dishes in the cheerful, rather old-fashioned kitchen. Outside I could hear the noise of a large animal digging in the run that enclosed one side of the house. It was one of the replacements for Per and Se, the two mastiffs that Land had kept for many years, at first no doubt for protection, but later, he was fond of saying, as irrefutable evidence of the existence of pure, unalloyed goodness per se.

I glanced out the kitchen window at the modest backyard and the garage at the end of the driveway that curved around the opposite side of the house where my car was parked. Just down the drive, an off-duty Cambridge policeman sat in an unmarked sedan. He had recognized me when I arrived and we greeted each other, veterans of shared annual meetings with their attendant weeks of evening rehearsals, ordeals to be remembered fondly because they were extraordinary and because they were over. The policeman was not dozing in his car. He was listening to a Red Sox game that was just audible over the sound of the mower, but his eyes were on Brattle Street. I passed again into the study, whose occupant still slept. Land was so protective of his family that he had once refused to tell a reporter the names of his daughters. Neither their pictures nor a picture of his wife had ever to my knowledge appeared in a Boston newspaper.

I sat down quietly and looked at him. He was no longer Chairman of the Board, Chief Executive Officer, President, Chief Operating Officer, or Director of Research. He had resigned and retired. He had sold his stock. His last tie with Polaroid was a contract which guaranteed him that the office and study at Osborn Street he had occupied for forty years would be his for the rest of his life, "and six months longer," he told me with a glint in his eye. I had left as well, he in August, I in October of 1982. I didn't have to ask him if he had regrets. He didn't have to ask me. We had both been at Polaroid for too long, Land for all his life, I for twenty-four years. But, of course, I told myself, the point is that only change is unchanging. We both had a longer ride than most people get.

Land ran his company longer than any of America's great business leaders, longer than Thomas Edison, longer than Henry Ford, longer than George Eastman. Giving it up had been the hardest thing he had done in his life. It had been an emotional trauma that engulfed everyone near him, from the Cambridge policeman in the driveway to the officers and board members of the company. None of us escaped. We watched as Land tore himself away from the most important thing in his life. The lines in his face were graven deeper than they had been, his silences lasted longer, his eyes more often focused inward. He accomplished this surgery on himself as he did most things, in his own personal, unexpected, passionate, and enigmatic way. He had written something in one of the annual reports in the seventies that was hovering in the back of my mind, but I couldn't bring it forward.

In 1940 he had been named one of the National Modern Pioneers by a group headed by Karl Compton. It was a singular honor. He was thirty-one. He had worked without ceasing, without deviating, for fourteen years since boyhood to become — what? A pioneer was as good a name as I could put to it. He had wanted to create new things; the polarizer and the instant camera would remain the best known. But perhaps his most original invention had been his company. It was no less the product of a conscious process of experimentation and insight and repeated failure and creation and ultimate success than had been the other inventions. In the slough of the Depression he was already shaping the idea of a new sort of corporation whose characteristics were so unusual as to be bizarre, almost ludicrous.

At a time when steel companies, automobile factories, and textile mills were slowing to a halt, spilling workers into the streets, he was talking and thinking and writing about a company founded on science that would design new products not imagined by the public, which would be attracted to the products because they filled a hitherto unperceived need. He wanted a company to create an environment for art at a time when many were worried about meeting the next payroll. He talked about a company where the work life would be so satisfying that workers would look forward to the day's beginning and regret its end, while sweatshops were in their heyday and unions fought to establish basic rights on the job. These were the ravings of a pioneer.

Not many took him seriously except some of those who worked with him and a few who, like Compton in 1940, listened attentively. As a Modern Pioneer, he was not very articulate in front of a large audience. He communicated well face to face and by writing, and painstakingly rewriting, until the words satisfied him. The ultimate communication of his ideas did not come until after the war, when he discovered photography as the medium through which he could most fully express the idea of the company. He ran the Polaroid experiment for fifty years.

He, of all people, should know well that no line of experimentation has an end. It always leads to other ideas, to other avenues, in this case to other people. I knew he felt that the experiment of his company had failed, because it was no longer his to pursue. I didn't agree. I felt it had succeeded in his terms and his tenure. Whether it succeeded or failed in someone else's term was irrelevant. To me. Not to him, I was sure. Land's ego at least equaled his intellect; both were immense, world-class. It was another attribute, however, his humanity, that ultimately made him fascinating to me. I had known other egos and other intellects. Land was a man who had lived more than anyone else I had known. He had created his life as he created his company. He was an initiator. Now he would no longer create at Polaroid. Neither would I, for that matter.

Land opened his eyes. He looked into me. I had the feeling of being examined, interviewed. "You were asleep, Din," I said. "I was a little concerned."

"Nonsense. I was resting my eyes for a moment. Why would you think I was asleep?"

"Well, I spoke to you and you didn't answer."

"I was thinking." He smiled his charming little-boy smile. "There is nothing more refreshing than thinking for a few minutes with your eyes closed."

"I suppose that's how you survived all those board meetings." I rose to take my leave. "Din, what was it you wrote in one of your shareholder letters about the future? About the past and the future? I can't bring it to mind."

The smile disappeared. He brought it to mind instantly. " 'The present is the past biting into the future,' " he said. "Why do you ask?"

Acknowledgments

The material, published and unpublished, that I used in the research for this book includes annual reports, periodicals, press releases, tapes, interviews, transcripts, and other sources. I am indebted to the following publications: the *Boston Globe,* the *Boston Herald,* the *Bay State Banner,* the *New York Times,* the *New York Post,* the *Wall Street Journal, Fortune, Life, Business Week, Time, Forbes,* and *Photo Dealer.*

The following books were particularly useful: Wyn Wachhorst, *Thomas Alva Edison* (Cambridge: MIT Press, 1981); Mark Olshaker, *The Instant Image* (Briarcliff Manor, N.Y.: Stein and Day, 1978); and Michael R. Beschloss, *Mayday* (New York: Harper & Row, 1986).

I am deeply grateful to all the people who shared their memories and experiences with me. The book would not have been possible without them. I also wish to thank Esther Newberg, Louise Desaulniers, Gerry Morse, Gordon Lewis, Elizabeth Rollins, Nasrin Harani, Adam Bolonsky, T. Brown, Sally Coxe, and Joanne Sayers for their contributions, assistance, and encouragement.

Finally, I want to thank the two people without whose extraordinary efforts there would have been, and could have been, no book: Peter Davison and Andrea Wensberg.

Index